MONASTIC EXPERIENCE IN TWELFTH-CENTURY GERMANY

Manchester University Press

MONASTIC EXPERIENCE IN TWELFTH-CENTURY GERMANY
The Chronicle of Petershausen in translation

Alison I. Beach, Shannon M. T. Li, and Samuel S. Sutherland

Manchester University Press

Copyright © Manchester University Press 2020

While copyright in the volume as a whole is vested in Manchester University Press, copyright in individual chapters belongs to their respective authors, and no chapter may be reproduced wholly or in part without the express permission in writing of both author and publisher.

Published by Manchester University Press
Oxford Road, Manchester M13 9PL
www.manchesteruniversitypress.co.uk

British Library Cataloguing-in-Publication Data
A catalogue record for this book is available from the British Library

ISBN 978 1 5261 2678 8 hardback
ISBN 978 1 5261 6697 5 paperback

First published 2020
Paperback published 2022

The publisher has no responsibility for the persistence or accuracy of URLs for any external or third-party internet websites referred to in this book, and does not guarantee that any content on such websites is, or will remain, accurate or appropriate.

Typeset by Newgen Publishing UK

CONTENTS

List of abbreviations	*page* vi
Map: Petershausen's religious landscape	viii

Introduction	1
The Chronicle of Petershausen	**23**
Prologue	25
Book One	38
Book Two	70
Book Three	97
Book Four	128
Translation of the Relics of St. Gebhard	151
Additional Entries	156
Book Five	177
Book Six	184
Appendix 1: *The Life of St. Gebhard*	191
Appendix 2: Concordance of book and chapter numbering	217
Bibliography	218
Index	226

ABBREVIATIONS

Abel and Weiland (1868)	*Casus monasterii Petrishusensis*, ed. Otto Abel and Ludwig Weiland. MGH SS 20:621–683 (Hanover, 1868).
ALH	The Annals of Lampert of Hersfeld, trans. I. S. Robinson (Manchester, 2015).
CBR	Chronicle of Berthold of Reichenau, in I. S. Robinson, *Eleventh-Century Germany: The Swabian Chronicles* (Manchester, 2008).
CBSB	Chronicle of Bernold of St. Blasien, in I. S. Robinson, *Eleventh-Century Germany: The Swabian Chronicles* (Manchester, 2008).
CBZ	*Ortliebi Chronicon*, in Luitpold Wallach, Erich König, and Karl Otto Müller, trans., *Die Zwiefalter Chroniken Ortliebs und Bertholds* (Sigmaringen, 1978).
CC:CM	*Corpus Christianorum – Continuatio Mediaevalis*
CCM	*Corpus Consuetudinum Monasticarum*
CFM	The Chronicle of Frutolf of Michelsberg, in T. J. H. McCarthy, trans., *Chronicles of the Investiture Contest* (Manchester, 2014).
COZ	*Bertholdi Chronicon*, ed. and trans. Luitpold Wallach, Erich König, and Karl Otto Müller *Die Zwiefalter Chroniken Ortliebs und Bertholds*. Schwäbische Chroniken der Stauferzeit 2 (Sigmaringen, 1978).
CP	Chronicle of Petershausen
Feger (1956)	*Die Chronik des Klosters Petershausen*, ed. and trans. Otto Feger. Schwäbische Chroniken der Stauferzeit 3 (Sigmaringen, 1956).
JL	Jaffé-Lowenfeld, *Regesta pontificum Romanorum*
Life of Gebhard	*Vita Gebehardi Episcopi Constantiensis*, ed. Wilhelm Wattenbach. MGH SS 10: 582–594 (Hanover, 1852).

ABBREVIATIONS

MGH DD	Monumenta Germaniae Historica, Diplomata
MGH Nec. Germ.	Monumenta Germaniae Historica, Necrologia Germaniae
MGH SS	Monumenta Germaniae Historica, Scriptores (in folio)
Mone (1848)	*Chronik von Petershausen*, ed. Franz Josef Mone. *Quellensamlung der badischen Landesgeschichte* 1 (Karlsruhe, 1848).
PL	*Patrologia cursus completus, series Latina*
REC	*Regesta episcoporum Constantiensium* 1 (Innsbruck, 1895).

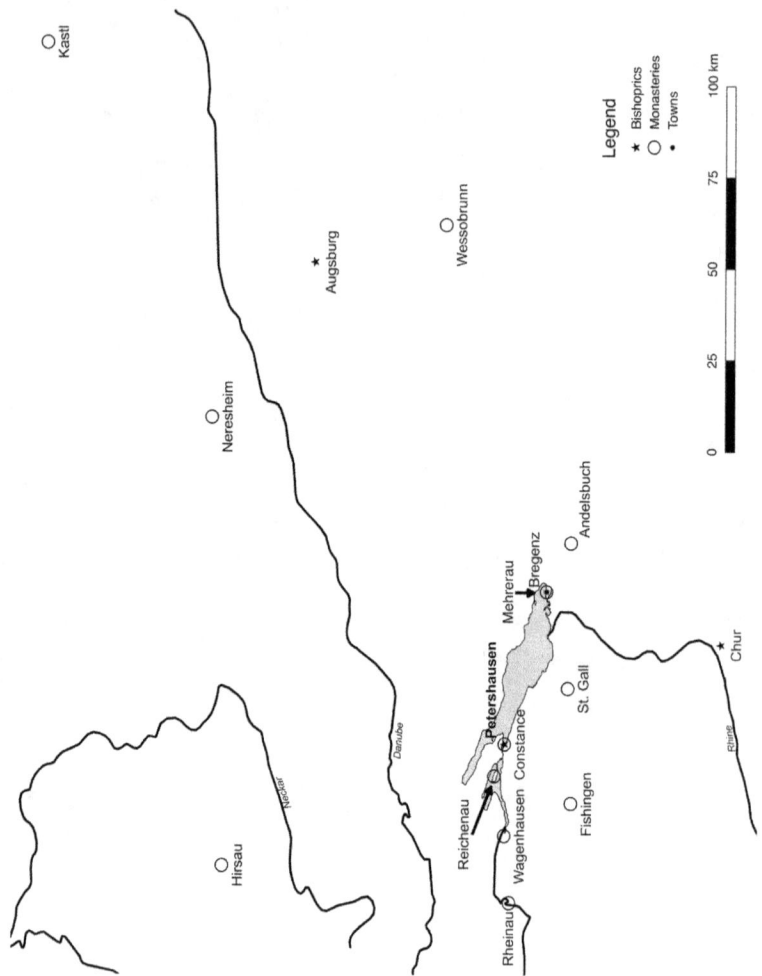

Map: Petershausen's religious landscape

INTRODUCTION

In 983, Bishop Gebhard II of Constance (r. 979–995) set out to establish a proprietary monastery not far from his episcopal precinct on the shore of Lake Constance.[1] Searching for just the right piece of land for this new community, the bishop and his companions set up camp in a swamp. Even after the search party was kept awake all night by the incessant croaking of frogs, the bishop still wondered if the spot had potential. When he asked what he should call the monastery if he were to build it there, one of his men, perhaps sardonic after a sleepless night, suggested the name *Ranunculorum Cella* – the Monastery of Little Frogs. Evidently not amused, Gebhard responded that he had no intention of building his community there "if it should be condemned with such a foul name."[2] And so the search continued. In the end, Gebhard selected a site just across the Rhine from the city of Constance in keeping with a consciously constructed parallel with the sacred topography of Rome.[3] The new monastery was the mirror of St. Peter's basilica in this landscape, and like St. Peter's, oriented with its apse to the west, a simulacrum that suggested a name much more pleasing to the bishop: Petershausen, literally the house of Peter. To secure that land, Gebhard arranged for an exchange with the present owner, the powerful monastery of Reichenau (f. 724). He endowed the community with lands from his own inheritance, travelled to Rome to secure relics and a papal privilege, and presided in person at the consecration in 992. Even after his death, Gebhard continued to watch over and protect his beloved monastery, working miracles at his tomb,[4] heroically rescuing

---

1 An episcopal proprietary monastery is a religious community that was under the lordship of a bishop. On the episcopal lordship of monasteries from the ninth to the twelfth century, see Susan Wood, *The Proprietary Church in the Medieval West* (Oxford: Oxford University Press, 2006), esp. 418–434.

2 Chronicle of Petershausen (hereafter CP) 1.9.

3 On the efforts of medieval bishops in German cities beyond the Roman *limes* to enhance their spiritual prestige through the creation of sacred landscapes that mirrored those of Rome or Jerusalem, see Alfred Haverkamp, "Cities as Cultic Centres in Germany and Italy During the Early and High Middle Ages," in *Sacred Spaces: Shrine, City, Land*, ed. Benjamin Z. Kedar and R. J. Zwi Werblowsky (New York: New York University Press, 1998), 172–191.

4 CP 1.55; see also Book 2 of the *Life of Gebhard*.

MONASTIC EXPERIENCE IN TWELFTH-CENTURY GERMANY

a drowning monk from a head-first fall into the crypt fountain,[5] and excoriating a monk-priest for his crimes against the community (such as claiming the biggest chalice for himself and filling it to the brim with wine before celebrating the Mass).[6] All of this is the predictable stuff of medieval monastic chronicles.

Historical annals and chronicles abound from German-speaking lands in this period, surely at least partly in response to the ecclesio-political disruptions that devastated the region. Some of the most notable examples come from the pen of Herman of Reichenau (c. 1013–1054), his continuator Berthold (c. 1030–1088), and Bernold of St. Blasien, who together documented events from 1000 to 1100. These Swabian chroniclers offer vital accounts of the shifting and violent landscape of eleventh-century Germany.[7] Beyond Swabia, the eleventh-century Annals of Lambert of Hersfeld (in the medieval Duchy of Franconia) constitute the most important narrative account of political events in the kingdom of Germany in the central Middle Ages. A so-called universal history, Lambert's Annals begin with the creation of the world and move into his own time. This is a particularly important source for the turbulent period between 1056 and 1077 – a source that the Petershausen chronicler himself seems to have had to hand when he compiled his own account of these events in Book Two. Still other chroniclers narrate the story of the conflict between popes and kings and emperors from the papal perspective. The contemporary chronicler Frutolf of Michelsberg provides the most important, sometimes eyewitness, account of many of the same events from the royal perspective, and his work was extended and adapted (including by Ekkehard of Aura) in the twelfth century.

Reaching for continuity amid the rapid religious and social change of the period – a period that for many monastic communities included profound internal change initiated in the name of correction or reform – the Swabian monk-chroniclers of the eleventh and twelfth

---

5 CP 3.15
6 CP 3.21
7 I. S. Robinson, trans., *Eleventh-Century Germany: The Swabian Chronicles* (Manchester: Manchester University Press, 2008); see also Hans-Werner Goetz, "Die schwäbischen Herzöge in der Wahrnehmung der alemannischen Geschichtsschreiber der Ottonen- und Salierzeit," in *Adel und Königtum im mittelalterlichen Schwaben: Festschrift für Thomas Zotz zum 65. Geburtstag*, ed. Aldres Bihrer, Mathias Kälble, and Heinz Krieg (Stuttgart: Kohlhammer Verlag, 2009), 127–144.

INTRODUCTION

centuries imagined historical narratives that insisted on connection to the past. At the Hirsau-affiliated monastery of Zwiefalten (f. 1089), the monks Ortlieb (writing between 1135 and 1137) and Berthold (writing between c. 1137 and 1138) cover much of the same territory as the Petershausen chronicler – with similar, albeit drier, accounts of the selection of a site for the monastery, the election of lay advocates, relic translations, as well as an impressive number of donations by noble patrons.[8]

Like Ortlieb and Berthold, or the author of the Chronicle of Ottobeuren (c. 1210), Petershausen's chronicler also sought to bolster the legal and economic welfare of his community by interweaving various charters and privileges – some interpolated or even forged – to suit present and anticipated needs.[9] It is, however, the colorful Ekkehard IV of St. Gall (980/990–1054), author of the *Casus Sancti Galli*, whose work most nearly resembles the CP. Just as will be seen in the case of the anonymous monk-author of the CP, Ekkehard enlivens his narrative of events at St. Gall from 870 to 972 with vivid anecdotes that reflect something of life within the monastery: conflicts between abbots and monks, divine punishment, miracles, abbatial abdications, devastating fires, and extraordinary deaths.[10] Like these other chroniclers, the author of the CP constructed a community identity on the imagined foundation of a shared past, creating cohesion in the present, often drawing on familiar recycled and repurposed tales of contemporary monastic histories.[11]

What truly sets the author of the CP apart from the rest, however, is that he continued the work sporadically for some thirty years, from c. 1136 to c. 1164, shifting from retrospective historian to contemporary witness and critic. He speaks with a clear and often feisty voice, revealing a perspective that shifts over time in response to conditions and events both within the monastery and in the broader religious,

---

8 For the Chronicle of Zwiefalten, see COZ and CBZ; for the text of the Chronicle of Ottobeuren, see MGH SS 23: 609–630. To date, there is no English translation of either of these Latin chronicles.

9 See, for example, CP 1.27 and 2.2, with (possible) interpolations regarding the right of the monastery to elect its advocate.

10 Ekkehard IV of St. Gall, *Casus Sancti Galli*. MGH SS 2: 75–162.

11 On the concept of "imaginative memory," see Amy G. Remensnyder, *Remembering Kings Past: Monastic Foundation Legends in Medieval Southern France* (Ithaca, NY: Cornell University Press, 1995), 2–3.

social, and political landscapes in which it was embedded. The CP begins as a narrative of the triumph of reform; men from Hirsau arrive and take charge, and a wonderful new abbot, Theodoric (r. 1086–1116), deftly implements the mandated changes. But this narrative of triumph gradually morphs into a narrative of cultural trauma. Subsequent abbots and monks fail to live up to the promises of the reform and the violence of the surrounding landscape finds its way into the community. The chronicler speaks with unexpected candor, often in the first person, as bishop-proprietors clash with the monks, advocates attack with their men, the cellarer pawns precious liturgical vestments, and a monk steals and hides the silver. The interpretation of frightening dream-visions divides the community. Two of the lay brothers beat the cellarer with clubs when he refuses to provide them with needed supplies. And after God permits the total destruction of the community in a massive fire – a horrifying inversion of the holy flames of Pentecost – the chronicler lays the blame right at the feet of the monks themselves.

The Petershausen chronicler's decision to remain anonymous also distinguishes him from many of his better-known contemporaries. A number of internal clues, however, suggest that this remarkable author may well have been the monk who would become Abbot Gebhard I (r. 1164–1170/1173). His striking level of interest in all things liturgical – from vestments, to books, to processions – suggests that he was the community's cantor, the individual charged with oversight of all aspects of the liturgy as well as the production and keeping of books.[12] Further, as recent studies have demonstrated, it was not uncommon for the cantor to do double duty as community historian.[13] Another clue comes from the often-bewildering parade of Gebhards across the folios of the Chronicle, a reflection of the monastery's long connection to the family of its founding bishop. The chronicler himself claims many of these Gebhards as relatives, noting, for example, a forefather (*avus*) named Gebhard among the monks at Petershausen at the end of the

---

12 For a more complete discussion of the identity of the chronicler, see Alison I. Beach, *The Trauma of Monastic Reform: Community and Conflict in Twelfth-Century Germany* (Cambridge: Cambridge University Press, 2017), 158–162; Alison I. Beach, "Shaping Liturgy, Shaping History: A Cantor-Historian from Twelfth-Century Petershausen," in *Medieval Cantors and Their Craft: Music, Liturgy, and the Shaping of History, 800–1500*, ed. Margot Fassler, Katie Bugyis, and Andrew Krabel (Woodbridge: Boydell & Brewer, 2017), 297–309.

13 Fassler et al., *Medieval Cantors and Their Craft*.

INTRODUCTION

eleventh century[14] and referring several times to his uncle Gebino (a diminutive form of the name Gebhard), a fellow monk at Petershausen who left the community to serve as Abbot of Wagenhausen (r. 1127–1134) and Fischingen (r. c. 1135–1138).[15] Gebhard was indeed a very common name within Gebhard II's family line: the powerful counts of Bregenz, the ruling comital family of the Voralberg from the tenth to the twelfth century.[16] Both a noble lineage of this sort and a familial connection to the founder further support the argument that the chronicler served as cantor, a position that suggests a high status within the monastery and one that often served as a springboard to the abbacy.[17] The timing for this attribution is also right; Gebhard I became abbot in 1164, just when the hand, tone, and style of the CP signal a change of scribe-author. It may be that cantor-historian-turned-abbot Gebhard I finally handed the ever-expanding manuscript over to a continuator, perhaps his successor as cantor, after devoting some thirty years of work to the text.

The Hirsau reform

The pivotal event witnessed in the CP is the arrival in 1086 of a group of outsiders, dispatched from the monastery of Hirsau at the behest of still another Gebhard: Bishop Gebhard III of Constance (r. 1084–1110). The new bishop had himself been a monk at Hirsau, the center of an influential eleventh- and twelfth-century movement for monastic reform.

Hirsau's own roots stretched back to 830, when Bishop Noting of Vercelli and Count Erlafried of Calw founded a small religious community dedicated to St. Aurelius just east of the River Nagold on the northern edge of the Black Forest. This little community would not last; monastic life there soon collapsed and the house was dissolved. The

---

14 cf. CP 3.14–3.16.
15 cf. CP 2.17, 3.38, 3.45, 4.32–4.34, and 4.40–4.41.
16 Helmut G. Walther, "Gründungsgeschichte und Tradition im Kloster Petershausen vor Konstanz," *Schriften des Vereins für Geschichte des Bodensees und seiner Umgebung* 96 (1978): 42–43. The CP is an important (although problematic) source for the history of the Bregenzer comital family. See Benedikt Bilgeri, *Bregenz. Geschichte der Stadt. Politik, Verfassung, Wirtschaft* (Vienna and Munich: Verlag Jugend & Volk, 1980), 22–31.
17 Felix Heinzer, *Klosterreform und mittelalterliche Buchkultur im deutschen Südwesten* (Leiden: Brill Publishers, 2008), 389.

5

impulse for a new founding would come only in the eleventh century, from none less than the great reforming pope Leo IX (r. 1049–1054), who commissioned his nephew, Count Albert of Calw, to revive the community. By 1065, the new house was ready to receive its first new monks, called from the monastery of Einsiedeln (f. 934), some 200 kilometers to the south in modern Switzerland. Troubles continued to plague the community, however, and in 1069 the count found it necessary, allegedly with the full agreement of the monks, to depose Abbot Frederick. It was then that William (c. 1030–1091) was called from the monastery of St. Emmeram in Regensburg to serve as Abbot of Hirsau, although he refused to accept ordination as abbot until 1071 in response to lingering doubts about the legitimacy of Frederick's deposition at the hands of the monastery's lay proprietor.

Almost as soon as the struggle between Emperor Henry IV and Pope Gregory VII for control over the investiture of bishops led to a major break between the two in 1076, the monks of Hirsau and its affiliates stepped forward as vigorous supporters of the papal cause, delivering fiery sermons and building a reputation as agitators and rebels.[18] Partly fueled by anti-imperial sentiment among the bishops and some of the nobles of Swabia, the reform gained momentum in the late eleventh century, and the Hirsau-oriented communities that increasingly dotted the landscape of southern Germany functioned as centers of support for the papal cause. Petershausen's papal orientation in the great clashes of the late eleventh and twelfth century was fixed by its bishop-proprietor and their association with the reformers from Hirsau.

But the lay nobles who functioned as monastic advocates (the individuals charged with seeing to a monastery's material welfare in the secular world) were freer to switch sides. A change in allegiance could turn a patron into an adversary, or an advocate into an aggressor. A hostile episcopal patron could also bring disaster – a fact made painfully clear at Petershausen during the episcopacy of Ulrich I. One of the most valuable aspects of the witness of the CP is its frank portrayal of the ways in which the supra-regional and regional violence associated with this protracted struggle played out at the most local level.[19]

---

18 On Hirsau monks as anti-imperial preachers, see Phyllis G. Jestice, *Wayward Monks and the Religious Revolution of the Eleventh Century* (Leiden: Brill Publishers, 1997), 249–265.

19 See esp. Book Three of the Chronicle.

INTRODUCTION

Enthusiastic medieval and early modern praise for William painted him as a model reformer and Hirsau as a refuge of "true religion" in a broken world. For the Petershausen chronicler, William was a man "pleasing both to God and men because he was extremely learned and most zealous in regular discipline, humble, gentle, a despiser of the world, and a most diligent lover of monks and of all virtue."[20] Almost four centuries later, Johannes Trithemius (1462–1516), Abbot of Sponheim and of St. Jacob in Würzburg, praised William's great learning (including the advanced liberal arts of the quadrivium, and particularly music, mathematics, and astronomy) and his benevolence toward the needy of all sorts. For Trithemius, William was a heroic rescuer of monastic life, a model of spirituality, and the ideal abbot.[21]

Modern scholarship, by contrast, has tended to dismiss the Hirsau reform as merely political – an impression surely reinforced by contemporary representations of rabble-rousing Hirsau monks preaching to crowds of laymen in support of the papal cause. The Hirsau movement is also frequently relegated to the status as a somewhat uninteresting derivative – a "German Cluny" – or criticized as entirely dominated by William's "philistine narrowmindedness," a personality flaw that led to the operation of communities regimented to the point of dictating "proper toilet habits or the time for cutting fingernails."[22] Such impressions, while not entirely wrong, have prevented a full picture of the spiritual dimensions of the movement from coming to the fore, particularly in English- and French-speaking academic circles. The CP enriches our understanding of monasticism within Hirsau's reforming orbit and provides a useful corrective to these rather narrow views of the movement.

What, then, was the Hirsau Reform, and what can be said about its goals and core spiritual ideals? According to the unrelenting rhetoric of praise that emerged from Hirsau's expanding reforming circle, William worked tirelessly to restore apostolic simplicity to monastic life, first locally and then regionally. At the heart of his plan was the goal of securing the freedom (*libertas*) of the monastery from all secular

---

20 CP 2.49.
21 Klaus Schreiner, "Hirsau und der Hirsauer Reform. Spiritualität, Lebensform und Sozialprofil einer benediktinischen Erneuerungsbewegung im 11. und 12. Jahrhundert," in *Hirsau. St. Peter und Paul. 1091–1991* (Stuttgart: Konrad Theiss Verlag, 1991), 159.
22 Schreiner, "Hirsau und der Hirsauer Reform," 161.

interference, including the kind of heavy-handed intervention seen in Albert's ousting of Abbot Frederick. In the wake of further struggles with the counts of Calw, William succeeded in securing a royal charter from Henry IV in 1075 that documented Albert's surrender of all of his rights over Hirsau and its possessions, recognized the rights of its abbots as the community's sole administrators, and assured the monks' right to the free election of their abbot in accordance with the Rule of St. Benedict.[23] This document, often called the Hirsau Formulary, was held up as normative within Hirsau's wider reform network. Not long after, William requested a copy of the customs of Cluny from Ulrich of Zell, an old friend from their shared time as students at the monastery of St. Emmeram. Ulrich had been a monk at Cluny since 1061, and the customs that he sent to Hirsau, along with his prefatory letter (*epistola nuncapatoria*), would provide considerable inspiration for the *Constitutiones Hirsaugienses* (Constitutions of Hirsau), which William would compile in the 1080s.[24] Customaries prior to this period had served mainly as inspirational sources, but the Hirsau monks were among the first to impose a written customary on the communities in their widening circle of monasteries.[25] Indeed, the survival of numerous manuscripts containing the *Constitutiones*, many copied at Hirsau itself, suggests strongly that this customary was a primary instrument of reform, and one that was intended to be normative.[26] Armed with manuscripts containing these texts, the monks spread their form of monasticism across the region as well as to places as far away as Admont (Austria) and Moggio (northern Italy), both intervening in previously established monastic houses and founding new ones.[27] By

---

23 H. E. J Cowdrey, *Pope Gregory VII, 1073–1085* (Oxford: Clarendon Press, 1998), 255–256. For the text of the diploma, see MGH DD H.IV, 6: 359–362; on lingering questions about the authenticity of this text, see Schreiner, "Hirsau und der Hirsauer Reform," 161.

24 Isabelle Cochelin, "Customaries as Inspirational Sources," in *Consuetudines et Regulae: Sources for Monastic Life in the Middle Ages and the Early Modern Period*, ed. Carolyn Marino Malone and Clark Maines, Disciplina Monastica 10 (Turnhout: Brepols Publishers, 2014), 41. For an edition of the Constitutions of Hirsau, see CCM 15, ed. Candida Elvert and Pius Engelbert.

25 Cochelin, "Customaries as Inspirational Sources," 35; Beach, *Trauma of Monastic Reform*, 24–25.

26 Beach, *Trauma of Monastic Reform*, 14–15, 46–48.

27 This account of the history of Hirsau and the reforming work of William is based on Klaus Schreiner, *Gemeinsam Leben: Spiritualität, Lebens- und Verfassungsformen klösterlicher Gemeinschaften in Kirche und Gesellschaft des Mittelalters*, ed. Mirko

INTRODUCTION

the time the movement lost its momentum around the middle of the twelfth century, the total number of communities with connections to Hirsau was well over 100.[28] Beginning in 1086 under Abbot Theodoric, and continuing to a lesser extent under Abbot Conrad, Petershausen's own influence expanded through a series of initiatives to reform extant communities and to found new ones. Some of these endeavors, as the CP shows, were more successful than others.[29]

The reformers called for the strict observance of the Rule of St. Benedict, with liturgical, communal, and individual life further governed by the regulations set forth in the written customs of Hirsau. The religious life, properly lived according to the Hirsau reformers, required – at least as an ideal – a radical retreat from the secular world into a life oriented toward the love of God and one's fellow monks in accordance with the Rule of St Benedict.[30] William's *Constitutiones* did, as some critics have noted, regulate nearly all aspects of daily life – from the reception and training of novices, to the details of the daily monastic liturgy, to the specifics of funerals and the office for the dead, and just about everything in between (including rules for proper hygiene).[31] It is important to note, however, that in some places the arriving reformers were quite tolerant of the persistence of some local custom.[32]

The reforming agenda associated with Hirsau indeed aligned quite neatly with contemporary Church politics. While there had been calls for reform from clerical circles since the Carolingian era, that rhetoric

---

Breitenstein and Gert Melville (Berlin and Münster: LIT Verlag, 2013). Earlier studies of Hirsau include Hermann Jakobs, *Die Hirsauer. Ihre Ausbreitung und Rechtsstellung im Zeitalter des Investiturstreites*, Kölner historische Abhandlungen 4 (Cologne and Graz: Böhlau Verlag, 1961).

28 A definitive list of Hirsau-affiliated monasteries remains a *desideratum*. Jakobs, *Die Hirsauer* provides a starting point, but a critical evaluation of the sources is required before any reliable count is possible; for the perils of identifying "reform filiations" along the model of Kassius Hallinger's Gorze-Kluny, using Petershausen as an example of a "mother house," see Beach, *Trauma of Monastic Reform*, 93–115.

29 These expansions, with all of their problems, failings, and reversals, are detailed in CP 3.24–3.27 (Andelsbuch/Mehrerau), CP 3.27, 4.20, and 4.40 (Wagenhausen), CP 3.33 and 3.37 (Kastl), CP 3.38 and 3.40 (Neresheim), and 4.40–4.41 (Fischingen).

30 Schreiner, "Hirsau und der Hirsauer Reform," 164–165.

31 Beach, *Trauma of Monastic Reform*, 25.

32 On this tolerance and its potential repercussions for local liturgical practice, see Beach, *Trauma of Monastic Reform*, 26.

sharpened and intensified in the eleventh century.[33] As the so-called Gregorian reformers insisted on a clear distinction between the lay and ecclesiastical spheres, the Hirsau reformers sought freedom from lay interference in the operation of monasteries. In both contexts, the ritual of investiture, in which a priest, bishop, or abbot was bestowed with the ring and staff that symbolized his office, became a flashpoint.[34] The ritual act of conferring the ring and staff was freighted from both sides, for as Maureen Miller puts it, "everyone recognized that power over ecclesiastical appointments meant power over the church."[35] The conflict between lay nobles, who were determined to establish or maintain control over the churches and monasteries in their territories, and the advocates of reform, who were determined to free the Church from them, crystalized around the symbolic process of investiture, and conflict and even violence ensued. Further, the drive of eleventh-century Church reformers to sharpen the distinction between the clerical and lay spheres, rooted in concerns about the pollution of the Church through clerical sexuality and simony, was mirrored in the calls of the Hirsau reformers for full separation from the secular world, as seen in attempts at enforcing strict claustration for both sexes. The Petershausen chronicler contrasted the spiritual safety of the "port" of Hirsau monastic life with the "shipwreck" of the broader (unreformed) church at the time.[36]

The Hirsau reformers also responded to new waves of lay piety, sometimes expressed in lay interest in retreat, at least partial, from the world. William made space at Hirsau for a new kind of religious man – the

---

33 Maureen C. Miller, "Reform, Clerical Culture, and Politics," in *The Oxford Handbook of Medieval Christianity* (Oxford: Oxford University Press, 2014); on monastic reform in south Germany in the eleventh century, see the useful overview in T. J. H. McCarthy, *Music, Scholasticism and Reform: Salian Germany, 1024–1125* (Manchester: Manchester University Press, 2009), 11–42; on monastic reform more broadly, see Steven Vanderputten, "Monastic Reform in the Early Tenth to Twelfth Century," in *The Cambridge History of Medieval Monasticism in the Latin West*, ed. Alison I. Beach and Isabelle Cochelin, 599–617 (Cambridge: Cambridge University Press, 2020).

34 The classic work on the investiture crisis in English remains Uta-Renate Blumenthal, *The Investiture Controversy: Church and Monarchy from the Ninth to the Twelfth Century* (Philadelphia: University of Pennsylvania Press, 1988). For an introduction geared toward students, see Maureen C. Miller, *Power and the Holy in the Age of the Investiture Conflict: A Brief History with Documents* (Boston: Bedford/St. Martin's, 2005).

35 Miller, *Power and the Holy in the Age of the Investiture Conflict*, 16.

36 CP 2.28 and 2.48.

INTRODUCTION

bearded brother (*frater barbatus*). These were adult converts (sometimes called *conversi* in contemporary sources), drawn primarily from the nobility, whom Karl Leyser considered to be "Hirsau's most startling innovation."[37] The bearded brothers lived in parallel with the choir monks, participating in some aspects of the liturgy while focusing on the manual labor that was needed to buffer the monks from the world outside the monastery. According to Bernold of St. Blasien, the more noble these men had been in the world, "the more they desired to be employed in the more contemptible offices." "Those who were formerly counts or margraves in the world," he continued, "now considered it the greatest delight to serve the brethren in the kitchen or the mill or to graze their pigs in the field."[38] That the CP includes accounts of two violent attacks on the monks by the monastery's bearded brothers suggests, however, that these men were not as content with their menial lot as Bernold claimed.[39] These men could also take charge of the less lowly business of running the monastic community, including managing its more worldly affairs, playing a sort of hinge role between monastery and the world beyond.

Hirsau spirituality was also notable for its strikingly positive assessment of female spiritual potential, influenced by the thinking of contemporary theologians and biblical exegetes such as Rupert of Deutz (d. 1129) and Gerhoch of Reichersberg (d. 1169). Rupert went so far as to argue that, while women differed from men in physical sex, they were equal spiritually. "For the substance of woman differs in no way from the substance of man except for sex," he argued, "since she is not less rational, nor is she less at liberty to aspire to similitude with the Creator, as was already stated above where scripture, speaking of this creation, says: *Male*, it says, *and female he created them*."[40] The

---

[37] Karl Leyser, "The German Aristocracy from the Ninth to the Early Twelfth Century. A Historical and Cultural Sketch," *Past & Present* 41 (1968): 45.

[38] MGH SS 5: 439; CBSB, 272. There were also unfree servants at Petershausen and other contemporary monastic communities, but there is no evidence for the interaction between these and the noble bearded brothers who engaged in menial manual labor within the community, like the bearded brother Lanzalin, who worked as assistant to the gardener (CP A.15). More research is needed into this underexplored social space within Hirsau-affiliated monasteries.

[39] CP 4.11 and 5.7.

[40] Rupert of Deutz, Commentary on Genesis 2: 1603–1609. CC:CM 21: 226; trans. Giles Constable, *The Reformation of the Twelfth Century* (Cambridge: Cambridge University Press, 1996), 66.

CP's strong defense of dual-sex monasticism, rooted in the presence of women among the disciples in the Gospels, is often cited in secondary literature as an example of this sort of positive attitude toward the spiritual potential of women.[41]

Many monasteries associated with Hirsau housed women alone, while others, like Petershausen, combined men and women, quartered separately, under a single abbot. Some communities, including Zwiefalten and Admont, also organized sub-communities of lay sisters (*conversae*), although there is no clear evidence for their presence at Petershausen. Women of the high nobility could certainly also enhance the social prestige and economic stability of a monastic community. While Petershausen's chronicler claimed no such bragging rights, Ortlieb of Zwiefalten proudly noted that his community was home to a multitude of highly noble women – women who "shone more brightly than the stars according to worldly nobility, but even more brightly and dazzlingly according to religion."[42] Such high-status women continued to work their connections and marshal family wealth on behalf of their communities, so that while the logistics of preventing contact between the sexes in double monasteries were complex and often fraught, many houses went out of their way to attract high-status women.

Another key characteristic of Hirsau-oriented monasticism was the intensification of the liturgy, a set of rituals for which the details, as noted above, had been worked out at Hirsau itself and transmitted in manuscripts in the hands of the arriving reformers. At Petershausen, this increased emphasis on liturgy was also visible in the addition of chapels and in the extension of spaces of liturgy to accommodate more singers and longer processions.[43] The Petershausen chronicler identifies sixteen new liturgical books acquired for the monastery during the abbacy of Theodoric, the first reformer from Hirsau.[44] When monks were sent from Petershausen to populate the newly founded community of Fischingen, they brought with them at least eight service books, probably copied at Petershausen following models with origins

---

41 cf. CP P.9.
42 COZ, 88.
43 For such expansions in the wake of the reform, during the abbacy of the Theodoric, see CP 1.21, 3.12, 3.13.
44 CP 3.49.

INTRODUCTION

at Hirsau itself.[45] The production of books, wherever it was carried out, required not only work space and materials, but also highly trained women and men to do the copying.

The Hirsau reform, like its initiator William, was indeed profoundly bookish, a characteristic also clearly reflected in the remains of book collections from a number of affiliated communities.[46] Contemporary library lists and a number of extraordinary book collections that survive attest to communities in which the study of the Bible was a center-point of spiritual life. The most striking example is the monastery of Admont, a community that came into Hirsau's orbit in 1115, from which more than 200 twelfth-century books, many of which were geared toward biblical interpretation, have survived.[47] The twelfth-century list of Zwiefalten's collections suggests a similar scope and focus on biblical study.[48] A book inventory from mid-twelfth-century Lippoldsberg (Lower Saxony), originally colonized by women from Schaffhausen (an influential node in the expanding Hirsau network located close to Lake Constance in modern Switzerland) shows that the women there owned a remarkable variety of texts, many of which would have been used for the study and exegesis of the Bible.[49] Surviving letters that the nuns of Admont exchanged with regional experts in biblical exegesis, including Gerhoch of Reichersberg, attest to the active use of such books; the women of Admont read, studied, copied, and exchanged manuscripts, reaching out for guidance beyond the community when they had unanswered questions. In the mid-twelfth century, Abbot Irimbert (r. 1137–1165) added books containing his own biblical sermon-commentaries on several Old Testament books

---

45 On books as conduits of the Hirsau reform, see Beach, *Trauma of Monastic Reform*, 45–48.

46 Increased book production, while characteristic of Hirsau communities in the wake of reform, was not unique to this particular reforming context. See Raymund Kottje, "Klosterbibliotheken und monastische Kultur in der zweiten Hälfte des 11. Jahrhunderts," *Zeitschrift für Kirchengeschichte* 80 (1969): 145–162.

47 Alison I. Beach, *Women as Scribes: Book Production and Monastic Reform in Twelfth-Century Bavaria* (Cambridge: Cambridge University Press, 2004).

48 Constant Mews, "Monastic Educational Culture Revisited: The Witness of Zwiefalten and the Hirsau Reform," in *Medieval Monastic Education*, ed. George Ferzoco and Carolyn Muessig (London and New York: Leicester University Press, 2000), 182–197.

49 Julie Hotchin, "Women's Reading and Monastic Reform in Twelfth-Century Germany: The Library of the Nuns of Lippoldsberg," in *Manuscripts and Monastic Culture: Reform and Renewal in Twelfth-Century Germany*, ed. Alison I. Beach (Turnhout: Brepols Publishers, 2007), 153.

to Admont's library, relying on the women of the community to serve as his copyists and editors.[50] The exceptional visibility of Admont's female scribes, as well as of those from Wessobrunn and Zwiefalten, reflects both the importance of literacy – and particularly the ability to copy books – within reformed communities and the fact that women could be fully engaged in that literate culture, both as consumers (as devotional readers and hearers) and as producers (as scribes and exegetes in their own right).[51]

The social landscape of medieval Swabia

The Chronicle also provides a fascinating window on the social structure of this region of Germany in the high Middle Ages, from the unfree inhabitants of lands owned by the monastery to the women and men of the highest nobility. The chronicler's imaginative genealogy places its founder Gebhard II in the illustrious line of Charlemagne, claiming that it was the great emperor himself who had granted Gebhard's ancestors lands in Alemania, including, staking an ancient claim to the contemporary family seat in Bregenz.[52] The attention that he pays to the most powerful comital family in the region – including several vivid accounts of the doings of Countess Bertha of Bregenz – adds further weight to the argument that this family held personal interest for him.[53] The folios of the CP are also populated by lesser men – the up-and-coming nobles of twelfth-century Swabia. We encounter less powerful counts maneuvering for control of monasteries, moving from the now-prohibited role of lay proprietors into their newly negotiated role as advocates.[54]

---

50 Shannon M. T. Li, "Irimbert of Admont and His Scriptural Commentaries: Exegeting Salvation History in the Twelfth Century" (PhD Dissertation, Ohio State University, 2017).

51 On Zwiefalten's female scribe Mathilda of Neuffen, see Alison I. Beach, "'Mathild de Niphin' and the Female Scribes of Twelfth-Century Zwiefalten," in *Nuns' Literacies in Medieval Europe: The Hull Dialogue*, ed. Veronica M. O'Mara, Patricia Stoop, and Virginia Blanton, 33–50 (Turnhout: Brepols Publishers, 2013).

52 Josef Zösmair, "Geschichte Rudolfs des letzten der alten Grafen von Bregenz (1097–1160)," *Schriften des Vereins für Geschichte des Bodensees und seiner Umgebung* 44 (1915): 25.

53 On Bertha of Bregenz, see CP 3.26 and 4.11. Her involvement also was notably omitted from CP 5.7.

54 On monastic advocates, see Jonathan Lyon, "Noble Lineages, Hausklöster and Monastic Advocacy in the Twelfth Century," *Mitteilungen des Instituts für Österreichische Geschichtsforschung* 123 (2015): 1–29.

INTRODUCTION

While the CP has long attracted considerable attention among German-speaking scholars for this inventive genealogy, those below the ranks of comital families have gone largely unnoticed. Here we meet the ministerials, men of the lower nobility, a knightly class of mostly unfree origins. Although technically servile, ministerials at this time held an important place as the upper knightly class. In a complex evolution spanning particularly the tenth through the thirteenth centuries, ministerials in southern Germany largely displaced the lower nobility before being subsumed in turn into the increasingly privileged class of knights, which was also of mostly servile origin.[55]

The majority of the lay population of Swabia at this time was, of course, neither noble nor knightly. The majority were free commoners on the one hand and unfree individuals of various conditions on the other.[56] Among the free commoners who continued to comprise the majority of the population in most of southern Germany, we find the usual division between a majority of rural peasants and a minority of urban burghers engaged in various occupations. It is the latter that the CP most often mentions, which is not surprising given Petershausen's close proximity to Constance. As for the servile population, the social reality in southern Germany had become quite complex by the twelfth century, featuring a number of distinct gradations of servitude. Many monastic *familiae* included variously among their ranks ministerials,

55 On ministerials, see John B. Freed, *Noble Bondsmen: Ministerial Marriages in the Archdiocese of Salzburg, 1100–1343* (Ithaca, NY: Cornell University Press, 1995), esp. 2–4, 50–54.

56 The dimensions of medieval unfreedoms is a matter of active and lively discussion among historians of medieval slavery and has been the subject of a number of recent conferences, including thematic threads at the Twenty-Third International Medieval Congress (Leeds, UK, 2016) and the Ninety-Third Annual Meeting of the Medieval Academy of America (Atlanta, GA, 2018), as well as a dedicated conference hosted by Binghamton University entitled "Medieval Unfreedoms: Slavery, Servitude, and Trafficking in Humans before the Trans-Atlantic Slave Trade" (Binghamton, NY, 2018). The model of Swabian society presented in this introduction is derived principally from an examination of contemporary *libri traditionum* in neighboring Bavaria, with which the Chronicle of Petershausen seems to accord. See Samuel S. Sutherland, "Mancipia Dei: Slavery, Servitude, and the Church in Bavaria, 975–1225" (PhD Dissertation, Ohio State University, 2017). For other recent and forthcoming contributions to the discussion of medieval slavery and unfreedom, see Alice Rio, *Slavery After Rome, 500–1100* (Oxford: Oxford University Press, 2017); Reuven Amitai and Christoph Cluse, eds., *Slavery and the Slave Trade in the Eastern Mediterranean (c. 1000–1500 ce)* (Turnhout: Brepols, 2018); and Thomas J. Macmaster, ed., *A Cultural History of Slavery and Human Trafficking in the Pre-Modern Era (500–1450)*, (London: Bloomsbury Academic, forthcoming).

other privileged *servi* not of ministerial rank, *censuales, coloni*, serfs, and some slaves. Some churches and monasteries in Swabia and Bavaria accumulated large networks of *censuales* through donations by lay commoners and nobles of serfs or slaves who were elevated into this improved status in the process, supplemented by periodic self-donations of formerly free members of society. These *censuales*, or tributary freedmen as they appear in the CP, were contrasted in monastic cartularies both with free and with servile conditions, existing somewhere in between. They held a sort of contingent freedom, permitted to live and work where and how they pleased provided that they and all their posterity made annual, individual payments to the church or monastery to which they belonged. If any should fail to pay, as happened at least occasionally, they would default into "daily servitude" or slavery.[57]

Coloni, who lived on lands owned by their lords with limited obligations of periodic dues in kind, had formerly possessed a similar kind of ambiguous freedom, but came by the twelfth century to be largely assimilated with the growing ranks of *servi manentes*, or serfs. These serfs of a more generic variety existed in a newer and less tightly defined class, similarly tied to the land of their lords on individual tenancies. While classed as unfree laborers, the labor obligations and regular dues of serfs were defined and limited by custom. Slaves, unlike serfs, were considered chattel property to be bought, sold, traded, or donated independently of land or even family and could be put to work in virtually any capacity without limitation. In the cartularies of neighboring Bavaria, the terms *servus cottidianus* or *servus praebendarius* were often (although not consistently) used to distinguish these slaves from serfs, who were still for the most part called by the old Latin terms for slaves that had since become quite flexible: *servus, famulus, ancilla*, or *mancipium*.[58]

Each of these groups – ministerials, *censuales, coloni*, serfs, and slaves – feature in the CP at various points. A number of the charters in the

---

57 On *censuales*, see Stefan Esders, *Die Formierung der Zensualität: Zur kirchlichen Transformation des spätrömischen Patronatswesens im früheren Mittelalter* (Sigmaringen: Jan Thorbecke Verlag, 2010); Knut Schulz, "Zum Problem zur Zensualität im Hochmittelalter," in *Beiträge zur Wirtschats- und Sozialgeschichte des Mittelalters. Festschrift für Herbert Helbig zum 65. Geburtstag*, ed. Knut Schulz (Cologne: Böhlau Verlag, 1976), 86–127; Philippe Dollinger, *L'évolution des classes rurales en Bavière, depuis la fin de l'époque carolingienne jusqu'au milieu du XIIIe siècle*. (Paris: Belles Lettres, 1949). As of yet the class of *censuales* in southern Germany has received little attention in English literature.

58 Sutherland, "Mancipia Dei."

INTRODUCTION

Chronicle mention unfree laborers, probably serfs, transferred along with their land. Other narrative accounts of donations and endowments are more varied. In the early years of the monastery, Bishop Gebhard II donated variously ministerials, knights, and serfs tied to specific lands, as well as servants to dwell in the monastery whose condition maps comfortably onto that of the *servi cottidiani* described in Bavarian cartularies, and others would donate additional individuals of various conditions in the years to come.[59] Domestic servants appear sporadically and in passing throughout the CP as the chronicler, while narrating some anecdote, deigns to mention the existence of the usually invisible servants living and working at the monastery or in the household of the bishop.[60] These offhand comments and unusually colorful anecdotes interspersed throughout the CP that mention these women and men are particularly valuable for the study of monastic servants, slaves, and other *familiares*, offering a lens into the social condition of servile classes quite different from and fruitfully complementary to the rich cartulary evidence of neighboring Bavaria.

The manuscript and its makers: University of Heidelberg, *Codex Salemitani* IX 42a

The CP survives in a single copy, preserved within a manuscript now owned by the University of Heidelberg. The medieval books from Petershausen that survived until its dissolution under Napoleon in 1803 were moved briefly to the nearby Cistercian monastery of Salem. When Salem was secularized in its turn later that year, the 442 manuscripts of the combined collection fell to the Margraviate of Baden (elevated in that same year to an Electorate). In 1827, Grand Duke Louis I of Baden (1763–1830) sold the entire collection to the University of Heidelberg.[61]

The text of the CP is one of two codicologically and paleographically distinct components that comprise *Codex Salemitani* IX 42a, both produced at Petershausen during the twelfth century.[62] The first codicological

---

59 CP 1.11, 1.32, 1.34, 1.35, 3.26, 4.5; *Life of Gebhard* 1.19, 1.20

60 See, for example, CP 2.5, 2.20, 3.21, 4.22.

61 Wilfried Werner, *Die mittelalterlichen nichtliturgischen Handschriften des Zisterzienserklosters Salem* (Wiesbaden: Reichert Verlag, 2000), LVII.

62 For a full description of the manuscript and its contents, see Beach, *Trauma of Monastic Reform*, 254–259.

unit, quires 1–4 (ff. 1r–34v), was copied by a single scribe into uniform gatherings of four bifolia. All of these texts, with the exception of a florilegium on ff. 20r–34v, are connected to Petershausen's patron saints, Gebhard II and Gregory the Great. That the various texts in this section of the manuscript flow together across the gatherings suggests that they were originally conceived and produced as a single unit that was likely used for performing the office on the feast days of these two figures so central to the community.

The Chronicle itself comprises the second codicological unit, consisting of nine quires (5–13) that are mainly the work of the chronicler himself.[63] The underlying physical structure of this section of the manuscript offers a wealth of evidence for the process of compiling the text. The chronicler copied the text on folios 35r–83v into uniform gatherings of four bifolia. In this section of the text, completed in 1136, he looks back on the long history of the monastery, first imagining the deep family history of Petershausen's founder and culminating with a vivid account of the translation of his relics and his canonization in 1134. Throughout the following twenty-three years (1136–1159), he continued to add material, appending new parchment as needed to make space for additional anecdotes and accounts of current events within the monastery. Both the hiatus in adding new material and the wear evident on the last folio of quire 8 correspond with the catastrophic fire that destroyed much of the monastery in 1159. Quire 8 ends with the chronicler's account of the fire, and much of the text has been rubbed away, suggesting its last folio (90v) was exposed to the difficult living and working conditions experienced in the wake of the fire. It would not be until c. 1164 that a new voice and hand would continue the work, followed by minor continuators, down to the final twelfth-century entry in 1179.

That two early modern visitors to Petershausen – the German scholar Hermann von der Hardt (1660–1746) and theologian, historian, and scholar of music and liturgy Martin Gerbert (1720–1793), Abbot of St. Blasien in the Black Forest – were shown the book with great ceremony during their visits to the monastery suggests the community's continued reverence for the CP, even well into the early modern period.[64]

---

63 For a full account of differing opinions regarding the identification of the Chronicle as the autograph of its author-compiler, see Beach, *Trauma of Monastic Reform*, 14–16.

64 The university is now in the process of digitizing its manuscript collections. *Codex Salemitani* IX 42a: https://doi.org/10.11588/diglit.605; *Codex Salemitani* IX 9 (a fifteenth-century manuscript containing the earliest extant version of the

INTRODUCTION

About this translation

This translation relies on the Latin editions of the Chronicle published by Otto Abel and Ludwig Weiland[65] and Otto Feger.[66] With two reliable modern printings of the Latin, it seemed to us unnecessary to retranscribe the text from the manuscript. In cases in which the reading in these editions was ambiguous or appeared questionable, we turned for clarification or correction to the original manuscript. While the chronicler was clearly a competent writer of Latin, he was no great stylist; we have tried to strike a balance between respecting his distinctive authorial voice, along with several of his less-appealing habits (such as the frequent repetition of particular phrases), and producing a readable and enjoyable translation. We have kept quite close to the text, avoiding aggressive colloquializing, while again striving for readability. One major change that we have made is to abandon the conventional numbering of the various books in order to reflect more clearly the chronicler's own intentions and authorial process. To minimize confusion, we have included the book and chapter numbers in Abel and Weiland (1868) and Feger (1956) in parentheses following our revised numbers. There is also a concordance of book and chapter numbers in Appendix 2.

Contemporary marginal and interlinear additions of more than three words are given in square brackets. Passages that have been erased, struck out, or otherwise damaged are given in curly brackets. Where possible, we have anglicized proper names for ease of reading following the *Dictionary of Medieval Names from European Sources*.[67] The original forms of names that have been anglicized are given in parentheses in the index. It should be noted that some personal names are spelled in two or three different ways in the original text as the chronicler himself was not consistent in his transliteration of Germanic names. Our decision to index the standardized form followed by the original, including all variants that appear in the text, seemed the best way to reduce confusion on the part of the reader while also preserving some sense of the variation. For the names of places, we have generally used the

---

twelfth-century *Life of St. Gebhard*): https://doi.org/10.11588/diglit.7328 (Date of last access: 22 December 2019).

65 Abel and Weiland (1868).
66 Feger (1956).
67 http://dmnes.org (Date of last access: 22 December 2019).

forms and identifications given in Feger (1956). Our translations of the chronicler's passages from the Bible are taken from the Douay-Rheims translation of the Vulgate, with occasional interventions to modernize the language. We have retained the Latin for words that lack satisfactory English translations (e.g., *pagus, custos*); these are given in italics.

Our annotations to the text are geared toward English readers. Our intention has been to offer vital context for readers of the CP rather than to provide exhaustive bibliography on particular topics or events. We have made our best effort to identify known figures, and their life or regnal dates are given in parentheses at their first appearance in the text. If no dates are provided, they are unknown. Here again, we relied in many cases on the footnotes in Feger (1956), making updates and corrections where needed. Historical background for certain events and concepts is also provided, as well as commentary on passages that may be confusing or misleading. We have tried, when possible, to provide suggestions for further reading in English in the footnotes, but any student or scholar with a serious interest in the political, social, or religious landscapes of medieval Swabia will need to engage the extensive literature in German.

This translation began modestly, in an informal medieval Latin reading group at the Ohio State University in the spring of 2013. Over good Belgian ale (particular thanks here to Kyle Shimoda), the group took a first shot at translating the Preface, and although we have since thoroughly revised the fruits of that initial effort, we are grateful for the impetus to prepare a formal translation of the entire text. We have also benefited from the generous advice and warm encouragement of many colleagues. Chuck Atkinson, Patrick Geary, Drew Jones, Lori Kruckenberg, and Andreas Odenthal all offered their expert assistance with the translation of the sometimes-baffling language of charters, chirographs, and various things liturgical. We owe particular thanks to Carin Ruff for checking our translation and sparing us from any number of errors (those that remain are, of course, our own), and to Giles Constable, who has been an enthusiastic supporter of the project from the start, insisting that this fascinating and lesser-known twelfth-century chronicle was worthy of a standalone translation into English. Alison's year as a member of the School of Historical Studies at the Institute for Advanced Study in 2013–2014 offered an ideal setting for long and invaluable conversations with Giles about the images of monasticism that were emerging from the text, as well as time

INTRODUCTION

and space to focus without distraction on the translation. Finally, we would be remiss not to thank the chronicler himself, whoever he was, for sharing Petershausen's experiences as a community in the wake of reform. His is a voice that we have come to know well as he has variously fascinated, frustrated, and amused us over the years. We dedicate this translation to him, with the hope that we have done justice to his voice and to the monastic experience that it reveals.

THE CHRONICLE OF PETERSHAUSEN

PROLOGUE

Introduction

The prologue to the CP opens a window on the religious landscape of the Middle Ages, offering a vital witness to the spiritual values espoused by Hirsau-oriented monks in the early decades of the twelfth century. This opening book of the Chronicle reads as a kind of manifesto – a forceful assertion of the apostolic foundations of traditional cenobitic monasticism in the Hirsau mode, and may indeed have been written originally as a standalone treatise on religious life. The monks' habit, tonsure, retreat from the world, strict enclosure, and the election of the abbot by the community were all, as the chronicler argues, grounded in scripture. The chronicler's tone here is noticeably defensive as he decries those who would criticize cenobitic monasticism – and thus religious life at Petershausen – by denying or ignoring its apostolic authority.

This apologetic posture is not at all surprising for a Benedictine monk writing in the early decades of the twelfth century. While the Rule of St. Benedict had dominated the monastic landscape of the Latin West since the Carolingian era, traditional monks now found themselves in the midst of a new evangelical turn. Fresh interpretations of the life of the apostles – the *vita apostolica* – had begun to pose a serious challenge to the spiritual dominance of traditional monasticism. Monks and nuns who followed the Rule of St. Benedict had long held, without much contradiction, that they imitated the apostles in their communal living, retreat from the world, and rejection of private property. But this new apostolicity challenged the received interpretation of the life of the apostles, in part through its insistence that preaching out and about in the world was one of the key activities of the true apostolic life.[1] Enthusiasm for

---

1 For more on this movement, see the classic essays by Marie-Dominique Chenu, "Monks, Canons, and Laymen in Search of the Apostolic Life," and "The Evangelical Awakening," in *Nature, Man, and Society in the Latin West*, trans. Jerome Taylor and Lester K. Little (Chicago: University of Chicago Press, 1968), 202–38 and 239–269. On the discord that the movement created, see Ernest W. McDonnell, "The 'Vita Apostolica': Diversity or Dissent," *Church History* 24 (1955): 15–31. The classic survey of the institutional and spiritual transformations of twelfth-century religious life is Giles Constable, *The Reformation of the Twelfth Century* (Cambridge: Cambridge University Press, 1996).

this new approach to the *vita apostolica* led to the proliferation of religious movements, and treatises calling for Church and monastic reform increasingly took up this newly focused model of the primitive church.[2] New groups of regular canons, like the Premonstratensians, whose founder dreamed of a new workforce of preachers, had begun to shift the balance from retreat from, to embrace of, the world. Conversion turned outward.

All of this sparked debate and conflict about precedent and authority, and old and new institutions alike searched for biblical models to imbue their orders and ways of life with a sense of dignity and authority. While the most common association was with the apostles, parallels were also drawn with Christ and Old Testament priests and prophets. And these associations were more than just inspirations – religious groups saw themselves as actually embodying these models.[3] This increasing competition among groups prompted urgent attempts to justify, organize, define, and classify – just as seen here in the prologue to the CP. The landscape that the chronicler paints for us is populated not only by monks, but also by bearded lay brothers, religious women, canons, bishops, rural and village priests, virgins, hermits, recluses, pilgrims, and beggars, with each group categorized in its turn by a *modus vivendi* grounded in scripture. He argues that despite the differences among these various callings (and certain present-day abuses), they together comprise a Church united in faith and dignified by the same apostolic authority.[4]

The focus and style of the prologue are similar to several other contemporary treatises on the religious life, notably the anonymous *Libellus de diversis ordinibus et professionibus qui sunt in aecclesia* and the *Tractatus de professionibus monachorum*, which was written by a monk of Bec.[5]

---

2 For example, see Peter Damian, *Contra clericos regulares proprietaries* (PL 145), Rupert of Deutz, *De vita vera apostolica* (PL 170), and Bernard of Clairvaux, *De moribus et officio episcoporum*, in *Bernard of Clairvaux: On Baptism and the Office of Bishops*, trans. Pauline Matarasso (Kalamazoo, MI: Cistercian Publications, 2004), 37–82.

3 On the use of biblical models in group formation, see Caroline Walker Bynum, "Did the Twelfth Century Discover the Individual?" in *Jesus as Mother: Studies in the Spirituality of the High Middle Ages* (Berkeley: University of California Press, 1982), 82–109.

4 CP P.24.

5 Giles Constable and Bernard Smith, eds., *Libellus de diversis ordinibus et professionibus qui sunt in aecclesia* (Oxford: Clarendon Press, 1972); Giles Constable, trans., *Three Treatises from Bec on the Nature of Monastic Life* (Toronto: University of Toronto Press, 2008), 29–105.

The author of the *Libellus*, who identifies himself as a canon, systematically treats different religious orders, starting first with hermits, then monks near laymen, monks far from laymen, secular monks, canons far from laymen, canons near laymen, and finally secular canons among laymen. Each group is associated with an Old or New Testament model, for the latter more often Christ than the apostles. Just like the Petershausen chronicler, the author of the *Libellus* stresses the unity amid all of this diversity, arguing that each group contributes in its own way to one Church. Although the author of the *Tractatus* focuses more narrowly on the variety within the monastic life itself, he too ascribes apostolic authority to the monastic way of life and considers the apostles to be the first monks. Although there is no way to know if the CP had access to these or similar works, their common approach to classification and justification through models drawn from the Bible certainly helps to place the CP and its author within the broader context of twelfth-century institutional and spiritual concerns.

HERE BEGINS THE PROLOGUE TO THE FOLLOWING BOOK

P.1. THAT EVERY INSTITUTION OF MONKS IS TAKEN FROM THE ACTS OF THE APOSTLES. Before writing the story of the monastery of blessed Pope Gregory, which is called the House of Peter, I will first note with what great dignity of authority the institution of monasticism shines forth. For some doubt or are altogether unaware of the origins of this sacrosanct form of religious life, and many therefore disparage it as though it were invented by ignorant men and supported by no authority. I will show absolutely clearly to those who misunderstand to such a degree, namely those who think that this sacred institution lacks authority, that these things had their beginning in the very founders of the Church – the holy apostles. For every institution of cenobitic life, if sought diligently, is unmistakably found in the Acts of the Apostles.

P.2. THAT THE DEPORTMENT OF MONKS IS TAKEN FROM THE DEPORTMENT OF THE CHERUBIM. For this holy way of life is raised up by six wings, just as the cherubim are raised from earth to heaven. These wings are contempt of the world, obedience, separation from worldly tumult, silence, meditation on divine reading, and diligent prayer. And this is the fullness of knowledge, which without a doubt raises on high, as though on wings, anyone filled with it by divine gifts.

P.3. The monks' habit itself clearly represents these six wings, since it was written of the cherubim: *the one had six wings, and the other had six wings:* two they extended over their heads, *with two they flew,* and with two they covered their bodies [Isa. 6:2]. So also is the monks' garment extended over the head from both sides: this is the cowl. The wide sleeves extend over the arms like the wings with which the cherubim fly, and they conceal the lower body like the wings that hide the bodies of the cherubim. So much for the angelic habit of monks.[6] Since I said above that these six wings are contempt of the world, obedience, a more secluded life, silence, meditation on divine reading, and diligent prayer, and that all of these things are taken from the life of the apostles, let me now explain how all of these things may be found in their acts.

P.4. ON CONTEMPT OF THE WORLD. Indeed, let the Apostle Peter say how they left the world behind: *Behold, we have left all things*; and how they obeyed Christ: *and have followed thee* [Matt. 19:27].

P.5. ON RECLUSION AND THE NAME OF MONKS. Indeed, the evangelist bears witness to the manner in which they separated themselves from the tumult of the world, saying: *Now when it was late that same day, the first of the week, and the doors were shut, where the disciples were gathered together, for fear of the Jews, Jesus came and stood in the midst, and said to them: Peace be with you* [John 20:19].[7] *When,* he says, *it was late* (*late*, that is, when the end of the world was drawing near) the disciples of the Lord were first *gathered together,* because while God had always had his own worshippers from the beginning of time, no one before this

---

6 Employing the image of angelic wings to describe the monastic habit was common, particularly in the twelfth century. See Klaus Schreiner, "Mönchtum zwischen asketischem Anspruch und gesellschaftlicher Wirklichkeit. Spiritualität, Sozialverhalten und Sozialverfassung schwäbischer Reformmönche im Spiegel ihrer Geschichtsschreibung," *Zeitschrift für württembergische Landesgeschichte* 41 (1982): 260–63; Giles Constable, "The Ceremonies and Symbolism of Entering Religious Life and Taking the Monastic Habit, from the Fourth to the Twelfth Century," in *Segni e riti nella chiesa altomedievale occidentale, 11–17 aprile 1985,* ed. Centro italiano di studi sull'alto Medioevo (Spoleto: Presso la sede del Centro, 1987), 818–819.

7 The chronicler sees the account in John 20:19 as an anti-Jewish metaphor indicating the beginnings of monastic enclosure. The Jews here are comparable to vices, from which monks seek separation. Such an analogy was in keeping with other contemporary exegesis. Schreiner, "Mönchtum zwischen asketischem Anspruch und gesellschaftlicher Wirklichkeit," 264–265.

is said to have secluded himself on account of his love of God. Most are said to have led a religious life in the secular world. But at the end of the world, after the Lord Jesus showed his love by dying for us, since we were still sinners, immediately, from the day of the Sabbath, *the doors were shut, where the disciples were gathered together, for fear of the Jews* – that is, on account of their fear of the vices causing tumult in the world. Indeed, they repaid Christ's love for them, for just as he made himself powerless over his own body (to speak in human terms) – for although almighty, he made himself powerless, fastened on a cross with nails for the sake of men – thus men make themselves powerless with respect to their own will by binding themselves together and by allowing neither mind nor body the free will to wander. Nowhere do we read before this that the disciples of Christ had shut themselves up, since they were sons of the bridegroom in joy as long as the bridegroom was with them. The bridegroom was taken away from them and immediately *on that same day* they were shut up as though in prison. Behold, the way of life of those who desire to soldier for God, removed from the strife of the world, was consecrated to God by the apostles as though first fruits. The name of monks originated here, because the Greek work "monk" means solitary in Latin. *I am alone*, says the Psalmist, *until I pass* [Ps. 140.10]. But how could David say that he was alone, since he was governing the Israelite kingdom? Because while he passed his life among the multitudes, occupied with their worldly business, he nevertheless always meditated internally on heavenly things. This is why he was *alone* – because he meditated alone among many people; thus the Apostle, out among the people, affirms: *Our way of life is in heaven* [Philem. 3.20]. Hence cenobites too, although they always live in community, are nevertheless without a doubt in solitude. How is it that they are gathered together in the same place and not segregated from one another, but are not permitted to speak with one another? They are both together and alone, because there is such silence and such peace and concord among the many living together that it is as though one man were living alone.

P.6. ON THE CLOISTER. Indeed, the *doors were closed on account of fear of the Jews*. For aside from the exterior gates (which are always kept closed in monasteries), so that no one tries to enter even when the gates are open, the interior *doors* are strengthened by such a great lock that one could seldom open them even if one wanted to do so. Does it not seem to you that the *doors* are completely *closed* when the mouth is kept from speaking, the ears from vain hearing, the hands from bad works, and the feet from aimless wandering? Whether he likes it or not, the monk will be bound to such an enclosure. *The doors*, he said, *were closed.* This is the origin of the word cloister, which, as I said, must always remain completely closed, inside and outside, without fail.

P.7. WHY MONKS ARE ENCLOSED. As I have said, this reclusion came about *on account of fear of the Jews*. What is this *fear of the Jews* if not the dread of inrushing vices? *Why*, says the Psalmist, *have the Gentiles raged, and the people devised vain things? The kings of the earth stood up, and the princes met together, against the Lord, and against his Christ* [Ps. 2:1–2]. And after this, he adds: *Let us break their bonds asunder; and let us cast away their yoke from us* [Ps. 2:3]. And what are the rages of the *Gentiles* if not the onslaught of countless vices? What are the battle lines of the kings and the assemblies of princes standing against Christ if not the powers and attacks of assailing demons against the health of souls? Their *bonds* are *broken asunder* and their *yokes* are *cast away* when the gates of the heart and body, as I said above, are closed off from vices by the sign of the Holy Spirit and no access is allowed to them so that they might abide in the monastery in the liberty of the glory of the children of God. For when the tongue is restrained so that it keeps silent even about good things and the other senses are similarly guarded so that they might not yield to vices, then truly the *doors are closed* so that enemies are not able to burst in.

P.8. WHAT IS THE FRUIT OF RECLUSION? When the gates are fortified by such enclosure, the Lord himself appears and offers the gifts of peace, as it is written: *Jesus came, the doors being shut, and stood in the midst, and said: Peace be to you* [John 20:26]. Behold he fulfilled by manifest deed what he had promised before the Passion, saying: *where there are two or three gathered together in my name, there I am in the midst of them* [Matt. 18:20]. The Lord himself, ascending into heaven, also gave this instruction to them, saying: *But stay you in the city till you be clothed with power from on high* [Luke 24:49]. Luke therefore testifies how studiously and devoutly they followed this command, saying: *All these were persevering with one mind in prayer with the women, and Mary the mother of Jesus, and with his brethren* [Acts 1:14]. Where, I ask, is there such constant prayer as there is in monasteries, where prayer is meted out nearly night and day in the work of God?

P.9. ON RELIGIOUS WOMEN. It should also be noted here that pious women soldiered for God equally with the holy disciples. And on account of this example, it is not blameworthy, but rather very laudable when religious women are received in the monasteries of the servants of God so that each sex, kept separate from the other, is saved in one place.[8]

P.10. ON THE ELECTION OF A SPIRITUAL FATHER AND THE NAME ABBOT. Also foretold in this happy gathering of the disciples of Christ is the general election of a father. For *Peter, rising in the middle of his brothers, said: Men, brethren* [Acts 1:15–16]: *Wherefore of these men who have companied with us all the time that the Lord Jesus came in and went out among us, Beginning from the baptism of John until the day wherein he was taken up from us, one of these must be made a witness with us of his resurrection* [Acts 1:21–22]. This should be noted in these words of the Prince of the Apostles, as the Apostle Paul also taught: a neophyte, that is, one newly baptized, should not be chosen for the office of teacher, but rather a man tested by long profession and witnessing to the virtues and teachings of Christ in all things. For how can anyone teach others what he himself has not yet begun to learn? And thus he who is ignorant will be ignored, because he who is judged to be ignorant of divine law should not be elevated to the place of teacher. He receives the name of father and ought therefore to offer the bread of doctrine to his sons. For the Apostle says: *For you have not received the spirit of bondage again in fear; but you have received the spirit of adoption of sons, whereby we cry: Abba (Father)* [Rom. 8:15]. As you see, *Abba* means *father*, and for this reason, the man appointed to preside over the monks is called abbot, that is, *father* – because good monks should not be oppressed like slaves under a cruel master, but cared for as dearest *sons* under a gentle *father*.

There! You have from apostolic authority contempt of the world, obedience, the assembly and seclusion of the brothers, as well as the general election of the father and the more secluded life.

P.11. ON MONASTIC OBSERVANCE. Regarding meditation, the constancy of prayer, and the silence of stillness, hear again what Luke reports in the Acts of the Apostles: *And they were,* he says, *persevering in the doctrine of the apostles, and in the communication of the breaking of bread, and in prayers* [Acts 2:42]. And further: *And all they that believed,*

---

8 This is a striking defense of the practice of organizing women and men into shared monastic communities, often called double monasteries. On the origins of such dual-sex communities, see Alison I. Beach and Andra Juganaru, "The Double Monastery as an Historiographical Problem," in *The Cambridge History of Medieval Monasticism in the Latin West*, ed. Alison I. Beach and Isabelle Cochelin, 561–578 (Cambridge: Cambridge University Press, 2020).

were together, and had all things in common. Their possessions and goods they sold, and divided them to all, according as everyone had need. And continuing daily with one accord in the temple, and breaking bread from house to house, they took their meat with gladness and simplicity of heart; Praising God, and having favor with all the people [Acts 2:44–47]. And then he says further on: *And the multitude of believers had but one heart and one soul: neither did any one say that any of the things which he possessed, was his own; but all things were common unto them* [Acts 4:32]. *For neither was there any one needy among them. For as many as were owners of lands or houses, sold them, and brought the price of the things they sold, And laid it down before the feet of the apostles. And distribution was made to every one, according as he had need* [Acts 4:34–35]. And a little bit later: *But of the rest no man dared join himself unto them; but the people magnified them* [Acts 5:13]. Which aspects, then, of every monastic observance do you see lacking in this regulation? For here we hear the Word of God, here the holy community, here the prayer, here the gathering of the brothers and the common life, here the despising and distributing of things according to the need of each, here perseverance in the Divine Office and almsgiving, here the common table and the joy and simplicity of the spirit, here the unceasing praise of God and the action of grace, here the unanimity and harmony of the multitude and the contempt for private property, and absolutely all things that are found in the rules of the fathers and observed in the customs of monasteries. All of these, I say again, are absolutely clearly seen in the Acts of the Apostles.

P.12. ON THE TONSURE OF MONKS AND CLERICS. About the tonsure of the brothers, moreover, Luke says: Priscilla and Aquila had shorn their heads in Cenchræ, for they had taken a vow [Acts 18:18, freely], since all who have taken a vow to serve God, whether at the altar or in the monastery, should shave their head. For our Lord Jesus Christ himself accepted the crown of thorns on his head when he was about to offer himself up as a sacrifice to the Father for us on the altar of the Cross, showing that he bore our sins in his body on the Cross. And scripture says elsewhere: they encircle me with the thorns of your sins.[9]

---

9 *Spinis peccatorum suorum circumdederunt me.* Although this is not a direct scriptural reference, some medieval authors attribute this phrase to the prophet Jeremiah. See, for example, Peter Damian (c. 1007–1072) *Contra Clericos Aulicos, opusculum* 22; the editor in PL 145 (col. 472), cites Lam. 3, although this does not appear to be correct. *Spinis peccatorum suorum circumdederunt me* could, however, be a general paraphrase of the biblical chapter.

Thus he was crowned, not in the substance of his own body, but with a crown of thorns. Because truly each person carries his own burden, we are rightly crowned from the hair of our own head. But that crown was placed upon our Lord Jesus Christ not as an honor, but as an insult, and so we must disfigure ourselves, suffering his reproach. And it should be noted that, just as Christ was crowned before he drew near to the altar of the Cross, so too should anyone who is going to offer his body and blood before the altar, or those who desire to offer themselves as a living sacrifice, first be marked with this same sign.

P.13. AGAIN ON THE TONSURE. Also in another way: just as the top of the head is exposed through tonsure, so ought our mind be stripped of earthy impulses through contemplation, and to appear pure and clean before God. But because it is impossible for man, encircled by this mortal flesh, always to be given over entirely to contemplation, a small circle of hair is worn around the head to show that man is disturbed at least somewhat, however minimally, by worldly thoughts. Secular clerics therefore wear a bigger circle of hair and shave a very small part, because they are still more assiduously devoted to the active than to the contemplative life.

P.14. ON GUESTSHOUSES. Nor should it be overlooked that even *xenodochia*, that is guesthouses, had their beginning at the time of the primitive Church. The evangelist Luke testifies thus: *And in those days, the number of the disciples increasing, there arose a murmuring of the Greeks against the Hebrews, for that their widows were neglected in the daily ministration. Then the twelve calling together the multitude of the disciples, said: It is not right that we should leave the word of God, and serve tables. Wherefore, brethren, look out among you... men of good reputation... whom we may appoint over this business... And they chose Stephen* as deacon and six others, and they *imposed hands upon them* and ordained them for this office [Acts 6:1–6]. Deacon in Greek means minister in Latin, and thus they were to minister to the poor, and when they were not occupied with this, they were also to proclaim the Word of God with the apostles.

P.15. THAT NOTHING OF RELIGION IS LACKING FROM MONASTIC DISCIPLINE. What aspect of sanctity, then, is missing from this holy form of religious life? Christ himself appears, just as I said above, and bestows gifts of peace, reveals the scriptures, breathes in his spirit, grants the power of remitting sins, and speaks and eats with them. The monks earn his blessing, and they see him ascending into heaven and sitting at the right hand of the Father. They see an angelic vision, the majesty of the Holy Spirit is revealed in a vision of fire, and they are given the knowledge of all languages.[10]

P.16. ON CANONS. So far I have explained by what authority the rule of monks arose, but now it seems fitting that I should also speak a little of canons, that is, regular clerics. Indeed, after he describes that quiet and tranquil life, endowed with special happiness and joy, which the apostles and other disciples of Christ led for fifty days after his resurrection, united in one place and sequestered as a community, living in the contemplation of the Lord, out of which we believe undoubtedly that the way of life of monks arose, just as I reported above, the evangelist Luke reports further: *And when the days of the Pentecost were accomplished, they were all together in one place: And suddenly there came a sound from heaven, as of a mighty wind coming, and it filled the whole house where they were sitting. And there appeared to them parted tongues as it were of fire, and it sat upon every one of them: And they were all filled with the Holy Spirit, and they began to speak with divers tongues, according as the Holy Spirit gave them to speak* [Acts 2:1–4]. And immediately they came out of their hiding places into public, preaching the Word of God with confidence and speaking of the mighty works of God in *divers tongues*. Thus on one day, three thousand Hebrews were converted to the faith of Christ, and on another five thousand. They all remained in harmony on the porch of Solomon, leading a communal life and following the teachings of the apostles [Acts 5:12, freely]. The bearded brothers today fulfill their role in the monasteries. Moreover, every day in the temple and out in the neighborhoods, the apostles were ceaselessly teaching and preaching Christ Jesus. The clerics who are called canons, who though gathered into a community nevertheless ceaselessly preach the word of God, imitate their zeal and way of life. They wear the clothing of apostles with dignity, lead the common life, obey the provost, guard the purity of heart and body, and lead those who are going astray back to the path of righteousness through preaching. And just as the disciples all gathered in harmony on the porch of Solomon next to the temple of the Lord, so too clerics or monks, and also religious women, build their dwellings around the oratory, and just like them they also abide

---

10 Here, the monks become the apostles at the Pentecost [Acts 2:1–4].

together daily in prayer and simplicity of heart, praising God and showing favor to all people.

P.17. ON THE NAME OF THE BISHOPS. They then ordained James, brother of the Lord, as bishop of Jerusalem,[11] showing that the church of God should by no means exist without leaders. For the bishop is called an overseer, and according to the prophet, the house of God should have a watchman who is able to have oversight and foresee the attack of the enemy.[12]

P.18. ON RURAL AND VILLAGE CLERICS. But this happy community of the disciples of Christ could no longer be hidden away in Jerusalem, since Christ wished to extend his church more widely throughout the world. And so he thought it right to prefigure another blessed way of life to be led in the church. For Luke says in these same Acts of the Apostles: *And... there was raised a great persecution against the church which was at Jerusalem; and they were all dispersed through the countries of Judea and Samaria* [Acts 8:1]. And further: *They therefore that were dispersed went about preaching the word of God* [Acts 8:4]. Rural clerics surely still fill the role of these men; like them, they are *dispersed* to various places and cultivate the vineyard of the Lord with great zeal. They carry out the care of souls, strive to unite the dispersed sons of God, and watch over God's flock. These men are thus the salt of the earth, the light of the world, the pillars of the church, the tongue of God, and the vicars of Christ through whom heaven is filled and the earth is illuminated.

P.19. ON HOLY VIRGINS. Concerning virgins, however, the Apostle says that he has no command from God, but he himself advises that they should without a doubt persist in virginity.[13] In fact, virginity exceeds the mandates of the Law, and for that reason, on account of human frailty, it is not commanded but advised. He who observes it surpasses human affairs and strives after the angelic. The leader and source of this way of life is the mother of all holiness herself. But we also read that the evangelist Matthew consecrated the queen of the Ethiopians,

---

11 This ordination is mentioned by Eusebius of Caesarea, *Ecclesiastical History*, 2.1.2–4 (referencing Clement of Alexandria, *Hypotyposes* 5) and 2.23.1–3 (referencing Hegesippus, *Commentaries* 5); and by Pseudo-Clement of Rome, *The Recognitions of Clement*, 1.43.

12 Ezek. 3:17, 33:1–9.

13 1 Cor. 7:25–40, esp. 39–40.

and the apostle Thomas consecrated the queen of the Indians to virginity for the Lord with a sacred veil.[14]

P.20. ON SOLITARIES. The solitary life is consecrated by John the Baptist or by our Lord Jesus Christ Himself, who after baptism fasted in solitude for forty days and forty nights, signifying that men of this profession should give their attention more completely to fasting. They should not be like solitaries of our time, who love to be thronged constantly by a mob of people with whom they never stop chatting. But just like Jesus himself, who remained entirely alone for forty days and nights, perfect solitaries should not allow themselves to be disturbed by people. For how can a person be called a solitary if he is not alone?

P.21. ON THE ENCLOSED. There really comes to mind no other model for the enclosed than the multitude of saints who endured imprisonment in the name of the suffering Christ, where many of them were worthy to be visited either by the Lord Himself or by angels. The enclosed thus imprison themselves for Christ, and in a certain way, bury themselves alive, hoping that if they die with Christ they might live again with him, and if they are buried with him, they might rise again with him. But in our times these people are considered reprehensible, because as soon as they are enclosed they want to be seen as teachers and prophets.[15] They falsely predict the future, attract a crowd, rarely pay attention to prayer or silence, desire to know all the affairs of the laity, and chat with these people and those people all day long. We thus condemn the enclosed and solitaries more than others, because they act as though their unjust behavior is lawful. For while clerics and monks sometimes violate what is just, they are nevertheless continually confined by the discipline of a master. Solitaries and the enclosed, on the other hand, since they enjoy free will, believe whatever they do to be holy and are deceived. For the intention is holy and good, but it is spoiled by liberty.[16]

---

14 The evangelical pursuits of Matthew are briefly referenced in Rufinus, *Ecclesiastical History* 10.9, and Socrates *Ecclesiastical History* 1.19. Thomas' missionary work in India is recorded in the *Acts of Thomas*.

15 The chronicler's dim view of contemporary *inclusi* accords with his critique of the enclosed men and women living at Petershausen in his own day (CP A.31).

16 Here the chronicler echoes first chapter of the Rule of St. Benedict, with its famous condemnation of sarabaites – "the most detestable kind of monks, who with no experience to guide them, no rule to try them *as gold is tried in a furnace* [Prov. 27:21], have a character as soft as lead," and whose "law is what they like to do, whatever strikes their fancy." On contemporary complaints about hermits and

P.22. ON PILGRIMS. The holy apostles themselves – who went around wearing sheepskins and goat pelts, needy and distressed, for whom the world was not worthy, wandering in solitary places, mountains, caves, and caverns in the earth – offer a model for pilgrims who set forth for the sake of God. These pilgrims, abandoning their fathers' homes, wander through the world hungry and thirsty, cold and naked, with no fixed residences, that they might become citizens of heaven and members of the household of God, who is rightly called the supporter of the poor and of pilgrims and of the needy, and the father of orphans, whom he allows to be consoled in his kingdom.

P.23. ON BEGGARS. Likewise the Gospel figure of Lazarus – who begged for crumbs but received nothing, and labored in hunger and thirst full of wounds and sores, and having all the pleasures in the house of the wealthy man before his eyes, nevertheless did not murmur against God, and because of this was led by the angels into the bosom of Abraham[17] – supports the practices of beggars. Therefore, he who receives alms and repays in prayer and does not accept more than he needs, is carried with the blessed Lazarus by angels into the bosom of Abraham.

P.24. THAT THE DIFFERENT PROFESSIONS AND WAYS OF LIFE AGREE ON ONE FAITH. I have briefly treated the various professions that exist in the church of God, lest anyone think that in them there is anything novel invented by modern men, since it would appear that all of them had their beginnings from the Lord himself or from his apostles, and lest anyone foolishly slander things that he knows possess such an abundance of authority. For although there are different professions and ways of life, one catholic faith graces each. Each one is rendered wholly pleasing to God, to whom, as we know, nothing is pleasing without faith. But whatever is founded in faith, built in hope, and offered to God with love, all these things are regarded with approval, cherished, and elevated to the heights of heaven by the one God himself and our Lord Jesus Christ in the Holy Spirit. Now that I have established these things, let us come, with God's help, to the main work.

HERE ENDS THE PREFACE

---

recluses and concern about the spiritual dangers that their unregulated behavior could pose, see Constable, *Reformation*, 62–64.

17 Luke 16:19–31.

BOOK ONE

Introduction

Book One, more than any of the other books that comprise the CP, is a work of creative memory. Writing around 1136, in the wake of a tumultuous period of reform, political disruption, and even exile, the chronicler weaves an historical narrative that answers his community's need for continuity with the past and security in the present.

The focus of Book One is the story of Petershausen's foundation by Bishop Gebhard II of Constance. The narrative is structured around the figure of Gebhard himself, with the chronicler first offering an account of Gebhard's ancestry and his early life and then turning to his role as monastic founder. The book ends with the bishop's death in 995 and his burial at Petershausen. The chronicler notes that while he had previously written a *Life of St. Gebhard* (included in translation as an appendix to this volume),[1] he is glorifying St. Gebhard again in this new text written to enhance the prestige of the monastery whose founding was the crowning achievement of Gebhard's life and that housed his body in death. While Book One contains many elements that are predictable in the Life of a monastic founder – a portentous birth, a precociously pious young adulthood, the performance of miracles to protect his monastery, and so on, it differs significantly in both structure and in content from the earlier *Life*, even when treating the same events.[2]

Among the additional biographical details that the chronicler provides in the CP is an imaginative account of the founder's illustrious descent from Charlemagne himself, situating Gebhard II within the powerful comital family of Bregenz (sometimes called the Udalrichinger in secondary literature).[3] By the chronicler's own time, the Bregenzer had

---

1 The chronicler acknowledges his authorship of the earlier hagiography in CP 1.6. He likely wrote this *Life of Gebhard* in connection with the founder's translation and canonization in 1034.

2 For a more detailed discussion of comparisons between the *Life of Gebhard* and CP, see pp. 191–192.

3 This is an imaginative account, indeed. Although the chronicler claims that Gebhard's ancestors were descended from Charlemagne's sister, Robert and Ulrich, the unnamed

THE CHRONICLE OF PETERSHAUSEN: BOOK ONE

become one of Swabia's most powerful families and Petershausen's most important patrons – surely a key reason for spinning this flattering (and thus historically unreliable) genealogy.[4] From the deep roots of this family, the chronicler moves to Gebhard's own father, Count Ulrich VI of Bregenz (d. 950/957), referred to here by his nickname Otzo.[5] After praising Otzo for his piety and recounting certain of his miraculous works, the chronicler introduces his four sons and their descendants. Here the chronicler pays particular attention to the division of the son's inheritance, and especially to the deceit of his son Liutfrid, who was to become Count of Winterthur and progenitor of Bishop Ulrich I of Constance (r. 1111–1127), with whom the monks of Petershausen would later have many conflicts.[6]

Following a brief discussion of Gebhard's miraculous survival of birth by excision (a birth story also recounted in the *Life of Gebhard*) and his early life, the chronicler turns to his efforts to found Petershausen. Here we are told the story of Gebhard's discovery and acquisition of the site for the monastery, the laying of its foundation in 983, as well as its construction and decoration.[7] The founding process culminates with Gebhard's consecration in 992 of Petershausen's basilica.

---

brothers of CP 1.2, were not her sons, but those of his brother-in-law by virtue of his marriage to Hildegard (758–783): Count Ulrich I (d. 807) of the nascent family line. See Bilgeri, *Bregenz*, 17–18; Zösmair, "Geschichte Rudolfs des letzten der alten Grafen von Bregenz," 25.

4 On the problems with the traditional label "Udalrichinger" for this family line, see Karl Schmid, "Zur Problematik von Familie, Sippe und Geschlecht, Haus und Dynastie beim mittelalterlichen Adel. Vorfragen zum Thema 'Adel und Herrschaft im Mittelalter,'" in *Gebetsgedenken und adilges Selbstverständnis im Mittelalter. Ausgewählte Beiträge. Festgabe zu seinem sechzigsten Geburtstag* (Sigmaringen: Thorbecke Verlag, 1983), 183–244. On the nobility of Swabia during the Investiture Conflict, see Thomas Zotz, "Der südwestdeutsche Adel und seine Opposition gegen Heinrich IV." In *Welf IV. – Schlüsselfigur einer Wendezeit*, ed. Dieter R. Bauer and Matthias Becher, Zeitschrift für bayerische Landesgeschichte 24, Series B (Munich, 2004), 333–359. See also Helmut Maurer, "Schwäbische Grafen vor den Mauern Roms. Zu Heinrichs IV. Eroberung der Leostadt im Juni 1083," in *Adel und Königtum im mittelalterlichen Schwaben: Festschrift für Thomas Zotz zum 65. Geburtstag*, ed. Aldres Bihrer, Mathias Kälble, and Heinz Krieg (Stuttgart: Kohlhammer Verlag, 2009), 193–204.

5 cf. CP 1.4.

6 On Otzo and his progeny, see CP 1.3–1.4. On the division of the inheritance, see: CP 1.5–1.6; cf. *Life of Gebhard* 1.9. The conflicts between Petershausen and Bishop Ulrich I of Constance were evidently numerous. See CP 3.39, 3.41, 3.42, 3.45, 3.48, 4.1, 4.6, 4.20, 4.23, and 4.25.

7 On the selection and acquisition of the site, see CP 1.9–1.12. On the construction of the monastery, see CP 1.16–1.24; cf. *Life of Gebhard* 1.11–1.12.

Like other Swabian chronicles, the CP includes the text of numerous charters and privileges, and it thus serves the dual purpose of chronicle and cartulary. Because no original archival documents survive from Petershausen during this period, most of these are preserved only in the CP, in some cases with significant interpolation. Some even appear to be outright forgeries.[8] These texts support the monastery's claims over various properties said to have been donated by its founder, but perhaps even more importantly, they support the monks' claims to particular rights, notably the election of their advocates. These charters and privileges work together with direct statements in Book One about the monastery's *libertas* – its freedom from all secular interference, a key goal of the Hirsau reformers. In CP 1.37, for example, the chronicler states boldly that Gebhard himself had stipulated that the monastery owe "no service, no tribute, no tax, no tolls, nor the performance of any duty at all, whether to the Roman pontiff, the emperor, nor even to the bishop of Constance, or to any person of whatever power or rank, but to God alone."

Book One also serves as a valuable witness to the relationship between the monastery and its servile population, as well as to the broader social landscape of Swabia during this period. In addition to the unfree laborers donated along with land, some are posted owning nothing except the houses in which they lived, while others are assigned to live in the monastery itself as *servi cottidiani* who live solely on rations provided by their masters.[9] Later, when more servants were required in the monastery, Gebhard removed a number of *servi cottidiani* from two donated estates and rehoused them in the monastery.[10] Unlike traditional serfs, *servi cottidiani* were not tied to the land and enjoyed no customary restrictions on the labor they owed to their masters. *The Life of Gebhard* also records that Gebhard reassigned a number of his own servants to the monastery to serve as cooks, millers, fullers, cobblers, gardeners, carpenters, and the like.[11]

---

8 CP 1.27, as a key example, is a strongly worded papal privilege from Pope John XV (r. 985–996). The text of this privilege, whose authenticity has been challenged, is included in both *Life* and Chronicle.

9 For those donated along with land in Book 1, see CP 1.8, 1.45. For the latter two categories, see CP 1.11. For *servi cottidiani*, see the general Introduction, pp. 16–17. Cf. *Life of Gebhard* 1.19, in which Gebhard reassigns a number of his own servants.

10 CP 1.34.

11 *Life of Gebhard* 1.19.

In addition to serfs and menial servants, Gebhard also donated unfree knights and ministerials for the defense of the newly founded monastery.[12] Gebhard nevertheless prudently withheld some of his most powerful ministerials for fear that they would do more harm than good; while nominally owned by the monastery, the powerful ministerials who belonged to a religious community could pose a threat to monastic property. The *liber traditionum* of the Bavarian abbey of St. Emmeram in Regensburg, for example, records several conflicts that arose in the twelfth century in which ministerials appropriated the monastery's dependents, claiming to have held them by legitimate benefice. In some cases, the abbot was forced to pay the offending ministerial in order to recover the lost dependents.[13]

Finally, thanks to the chronicler's sustained interest in the decoration and ornamentation of the monastery, and particularly in its liturgical books, textiles, and implements, Book One provides valuable detailed descriptions of the material culture of the monastery. He also includes the text of a number of grave inscriptions, which would otherwise have been lost in the great fire that destroyed the monastery in 1159 or in its final demolition in the nineteenth century.[14]

HERE BEGINS THE *CASUS* OF THE MONASTERY OF PETERSHAUSEN

Book One

1.1. ON THE DIVISIONS OF GAUL.[15] It has been said that there were three divisions of Gaul. One is called Long-Haired Gaul, or

---

12 CP 1.32, 1.35; cf. *Life of Gebhard* 1.20. For more information on servile knights, see also Benjamin Arnold, *German Knighthood, 1050–1300* (Oxford: Clarendon Press, 1985). On ministerials, see Freed, *Noble Bondsmen*, esp. 2–4, 50–54.

13 See *traditiones* 778, 884, 899, 928, and 951. Josef Widemann, ed. *Die Traditionen des Hochstifts Regensburg und des Klosters St. Emmeram*. Quellen und Erörterungen zur bayerischen Geschichte. Herausgegeben von der Kommission für bayerische Landesgeschichte bei der Bayerischen Akademie der Wissenschaften. Neue Folge, Bd. 8 (Munich: C.H. Beck'sche Verlagsbuchhandlung, 1942).

14 See, for instance, CP 1.16–1.23, 1.46–1.48, 1.51–1.55. For the inscriptions, see CP 1.19, 1.53–1.54; cf. *Life of Gebhard* 1.24. Another set of burial epitaphs is recorded in CP 2.24.

15 The names of these three divisions are well attested in classical sources, but they traditionally refer to different regions than the chronicler suggests here: *Gallia Comata* for the northern parts of Transalpine Gaul, *Gallia Bracata* (aka *Gallia Narbonensis*) for the southern portion of Transalpine Gaul (what is now the Languedoc and

Italy, which the Lombards and Romans inhabit, because long ago the Italians cared for their hair more diligently than other peoples. Or it is called Long-Haired, as in adorned, since it is adorned by the city of Rome, which held the most exalted rank in the empire of the whole world. Another is called Trouser-Wearing Gaul, which the Germans inhabit, because the Germans wear trousers, or breeches, more than other peoples. The third took the name Toga-Wearing Gaul, since the inhabitants of this province wore togas (that is, multicolored garments extending all the way to the heel) and even corrupted neighboring peoples with this rot. And indeed, as I said, these features once particular to each province are now universal.

1.2. ON THE ANCESTRY OF THE BLESSED GEBHARD. In the region of Gaul that was known as Toga-Wearing, there was a certain man graced with most noble lineage to whom the King of the Franks, who was also the Emperor of the Romans,[16] gave his sister in marriage. She bore two sons, both made famous by their lineage and also by their spiritual virtue.[17] Once they reached manhood and were rich in goods and most fierce in strength and arms, it happened that the poison of enmity crept in between them and the king of their province and infected their hearts to such a degree that it could not be contained until the hand of the sword[18] deprived the king of life. After the king was killed, these two brothers, fearing the hostility of their

---

Provence), and *Gallia Togata* for Cisalpine Gaul in northern Italy (not including the city of Rome). Cf. Cicero, *Orationes Philippicae* 8.9.27; Cicero, *Epistulae ad Familiares* 9.15.2; Cicero, *In Pisonem* 23; Pomponius Mela, *De Situ Orbis* 2.4.2, 2.5.1, 3.2.4; Pliny the Younger, *Naturalis Historia* 3.5 (.4), 3.19 (.14), 4.31 (.17); Catullus, *Carmina* 29.3; Lucan, *Pharsalia* 1.443; Juvenal, *Saturae* 8.234; Caesar, *De Bello Gallico* 8.24.3; 8.52.1. It is curious that the chronicler was aware of these ancient names but not their proper referents, and that he apparently assumed that the ancient Romans wore their hair long and did not wear togas (of which the chronicler clearly had a very low opinion).

16 See the chapter introduction for the chronicler's invocation of Charlemagne in his imaginative genealogy of Gebhard. This account of the founder's ancestry should be understood, not as an accurate accounting of Gebhard's background, but as the construction of a legitimizing pedigree.

17 These brothers are supposed to be Robert and Ulrich, traditionally not identified as the sons of Charlemagne's sister, but those of his brother-in-law by virtue of his marriage to Hildegard (758–783), Count Ulrich I (d. 807) of the nascent comital line, sometimes labeled the Udalrichinger, which claimed its own ancient connection to the Carolingian court by this tradition.

18 The phrase "the hand of the sword" may echo the language of Ps. 62:11 (*they shall be delivered into the hands of the sword...*).

fellow countrymen, took themselves to their uncle, the august emperor, who received them graciously and gave them many excellent estates in Alemannia. He gave them Bodman, Bregenz, Überlingen, Buchhorn, Ahausen, Teuringen, Heistergau, and Winterthur along with all their appurtenances, as well as others in Raetia Curiensis[19] and many other places that have been erased from memory by the passing of time. Thus enriched with such great gifts from the emperor, they visited these estates and brought them under their own rule, and lavishly gave gifts from them to the most noble men who had accompanied them. They gave Teuringen to one, Überlingen to another, and Buchhorn to another. Afterwards, they intermarried and were joined to these men by affinity.[20] Later, after the wrath of the Gauls that had burned against the two brothers because of the death of their king subsided, their neighbors and friends sent to them and asked them to return to their fatherland. One of them was won over by extensive pleading and returned, while the other, named Ulrich, remained in the province of the Alemanni and kept everything that had been given by the emperor, as do his posterity down to the present day.

1.3. ABOUT OTZO. From this seed, Otzo was born.[21] He was a pious and venerable count who lived in Bregenz, in a place that still shows the ruins of ancient habitation. [Here he took a wife named Diepirga,[22] who was very pious toward God and truly most noble toward the world.]

ABOUT THE BIRDS. This Otzo was so pious and worthy that even birds sensed his sanctity and would boldly fly to his table and take food from his hand, and when some departed satisfied, others would come to be nourished in turn.[23]

---

19 Raetia Curiensis, an early medieval province in central Europe with its administrative center in Chur, and which included parts of Vorarlberg, became part of the Duchy of Swabia in the tenth century. See Peider Lansel, *The Raeto-Romans* (Chur: Buchdruckerei Bischofberger, 1937), 15.

20 That is, affinity through marriage, a form of consanguinity.

21 Otzo was the nickname (CP 1.4) for Count Ulrich VI (d. 950/957), who was the first Udalrichinger count of Bregenz. See Bilgeri, Bregenz, 22–23.

22 The mother of Gebhard, d. 949 (cf. CP 1.6).

23 On encounters between saints and animals in medieval literature, see Robert Bartlett, *Why Can the Dead Do Such Great Things? Saints and Worshippers from the Martyrs to the Reformation* (Princeton, NJ: Princeton University Press, 2013), 390–398; David Salter, *Holy and Noble Beasts: Encounters with Animals in Medieval Literature* (Woodbridge: Boydell & Brewer, 2001).

MONASTIC EXPERIENCE IN TWELFTH-CENTURY GERMANY

ABOUT THE DEER. One day at dawn, a deer came out from the woods and knocked at the door of Otzo's dwelling with her hoof. When the doorkeeper opened the door and saw her, he announced that an animal was standing and knocking on the door. Otzo, guided by piety, recognized that the animal had been led there on account of some distress, and said to his servant: "Quick! Follow her and see if she wants something." He followed the deer without delay as she led him into the woods and showed him her offspring with its foot caught in a snare. Standing with her head bowed she began to plead, as it were, with a motion of her ears. The servant immediately freed the fawn's foot from the snare. The deer left rejoicing into the forest with her young, and the servant returned to his master and related to him what had transpired. With these and similar things, God often jested, as it were, with this venerable man, since the light-hearted man *that sheweth mercy* in the Lord *shall not be moved forever* [Ps. 111:5–6].[24]

[Another time, when the same venerable Count Otzo lingered at the court of the emperor,[25] a lion escaped from the cage one day, and following his nature, tore apart every place he could enter. Since no one dared approach the lion and all fled before him, certain men suggested to the emperor that he speak to the aforementioned man of God, Count Otzo, so that, with God's virtue, Otzo might calm the lion a little. For they said that they had learned from experience that he was so virtuous in the Lord that, if he wished, he could easily soften the lion's ferocity. When the emperor heard these things, he summoned Otzo without delay and humbly begged him on account of the urgent situation. Because of his humility, Otzo at first explained that he could not attempt such deeds, but in the end he gave in to all the supplicants who were present with the emperor and put himself in the path of the raging lion. When the lion saw Otzo, he immediately rushed at him with all of his ferocity as though about to rip him to shreds. But when Otzo received him with open hands, the lion suddenly forgot his ferocity entirely and prostrated himself before the man of God and began to lick his feet. Petting the lion, Otzo directed the lion's attendants to restrain and cage him without fear. When the emperor saw this, he was

---

24 The Douay-Rheims translation of the Bible renders *iucundus homo* as "acceptable is the man," but the chronicler seems to be making a pun here with *Deus quasi ioculabatur*.

25 The chronicler likely means to invoke Otto I for this fanciful tale, although he did not become emperor until 962, well after Otzo had died (in 950/957).

dumbstruck and went to Otzo reverentially saying: "Since I see that you act with God, I freely absolve you from all future service to the crown."]²⁶

1.4. ON THE PROGENY OF OTZO.

Otzo later had four sons, one named Ulrich, another Marquard, the third Liutfrid, and the fourth, truly the splendor of the whole family, Gebhard.²⁷ They called Ulrich "Otzo" on account of his charm, and [his son Ulrich]²⁸ fought in a battle that Emperor Otto [I]²⁹ waged against the Hungarians near Augsburg.³⁰ The father nobly enriched the monastery of Lindau³¹ from his estates and was reverently buried there, where he now rests in peace. His descendants still flourish near Bregenz. Moreover, his son Marquard was made count, and became very powerful through his friendship with Emperor Otto.³²

1.5. ON LIUTFRID AND HIS PROGENY.

When these four brothers wanted to divide the inheritance of their deceased parents among themselves, the aforementioned Liutfrid, since he was lazy and unwarlike and quite despicable in every other way, feared that he might be scorned by the brothers in the division because of his idleness. He thus began to consider how he could trick them so that they would not deny him part of the inheritance. Mulling over many possibilities and finally discovering a suitable plan for himself and his posterity, he spoke to one of his brothers without the knowledge of the others, saying: "You know, brother, that I am inferior to the rest of you, and I am clearly not at all suited to the affairs of the world. But if you go along with my plans, you will win no small profit for yourself and your posterity. For I love you more than my other brothers and I wish to live with you. Therefore, when the time comes for the division of our inheritance, take pains to make sure that Winterthur and its appurtenances are assigned to me,

---

26 This entire passage, which like CP 1.3 has the character of a conventional hagiographical anecdote, was added to the bottom margins of folios 40v–41r.
27 Count Ulrich VII of Bregenz (r. 955/7–972); Marquard (d. 955); Liutfrid, Count of Winterthur (d. c. 993).
28 Originally, this line read: "he fought in a battle that Emperor Otto waged against the Hungarians near Augsburg," but a (perhaps second) contemporary hand has added the words "his son Ulrich" above the line.
29 Emperor Otto I (r. 936–973; crowned emperor in 962).
30 This is the Battle of Lechfeld (955).
31 f. 817/822, a community of regular canonesses.
32 It was actually Ulrich, not Marquard, who succeeded Otzo as Count of Bregenz.

and know beyond a doubt that, if these things come into my possession, I shall deliver them to you, and afterwards I will live with you however you see fit. Take your own profit into consideration and follow my advice." He said the same things in secret to the second brother, and the third brother, with each one believing that he said these things because he loved him, and prompted by this hope, each brother surrendered to Liutfrid's influence. Because of these promises, when it came time for the division and the lot fell to each one, each hastened to fulfill Liutfrid's request, not knowing that he had made the same promise to the others. Since all agreed, the matter was decided easily and they confirmed Winterthur with its appurtenances for Liutfrid.[33]

Rightly overjoyed, he visited the excellent estates that were surrendered to him and brought everything under his rule. Having thus tricked his brothers with such cunning, he gave his attention to agriculture and amassed a small fortune. After he took a wife, he begat a son from her by the name of Albert, who crossed into Apulia with the blessed Pope Leo[34] and died there fighting on behalf of St. Peter against the Normans, who had invaded the region.[35] His daughter was Adalheid, whom Count Hartman the Elder of Dillingen took in marriage.[36] She begat for him Hartman the Younger and Albert,[37] who is still living, and who was made heir to all his paternal and maternal inheritance, and Ulrich, who was made Bishop of Constance,[38] about whom I may say a little bit later on,[39]

---

33 cf. the account of this division of inheritance in *Life of Gebhard* 1.9.
34 Pope Leo IX (r. 1049–1054).
35 Pope Leo IX organized an anti-Norman coalition, including a force of several hundred men from Swabia, and initiated a campaign in 1053 against the forces of Robert Guiscard (c. 1015–1085) in Apulia. The papal forces were defeated decisively by the Normans at the Battle of Civitate on 17 June 1053, and much of the Swabian force was killed. This disaster for the papal army dispelled any hope of expelling the Normans from Apulia and freed them to conquer the rest of southern Italy. The Normans eventually received papal recognition of their Italian holdings with the Treaty of Melfi in 1059. See G. A. Loud, *The Age of Robert Guiscard: Southern Italy and the Norman Conquest* (Harlow, England: Pearson Education Limited, 2000), esp. 117–119, 127–130.
36 Count Hartman I of Dillingen (d. 1121); married to Adalheid of Winterthur-Kyburg, who died in c. 1125 as a nun at the monastery of Neresheim (f. 1095); on the counts of Kyburg-Dillingen, see Maurer, "Schwäbische Grafen vor den Mauren Roms," 201–204.
37 Count Hartman II of Dillingen (d. 1134); Albert I (d. 1151).
38 Bishop Ulrich I of Constance.
39 CP 3.39, 3.41, 3.42, 3.45, 3.48, 4.1, 4.6, 4.20, 4.23, and 4.25.

as well as three daughters who now abide in the religious habit. One of these had borne Count Ulrich of Gammertingen and Albert of Achalm, both of whom are still alive.[40]

1.6. HOW GEBHARD GOT HIS INHERITANCE.

Gebhard, the youngest of the aforementioned brothers, but their jewel, was cut out of the womb of his deceased mother [Diepirga], and he was covered in certain wrappings up until the expected time of birth, and thus God spared his life for the salvation of many.[41] Writings attest of such people who have been excised, that if they survive, they should be considered blessed in this world.[42] And so he was nurtured and given over to learning, educated in Constance, and was there made a canon. Because I detailed his life in another work as well as I could,[43] I will now touch on it just briefly. In short, when his brothers distributed parts of their inheritance among themselves as described above, they said that as a cleric, Gebhard did not need his inheritance as he was rich enough from the resources of the church. When Gebhard heard this, he sought his portion with grave indignation.[44] A most eloquent and effective man,

---

40 Count Ulrich of Gammertingen (d. c. 1110); married to Adalheid of Dillingen, who died c. 1140 as a nun at the monastery of Zwiefalten (f. 1089).

41 This is a rare account of birth by excision: the cutting of the fetus out of the body of the mother. The *Life of Gebhard* and the rhymed office for his feast, both written in connection with his canonization in 1134 and both with connections to the chronicler himself, also mention his birth by excision from an unnamed mother. See *Life of Gebhard* 1.1. All similar accounts of this procedure describe the mother as already dead, and the Church required immediate excision so that the child could be baptized. Birth by excision was not performed as a medical procedure on living women until at least the fifteenth century. Steven Bednarski and Andree Courtemanche, "'Sadly and with a Bitter Heart': What the Caesarean Section Meant in the Middle Ages," *Florilegium* 28 (2011): 38–43; Samuel Lurie, "The Changing Motives of Cesarean Section: From the Ancient World to the Twenty-First Century," *Archives of Gynecology and Obstetrics* 271 (2005): 282–283.

42 The chronicler is perhaps referring to ancient belief that held that if a child survived excision from the womb, he was destined for a great future. For instance, the Hellenistic god of medicine Asclepius survived birth by excision, and Pliny the Elder reported the same for Scipio Africanus and an early Caesar (*The Natural History*, 7.9). Bednarski and Courtemanche, "'Sadly and with a Bitter Heart,'" 38; Lurie, "The Changing Motives of Cesarean Section," 281–82.

43 i.e., *Life of Gebhard* (specifically 1.9).

44 The timing of this division of inheritance is problematic. The story implies that the division occurred before the death of Marquard in 955, as it involved all four brothers. But Gebhard, who was born in 949, would only have been five or six when the original division was made, although the justification for withholding his share provided by the chronicler suggests that the division may have been made later, when he was already a cleric. According to the *Life of Gebhard* (1.2), Gebhard was

he threatened them to the utmost, saying that if they refused to surrender his hereditary right by their own free will, he would take up arms and defend it with his sword. When they heard this, they did reluctantly what they would not do voluntarily, and they surrendered his portion of the inheritance.

1.7. ON THE THINGS HE BEQUEATHED TO CONSTANCE. But because the law of God was in his heart, his course was not diverted by earthly riches. Instead, during the time of Bishop Conrad of blessed memory,[45] he bequeathed a part of his estates to the church of St. Mary in Constance, over which he made the following privilege:

1.8. PRIVILEGE OF OBERDORF.[46] "Let everyone, both present and future, know that I Gebhard, a rather unworthy brother of the holy church of Constance, considering the remedy of my soul, and also following the evangelical and apostolic teachings, with the consent of my brothers and by the hand of my advocate Ulrich, do bequeath the property under my rule, which I am known to possess by parental inheritance in the locations Oberdorf, Heggelbach, Billafingen, and Liggersdorf, with all the appurtenances pertaining to those same places – the buildings, unfree laborers, pastures, forests, running bodies of water, and everything mobile and immobile that appertains to those same places – to the holy community of the aforementioned church of Constance, for the brothers diligently serving God at this very place, over whose spiritual regimen Bishop Conrad, a man of the highest religion and doctrine, presides, with the condition that I, retaining that same property for myself, or another of my choosing from this same fraternity, thence pay an annuity each and every year henceforth for posterity on the feast of our holy and venerable father Pope Gregory, rendered to the aforesaid brothers, as the canonical rule will show. Done in Constance on 12 March, with the agreement of my aforementioned advocate Ulrich and other witnesses whose names are

---

handed over to the church as a boy to be educated, and the Life includes numerous stories of his youth that occur before he attains his inheritance (*Life of Gebhard* 1.9). At least as the chronicler understood the account, then, the three older brothers likely managed the original division of the inheritance without Gebhard's involvement. Presumably Gebhard's threats over the matter commenced later, after he had reached adulthood.

45 Bishop Conrad I of Constance (r. 934–975).

46 This is the earliest extant witness to the text of this charter. See Manfred Krebs, "Quellenstudien zur Geschichte des Klosters Petershausen," *Zeitschrift für die Geschichte des Oberrheins* 48 (1935): 486–487.

written below: Eberhard, Liutfrid, Hildebold, Chuzzo, Cozpret, Albert, Meribod, Liutpret, Sigbert, Hadebert, Dietger, Wern, Adalgod."

1.9. HOW HE SOUGHT A PLACE TO BUILD A MONASTERY. When it pleased him who had miraculously removed Gebhard from the womb of his mother and had called him through his grace to be a burning and glowing lamp in the house of the Lord, never submitting to flesh and blood to enjoy leisure or pleasure, but rather keeping in mind how he was called to labor in the vineyard of the Lord and cultivate and improve it, Gebhard began to investigate through the counsel of the Holy Spirit how he might shake himself free from the snare of this world as if a fawn,[47] in order that, like a Hebrew slave in the seventh year, that is after the agreed labors of this world, he, as a free man, might be able to observe the Sabbath forever.[48] Finally, he sought with every intention to discover how he could most pleasingly offer to Christ whatever he had or could acquire, and in the end he came to the following conclusion: nothing would be better for the benefit of his spiritual well-being than to build a monastery. And so he began to seek an appropriate location for this plan, where he could satisfy his desire. And when he spent the night in a certain place for this purpose, little frogs from the swamp disturbed him all night with their croaks. The next morning he inspected the location, and as he was considering whether the place would be useful for his intention, it is said that he asked by which name the monastery should be called, were it to be constructed there. One from his retinue immediately responded that it should be called the Monastery of Little Frogs, whose croaking happened to bother them through the night. But he replied, "By no means is it to be built in this place, if it should be condemned with such a foul name."

1.10. HOW HE ACQUIRED THIS PLACE. Because it is written that God *shall do the will of those who fear him and shall hear their prayer* [Ps. 144.19], he soon showed his servant Gebhard, so we believe, the place where he intended his wish to be fulfilled. The bank of the Rhine across from the city of Constance was pleasing for his plan, and although it was less suitable for building the monastery, he nevertheless thought it splendid. This place had formerly belonged to the monastery of

---

47 This may allude to CP 1.3, in which Otzo rescues an ensnared fawn.
48 This idea of the length of labor and freedom of Hebrew slaves is an allusion to Exod. 21:2 and Deut. 15:12.

Reichenau,[49] just as the land above and below that site still do, and at that time it was uninhabitable because it was damp like a swamp. The man of God, however, exchanged the property that he had in Zurzach for this same small place. The monastery of Reichenau did not receive all that it now possesses in Zurzach from the man of God, but only the part that was under Gebhard's rule and could be rightfully exchanged for this place.[50] After this exchange was legally confirmed, the man of God divided that same little estate into three small parts. One part he allotted to himself and his successors, the bishops of Constance, another to the canons of the same church, and the third for the construction of the monastery.

1.11. ON THE RIGHTS OF THE INHABITANTS OF THIS PLACE. And because the men whom he appointed to live there had nothing except the houses in which they lived, and were able to own neither fields, nor woods, nor pastures, for their support he assigned to all of them and to their posterity the privilege that the heriot[51] should not be taken from the dead, but that their descendants be allowed to keep everything that they left behind, and also that they might sail as much as their lords required, and that those who had the skill might fish. He assigned this same right to the servants of the monastery, with this exception: that these servants, because they possessed little by way of fields or meadows, ought to serve their masters daily and to receive rations from them.[52]

49 Reichenau, an island monastery on Lake Constance, founded in 724 by the itinerant monk Pirmin (c. 700–753), was one of the most powerful monasteries in the region.

50 The text of a charter documenting this exchange was inserted by a twelfth-century scribe into Petershausen's tenth-century Sacramentary (University of Heidelberg, *Codex Salemitani* IXb) on ff. 18v–19v. Manfred Krebs hypothesized that this charter was forged after the fire of 1159 to replace a document that was destroyed when the archives burned, with the forger borrowing and patching together language from the CP and the *Life of Gebhard*. See Krebs, "Quellenstudien," 513–515. For a digital facsimile, see https://doi.org/10.11588/diglit.604#0038 (Date of last access: 22 December 2019).

51 That is, the tribute due to a lord upon the death of tenant, paid from his belongings. A similar benefit appears in *Life of Gebhard* 1.19, suggesting that both accounts describe the same donation.

52 The reference to serving the brothers daily (*cottidie*) identifies these unfree laborers as *servi cottidiani* – members of the lowest social status in southern Germany who were essentially owned as chattel slaves and could be used without customary restriction for both agricultural and domestic labor. See CP 1.34, where unfree laborers (*mancipia*) are reassigned from donated estates to serve as domestics in Petershausen for daily service. The *servi cottidiani* described in this chapter are

1.12. ON THE CHAPEL OF ST. MICHAEL. He first built a small chapel there, which he dedicated on 29 July in honor of St. Michael, and in which he raised a dead man through prayer.[53]

1.13. ABBOT PEZILIN. HOW THAYNGEN WAS ACQUIRED. At first he had a certain Pezilin as abbot,[54] under whom he exchanged an estate in Thayngen and a small property in Epfendorf with the church of Constance, over which exchange he had the following privilege written:

1.14. PRIVILEGE OVER THAYNGEN. "In the name of the holy and indivisible Trinity. Let it be known to all those present as well as future, that I Gebhard, unworthy bishop of the church of Constance, with the hand of my advocate Chuzzo, made the following exchange with Abbot Pezilin of the monastery of St. Gregory, considering our common benefit: I traded that estate that the church I oversee is said to have in the village of Thayngen in the *pagus* of Hegau and the village of Epfendorf in the *pagus* of Baar, delivering it to him and to his monks to be held fully, indeed so that he, with the hand of his advocate Eberhard, might submit to me and to my successors to be held fully whatever the monastery that he oversees legitimately owns in the village of Lutwangen in the *pagus* of Albgau and in Repperweiler in the *pagus* of Eritgau. This exchange was made and confirmed in our presence, with the support of both advocates, mine and the abbot's, in Constance with the witnesses whose names are written in the following subscription present: Archpriest Meginzo; Dean Sigbod; Archdeacon Irinc; Archdeacon Gerard; Alberich, Gunderic, and many others. Done publicly in the holy synod of the church of Constance in the year of the Incarnation of the Lord 995 on a Wednesday in the seventh indiction."

1.15. THE FIRST MONK RUPERT. THEY ACCEPTED THE FIRST CUSTOMARY FROM THE MONASTERY OF ST. MEINRAD. The first monk Rupert came to the monastery to make his profession.[55] Gebhard decided that his monks would follow the

---

specifically *servi praebendarii* – those who were allowed a house and small garden but nevertheless depended on regular rations for subsistence. For more information on *servi cottidiani*, see Sutherland, "Mancipia Dei." Still useful is Dollinger, *L'evolution des classes rurales*.

53 cf. *Life of Gebhard* 1.12 for an extended account of the circumstances of this miracle.

54 Abbot Pezelin (c. 993–996). Probably identical with Abbot Perriger named in the privilege in CP 1.31 and identified as first abbot (in CP 1.50 and the *Life of Gebhard* 1.18. Abel and Weiland (1868) made this identification in their edition on 631, n. 17.

55 cf. *Life of Gebhard* 1.10, in which the monastery was first populated with twelve monks of unspecified origin.

regimen and norm of living of the monastery of St. Meinrad, which is called Einsiedeln,[56] because the monks of that monastery were then most pious. He constructed posts all around the place in order to dry the soil.

1.16. WHEN HE FOUNDED THE CHURCH. In the year of the Incarnation of the Lord 983, he laid down the foundation of the basilica and bestowed four gold pieces, which he placed beneath each corner of the church.

1.17. ON THE CRYPT. He made a crypt on the western side, in which he dug a well and built an altar in honor of St. Martin, which Gebhard III[57] later demolished on account of dampness.

1.18. ON THE CIBORIUM. He built a sanctuary above the crypt, in which he erected the main altar in honor of Pope St. Gregory, over which he built an exceedingly splendid ciborium.[58]

1.19. ON THE FOUR COLUMNS. After he had made four columns out of oak and had vines carved on them, he gathered the inhabitants of Constance together and addressed them saying, "I have four daughters, whom it behooves me to give over in marriage, but I cannot adorn them without your help. I convene you now for this cause, and I ask that you help me to acquire ornamentation according to your ability and inclination." And when all responded that they would most willingly do whatever he instructed, he ordered that the columns be brought forward and said that he wished them to be adorned with silver and entreated them to help him with this, which everyone did eagerly. With their help, he adorned the columns with the finest silver and he most tastefully built stone sculptures on these bases. {He positioned four arches above the columns, which he adorned on one side with gilded silver and on the other with gilded copper...} Above the arches, and also above the columns, he put a canopy of such size that it covered the entire ciborium. It had a round opening in the center, and this was covered with gilded copper on the inner ring, and it had a projecting rim adorned with silver below, which a certain abbot removed and replaced

---

56 Einsiedeln was founded in 934. St. Meinrad (c. 797–861) was a monk educated at Reichenau who went on to adopt the eremitic form of religious life. The monastery was built on the site of his hermitage by dedicated followers.

57 Bishop Gebhard III (of Zähringen) of Constance (r. 1084–1110).

58 In this context, a ciborium is a canopy, generally supported by four columns, that stands above the altar.

with lead. Moreover, the underside of this canopy was tastefully covered all over in gilded copper, with images of the four evangelists exquisitely rendered, as well as several other scenes. Silver panels were attached on the transverse arch of each of the four sides, and on each was inscribed one of the following verses in gold letters:

> *This meager work, completed with various techniques,*
> *bears to you, Gregory, the humble devotion of a servant,*
> *an unworthy bishop. By your prayers may you, kind father,*
> *together with the faithful people, unite him with the hosts of heaven.*

Above the opening in the canopy, a gilded pyramidal helm roof[59] was raised up on rounded wooden columns, and on top of this was a figure of a white lamb looking down upon the congregation.

1.20. ON THE PRINCIPAL ALTAR AND ITS SIDE PANELS. The altar itself was hollow, with a panel on the eastern side decorated with the finest gold and precious stones, and another on the western side completely covered in silver, which had in the center an image of St. Mary rendered exquisitely in the finest gold, weighing a talent, {which Abbot Berthold[60] removed, broke apart, and sold in pieces for grain during a time of famine}.[61] Various vessels containing saints' relics hung above the altar.

1.21. ON THE CHOIR. Many steps led up to the altar from the choir, which Abbot Theodoric removed when he expanded the choir.[62] In the middle of the top step there was a lowered space surrounded by square stones, which was as wide as the altar and which extended to the place where supplicants kneel at the altar. Near the altar there was a slab of green marble set into the floor, on which the kneeling celebrants kiss.[63] The choir was indeed quite small since it was diminished by these steps.

---

59 A helm roof is a steeply pitched roof with four sides that rise from a square base and converge at the top. See R. A. Stalley, *Early Medieval Architecture* (Oxford: Oxford University Press, 1999), 128.

60 Abbot Berthold (r. 1116–1127).

61 The final clause about Abbot Berthold's destruction of the panel was erased in the manuscript, perhaps because the account is repeated in CP 4.21, or perhaps by a later reader trying to minimize the chronicler's accounts of the destruction of objects bestowed by Gebhard II.

62 cf. CP 3.7.

63 For a history of liturgical kissing, and particularly the "kiss of peace" exchanged between celebrants during the mass, see Katherine Ludwig Jansen, *Peace and Penance in Late Medieval Italy* (Princeton: Princeton University Press, 2018), 164–165.

1.22. ON THE PAINTING. The walls of the basilica were also beautifully painted on every side, with scenes from the Old Testament on the left and from the New Testament on the right, and wherever the image of God was, he had a gold circle around his head. Out of affection, the bishop of Venice[64] had given Gebhard a full measure of Greek paint, which is called *lazur*, and which is the best paint by far, and this was spread all over the walls, as I myself saw.[65] Abbot Conrad[66] completely removed this painting, since by that point age had robbed it of its splendor. Gebhard made doors of incomparable splendor, and a very small portico in front of the church, which Abbot Theodoric enlarged and improved.

[**1.23. ON THE FOUNTAIN.** When the church was being decorated with different paints with the greatest zeal, it happened on a certain day that Gebhard left that place and delayed his return for some time. In the meantime, the treacherous painters deceitfully stole the best paints, went off into a nearby woodland, and hid them there, secretly burying them in the ground. When the holy bishop returned, the painters began to weigh the paints, rudely complaining that the work was delayed due to a negligent shortage of paint. Hearing this, the blessed man was silent for a while and then replied: "If we do not have enough, more must be acquired. Therefore come, follow me; perhaps the Lord in his kindness will give us that which you seek so that you can finish the work." And he led them without a guide to the place where they had hidden the paint, and there he drove his staff into the ground, saying: "Dig here in the name of God, and see if you find anything." Terrified with bad conscience, the painters dug into the ground. They uncovered the paint that they had hidden and reluctantly brought it forward. With a cheerful face, the man of God said to them: "Now hasten, dear sons, and work earnestly with this paint that the Lord

---

64 This refers to the Patriarch of Grado, Vitalis IV Candiano (r. 976–1017).

65 This refers to an intense blue paint whose pigment was produced by from costly lapis lazuli, which was mined only in Afghanistan in the Middle Ages. The use of the term "Greek" here likely reflects the transit of the stone from Afghanistan along the medieval silk routes through the Byzantine Empire, and especially to the grinding of the pigment there on its way into Western Europe. Recent research has confirmed the availability of lapis lazuli pigment in German-speaking areas as early as the end of the tenth century. See Anita Radini et al, "Medieval Women's Early Involvement in Manuscript Production Suggested by Lapis Lazuli Identification in Dental Calculus," in *Science Advances* 5, No. 1 (2019).

66 Abbot Conrad (r. 1127–1164).

revealed to us." Completely terrified, they departed, marveling among themselves at what had happened. And a fountain of the clearest water immediately burst forth from that same place and does not cease to flow to this day. The next day when the man of God sat at the table and these painters stood about gathered for work, they suddenly fell and lay prostrate as if dead. When this was announced with a great uproar to blessed Gebhard, still sitting at lunch, he calmly replied: "Let it be; they ought to atone a little, since they transgressed in the affairs of the saints." Saying this, he remained apart from the commotion until he withdrew from the table cheerfully. He then ascended the scaffold to the place where they lay as if dead, and prodded them with his staff, saying: "I will not pay you to lie here numb with sleep, so get up and work." And immediately lifting their heads, they rose healthy and began to work as if nothing had happened.]

1.24. WHEN HE DEDICATED THE CHURCH. In the year of the Incarnation of the Lord 992, in the fifth indiction, in the tenth year after he began to build, the blessed Bishop Gebhard himself dedicated the church that he built in honor of the blessed Pope Gregory on 28 October in great glory.

1.25. HOW HE ACQUIRED A SPECIAL PRIVILEGE. When he finally came to Rome, he was honored by Pope John[67] for his veneration so exceedingly that the pope not only gave him as great a privilege as he had requested, but also allowed him to put his hand on the body of the blessed Pope Gregory.[68] And it was granted to him that he could freely take away with him whichever of the sacred bones rose with one touch of the hand.

1.26. ON THE HEAD OF ST. GREGORY. Whence by the grace of God he lifted Gregory's head from his body with other magnificent relics. When Gebhard had obtained everything he wanted to his liking, he returned overjoyed.[69]

Today we find this beloved head in a reliquary, and while it was once very solid, it is now broken down thoroughly through old age and neglect. Formerly, as I heard, it had been enclosed in the altar of St. Peter in the southern side of the church, where his tomb was known

---

67 Pope John XV (r. 985–996).
68 Pope St. Gregory the Great (r. 590–604).
69 For the chronicler's account of Gebhard's dramatic escape from Rome, in the mode of a *furta sacra* (relic theft) with Gregory's head, see *Life of Gebhard*, 1.16–1.17.

to have been in Rome.⁷⁰ But it has since been removed from that altar and set above the altar of St. Mary, and the altar of St. Peter has thus remained empty and dishonored. For this reason, it was later restored and dedicated by Bishop Conrad of Chur.⁷¹ When we eventually opened this reliquary, we found within it a red container filled with the ashes of saints, among which we discovered a most beloved treasure – the head of the most holy Pope Gregory – but we grieved that it had been broken into small parts. We still do not know how this happened. We found many other relics in this same reliquary, however, which we hope to be of the same father, St. Gregory, both because we found only one label among them, and because they displayed the brightness of his other bones. We collected the intact bones and removed others, and we put the ashes back where we first found them. The reliquary itself was given to Mimmenhausen when a chapel was built there.⁷²

1.27. THE PRIVILEGE OF THE MONASTERY FIRST WRITTEN IN THE BOOKS, WHICH IS ALSO STILL PRESERVED IN THE MONASTERY. This is the privilege that blessed Gebhard received from Pope John XV over that same place:

"John, Bishop, Servant of the Servants of God, in the name of the holy and indivisible Trinity, the Father, the Son, and the Holy Spirit: we wish it to be known to all believers in Christ how Gebhard II, worthy of love, bishop of the holy church of Constance and our most beloved brother, came to Rome to pray at the house of Peter, the Prince of the Apostles, and of Paul, and before our presence, and reported to us how he, moved by the prompting of God, has constructed a church of cenobites in honor of blessed Gregory, confessor of Christ, on the bank of the river that is called the Rhine. In this place he most illustriously established the Rule of Abbot St. Benedict and his monastic brethren. There he most generously bestowed lands from his own estates, which came to him from his parents, as well as a portion from the estates of his sacred church, for the sustenance and income of those monks who cease neither day nor night to render praise to Christ diligently in that same holy monastery. For these things he has begged this indulgence of our humility, that this aforementioned place remain forever

---

70 On the architectural parallel consciously created between Petershausen and St. Peter's basilica in Rome, see p. 1 above.
71 Bishop Conrad I of Chur (r. 1122–1142).
72 CP 5.13 states that the monks built oratories in six villages, including Mimmenhausen, during the time of Abbot Conrad.

under the protection and defense of St. Peter, and of us and our pontifical successors, such that no one, neither king nor duke nor margrave, nor even the bishop who holds that episcopate at the time, nor any other person may dare to alienate or in any way remove from that holy monastery all those things that were granted by the aforementioned Gebhard; but we grant that they are to remain secure, stable, and fixed forever. And also by this apostolic precept, at the request of our aforementioned brother, we prohibit in the name of our Lord Jesus Christ anyone to be placed over this monastery other than he whom the brothers assiduously serving God there elect by common consent; the bishop should take care to confirm the elected man with the sign of blessing. The same procedure should also be observed for the election of an advocate. If, God forbid, it should ever happen that the bishop of this sacred church proves to be a heretic or schismatic, the brothers of the aforementioned monastery may by the authority of the Apostolic See have the power to seek ecclesiastical rites wherever they recognize a catholic bishop, and that the unjust bishop may not presume to inflict some injury on them concerning this. For if, although we do not expect it, anyone of whatever order or power is tempted to disrupt in some way those things that were bestowed upon the aforementioned monastery by our aforementioned brother, or if he wishes to take away from the right or domain of this monastery, unless he comes to his senses, he shall stand excommunicated from the body and blood of our Lord Jesus Christ and anathematized by all the sacred fathers and by us, and he shall not receive the viaticum at the end of his life, and even in death his name shall not by any means be recited during the solemnities of the Masses. Whoever through pious intention will stand as guard and keeper of this our precept shall forever deserve to attain the grace of benediction and eternal life from the Lord God and our Savior Jesus Christ. Amen. Written by the hand of John, the notary, regional, and official of the holy Lateran Palace. Given on 25 April by the hand of Bishop Gregory of the sacred church of Portus and Librarian of the Holy Apostolic See,[73] in the fourth year of the pontificate of our most sacred Pope John XV."[74]

---

73 That is, the dignitary of the Roman Curia in charge of the papal library and archives.
74 JL #3831 (dated 989). This papal privilege, like Gregory V's privilege of 996 (JL #3897, CP 2.2), is preserved only in the CP. It has been suggested that the sentence guaranteeing the monks the right to elect their advocate is a later interpolation. Other wording is also unusual in contemporary papal privileges (including

[1.28. HOW HE PRAYED AT THE SEPULCHER OF ST. ULRICH. When the blessed Bishop Gebhard was returning from the thresholds of the apostles[75] after receiving this privilege and the saints' relics, as described above, once he had crossed the Alps and arrived in Alemannia, he came to Augsburg and went to pray at the sepulcher of the most blessed Ulrich, the bishop of this same city,[76] who had departed from the world to God almost fifty years before. While he attentively prayed there, he heard a resounding voice, as if from the tomb, saying to him, "What do you seek or require, Gebhard?" As if hearing a familiar voice, he boldly responded, "Since I recently built a place that will be dedicated to the Lord, I ask that this place be graced by your patronage, and that some relics from your most sacred body be allowed to be brought there on account of your piety." To this, again as if from the tomb, the voice responded, "This cannot be done by any means, since I desire that my intact body await the last day in this place. And because you dared to disturb and batter me with your prayers, in consequence, when you reach the land of your monastery, you will know my wrath." After he heard this prophecy, Gebhard withdrew and returned to his own lands. When he arrived at the farthest part of the land that belonged to the monastery, behold, the spines of thorn bushes hanging over the road snagged the bishop's boot as he passed and wounded his shin. When he felt the pain from the wound, he said with a clear voice, "Behold, St. Ulrich has completed in deed that which he predicted in word." This wound afterwards increased in severity from day to day, and it could not be healed thereafter with any medicine until the end of his life.][77]

---

the above formulation, "John, the notary, regional, and official of the holy Lateran Palace"). Experts in diplomatics have argued that JL #3831 was so heavily altered by the chronicler that its original content was lost, and that JL #3897 was forged in its entirety. On the hypothesized modification and forging of these two papal privileges for Petershausen, see Ilse Juliane Miscoll-Reckert, *Kloster Petershausen als bischöflich-konstanzisches Eigenkloser. Studien über das Verhältnis zu Bischof, Adel und Reform vom 10. bis 12. Jahrhundert* (Sigmaringen: Jan Thorbecke Verlag, 1973), 62–65. See also Krebs, "Quellenstudien," 487–488.

75 "The thresholds of the apostles" is a phrase commonly used in the Middle Ages to refer to the city of Rome.

76 Bishop Ulrich I of Augsburg (r. 923–973), the first saint officially canonized by a pope (specifically Pope John XV, who also provided Petershausen with its papal privilege).

77 This account of a hostile encounter between the newly canonized (993) Ulrich of Augsburg and Gebhard II points to the animosity that had emerged between family lines by the time this part of the CP was written (c. 1136). As Petershausen's

THE CHRONICLE OF PETERSHAUSEN: BOOK ONE

1.29. ABOUT THE ARM OF THE APOSTLE ST. PHILIP. Emperor Otto[78] gave Gebhard a silver-covered reliquary that contained the arm of the apostle St. Philip with numerous other magnificent saints' relics. This arm was rediscovered during the time of Abbot Theodoric,[79] although shattered into pieces; afterwards, during the time of Abbot Berthold,[80] it was decorated with gold, silver, and jewels by Conrad (his chaplain at the time and later abbot)[81] and other brothers.[82] One joint from the fingers of Pope St. Gregory was enclosed in the base along with many other relics.

1.30. OTTO'S MOTHER WAS FROM GREECE.[83] The mother of the aforementioned ruler Otto had been brought from Greece, and when she came thence, she brought with her the aforementioned arm.

1.31. HOW WORNDORF WAS ACQUIRED.[84] At the request of Count Marquard, brother of the blessed Gebhard, this same emperor granted a certain small estate to the monastery, over which he wrote the following privilege:

"The privilege over Worndorf. In the name of the holy and indivisible Trinity. Otto, King by favor of divine mercy. Let it be manifest for the pious devotion of all the faithful, present and future, how we, on account of the petition and intervention of Count Marquard and for love of our faithful and venerable Bishop Gebhard of the church of Constance, who has often exhibited devoted service to us, give to the church of St. Gregory, honorably built in the location called Petershausen, over which the reverend and first Abbot Perriger now presides, from our property everything that we have in the villages called Worndorf and Krummbach, in the *pagus* of Goldineshundere, situated in the county

---

episcopal proprietor, Bishop Ulrich I of Constance – the son of Count Hartman of Dillingen and thus a direct descendent of the family of St. Ulrich of Augsburg – would later prove to be a thorn in the side of the monastery. See, for example, CP 3.45, 4.6, and 4.25. That Ulrich's Augsburg was allied with the emperor in the conflict over investiture, and Gebhard's Constance was allied with the pope, is also a point worth emphasizing.

78 Emperor Otto III (r. 983–1002; crowned emperor in 996).
79 Abbot Theodoric (r. 1086–1116).
80 Abbot Berthold (r. 1116–1127).
81 Abbot Conrad (r. 1127–1164).
82 cf. CP 4.10.
83 The Byzantine Princess Theophanu (c. 955–991), wife of Emperor Otto II from 972.
84 This royal privilege is edited in MGH DD O III, 126. See also Krebs, "Quellenstudien," 488.

of the same aforementioned Count Marquard. And we hand over to the aforementioned church the same property with all appurtenances duly pertaining to it, in grounds, buildings, cultivated and uncultivated lands, fields, meadows, plains, pastures, forests, hunting preserves, lakes and flowing rivers, fisheries, mills, roads and impassable areas, ingress and egress, acquired and to be acquired, and all other appurtenances that could yet be mentioned, for this reason: that this same property henceforth might forever remain unaltered under the rule of this church free from the objection of all men. And so that this donation of our Highness might remain inviolable in the future, we ordered that this document be marked with the impression of our signet, and we corroborated this with our own hand, as is shown below. The signet of the most glorious King Otto. I, Hildebold, bishop and chancellor in the place of Archbishop Willigis,[85] confirmed it. Given on 2 June in the year of the Incarnation of the Lord 993, in the sixth indiction, in the tenth year of the reign of Otto III. Transacted in the royal palace in Bürgel."

1.32. HOW THE BLESSED GEBHARD DONATED HIS KNIGHTS TO THE CHURCH.[86] All that he had or was able to acquire, Gebhard faithfully offered to his monastery for God, except for certain men among his ministerials, who were wealthy and powerful. He did not wish to hand them over because he prudently reckoned that they might be more of a detriment than an asset to this modest place.[87]

1.33. ON NEUHEIM. The blessed man obtained a rather respectable property in Neuheim in exchange for land in Markdorf.[88]

1.34. ON TÄGERWILLEN AND GOTTLIEBEN. A certain noble woman gave him her estate in Tägerwilen and Gottlieben, which was later enlarged twice. For in that location two vineyards were exchanged for two manorial estates, which Lord Adalgod of Märstetten gave to the monastery in the place called Ottenberg. [Moreover, another

---

85 Archbishop Willigis of Mainz (r. 975–1011).

86 cf. *Life of Gebhard* 1.20.

87 For the possible reason for Gebhard's concern, see p. 41 above. For some of the ministerials he did bequeath, see CP 1.35.

88 A charter documenting this exchange was entered into Petershausen's tenth-century sacramentary (University of Heidelberg, *Codex Salemitani* IXb) on f. 35r. This is an early thirteenth-century forgery. See Krebs, "Quellenstudien," 516. For a digital facsimile, see https://doi.org/10.11588/diglit.604#0071 (Date of last access: 22 December 2019).

manorial estate was acquired there during the time of Bishop Ulrich II[89] for which another excellent manorial estate near Stahringen was given.][90] Gebhard put the unfree laborers of these properties in the same monastery with the brothers so that they might serve them wherever necessary each day, just as those who had lived in this place, and so that they might haul dried wood from Neuheim and always be prepared for every service.[91]

1.35. ON MINISTERIALS. ON THE MEN OF ARBON. ON THE MEN OF BOHLINGEN. And while I am speaking so much about vassals, that is, about ministerials: Gebhard gave a certain Makko, forefather of Rudolf of Arbon and his line, and also the forebears of Hacho and his kin from Bohlingen, together with all the things that they possessed, to the church of Constance. Nevertheless, the aforementioned Makko, later going to Jerusalem, freed himself with certain gifts to the monastery, saying that he should not be bound to any service there because he had been the blessed man's own servant. Gebhard gave a certain man called Turand, of this same lineage, nobility, and wealth, whose posterity still lives in Owingen, to the monastery. He also conferred many poorer men to the monastery and assigned to all of them this duty: that they should ride with the abbot and serve him both at home and abroad, make their horses available either to the abbot or the brothers wherever necessary, defend the monastery to the best of their ability, and place themselves in the service of absolutely no one except the abbot and his monks alone.

[**1.36. ON THE ENDOWMENT OF THE MONASTERY.** These are the things that blessed Bishop Gebhard gave to the monastery from the inheritance of his parents or that he acquired from another source: Owingen, Sauldorf, Anslechiswilare, Altenrhein, Höchst and Brugg, Rot, Stetten, Mülheim, Walbertsweiler, Schlatt and Rinhart. He acquired one quarter of Epfendorf and Thayngen from the church of Constance in exchange for others of his properties, that is Lutwangen and Repperweiler, Eichstetten, Epfendorf, Neuheim, Tägerwilen, Gottlieben, as well as Dussnang, and Oberwangen, one of which he

---

89 Bishop Ulrich II of Constance (r. 1127–1138).
90 Petershausen's twelfth-century necrology names Gozzhalm as the donor of Stahringen. See MGH Nec. Germ. 1, 677 (27 November).
91 Like the laborers originally designated for the monastery, these are *servi cottidiani*. cf. CP 1.11, note 52.

obtained with the means of the diocese, the other with the means of the monastery; he also granted Oberdorf from the property of the diocese.]

1.37. ON THE LIBERTY OF THE MONASTERY. Blessed Gebhard stipulated that this monastery owe no service, no tribute, no tax, no tolls, nor the performance of any duty at all, whether to the Roman pontiff, the emperor, nor even to the bishop of Constance, or to any person of whatever power or rank, but to God alone. This place therefore remains inviolate up to the present day, and no one dares to defile it.

1.38. ON THE TAX OF OTHER MONASTERIES. Of course, other monasteries that are called free must pay a gold coin worth five *solidi* to Rome each year. The monastery of Petershausen, however, owes nothing to anyone – not to Rome, nor to Constance, nor to Mainz,[92] nor to the king, nor to the duke – except that it should be free to attend to regular religion.

1.39. ABOUT SERVICE ON THE FEAST OF ST. GREGORY. Of course, certain men are accustomed to claim that we ought to give a prebend to the brothers of Constance on the feast of Pope St. Gregory – for they know that this was established before the monastery was founded. Indeed, just as I said above, blessed Gebhard, before he was made bishop, gave the property that he had in Oberdorf, Billafingen, Heggelbach, and Liggersdorf to the church of Constance, and he himself received these as a benefice with the condition that either he himself or whoever might have this benefice after him should serve the brothers of the aforementioned church plentifully on the feast of St. Gregory.[93] After this, when he was made bishop, he founded the monastery and granted us the aforementioned estates with the same obligation that I stated in that matter, and he in turn assigned to the canons the duty that, three times a year, they should come as a community to that same monastery in a solemn procession and, taking turns, sing mass for his soul. And beyond this, on the feast of St. Gregory they should joyously sing a public mass for him with the brothers, and the monks should lead the choir and serve at the altar, and on that day, just as I said above regarding the aforementioned estates, the clerics should be given two talents and five *solidi* for service.

---

92 Mainz was the seat of the archbishop.
93 cf. CP 1.7–8, in which Gebhard promises the annual tribute attached to these lands to the canons of Constance.

{1.40. The proper measure of their service is this: first, three measures of grain for making loaves; then from the western table in the refectory, some fish, one half peck of millet pounded with a pestle, three urns of wine, and five *solidi* in coin. This is the service that was owed each and every year from the aforementioned properties. But Abbot Conrad reduced this to two talents and five *solidi* that ought to be given to them.}[94]

1.41. ABOUT AICHSTETTEN. There was a certain count named Adalhard, a pious, devout, and God-fearing man, and a relative of the blessed man Gebhard according to consanguinity of the flesh; he was not, however, from Swabia, but lived in a distant land. Many great estates in the *pagus* of Illergau – that is, near Aichstetten and Breitenbach, Rieden, Hausen, and Steinbach – fell into his rule through inheritance. Whenever this man came from his land and visited these estates (which he did very rarely), all of the inhabitants hastened to greet him with their little gifts, just as all serfs do for their lord. But because he was kind and merciful, he asked his attendants what these men were hoping for by doing these things. And when they responded that these were his men and that they had come with the greeting that was owed in order to visit him, he ordered, "Have each of them keep their gifts until I can inspect them for myself after lunch." Then, after all were fully and abundantly filled with food, he gave them back their gifts and allowed them to depart without taking anything from them. Thus they would rejoice that he came there. This count, then, gave his relatives in Bregenz an estate in Steinbach, which later came under the control of men in Kirchberg as a wedding gift.

1.42. ADALHARD GAVE BLESSED GEBHARD AICHSTETTEN, BREITENBACH, AND RIEDEN. This pious Count Adalhard gave his nephew, blessed Bishop Gebhard, all of his property in Aichstetten, Breitenbach, Rieden, and Hausen – some forty manorial estates – and more in cultivated fields and meadows (with the sole exception of the very extensive woods), the parish church with many tithes, and pastures, fisheries, and mills. The aforementioned Count Adalhard also legally handed over many tributaries with all of their possessions

---

[94] This entire chapter has been rendered illegible, perhaps after its stipulations for service to the church of Constance on the feast of St. Gregory were no longer valid. The act of striking through the text on f. 47r appears to have damaged the text on the reverse (f. 47v). We have used the Latin text from Feger (1956), which itself was based on the reconstruction in Mone (1848).

in ownership to his nephew, the venerable Bishop Gebhard, and the blessed man gave them with manifest devotion to his monastery, which he had built in honor of Pope St. Gregory, without any contradiction and before appropriate witnesses, to remain thereafter for the use of the brothers serving God there.

1.43. ABOUT DUKE BURCHARD. At that same time, since they had no earthly child, the devout Duke Burchard[95] and his wife Hadwig chose Christ as their heir, and accordingly founded a monastery in their castle on the mountain called Twiel,[96] where they handed over estates and all their appurtenances most sufficient for the sustenance of the monks, and divided the rest among other monasteries. The first abbot who ruled this monastery was a holy and venerable man called Walfrid.

1.44. ABOUT THE MONASTERY OF STEIN. This monastery was later moved from the mountain of Twiel by Emperor Henry[97] and established on the bank of the Rhine in a place called Stein.[98] And because that same king claimed all of Duke Burchard's possessions for himself as an inheritance, he took away many things from the same monastery and left only enough to suffice for a few brothers. Finally, he subjected this same abbey, as well as the things that belonged to it and those that he had taken away, to the diocese of Bamberg, which he himself had just founded.

1.45. HOW GEBHARD ACQUIRED EPFENDORF. After Duke Burchard died, his widow, the aforementioned Hadwig, gave the blessed man, her nephew Bishop Gebhard, the estate called Epfendorf for the support of the brothers serving God in his monastery, called Petershausen. The monastery possesses these even to the present day by the authority and privilege of Emperor Otto III. A quarter of this same estate belongs to the monastery of Stein.

Privilege over Epfendorf: "In the name of the holy and indivisible Trinity. Otto, King by favor of divine mercy. If we offer a favorable hearing to the pious petitions that the priests pour into our ears for

---

95 Duke Burchard III of Swabia (r. 954–973).
96 The castle monastery is also known as Hohentwiel. The original monastery, founded in 970, was dedicated to St. George and St. Cyril.
97 Emperor Henry II (r. 1002–1024; crowned emperor in 1014).
98 The relocation took place around 1007.

the churches entrusted to them, we believe that this will doubtless be beneficial to us for the condition of our present kingdom and for the reward of eternal blessedness. Wherefore let the skilled diligence of all my faithful subjects, both present and future, know how Lord Gebhard, venerable bishop of the holy church of Constance, coming before our royal Highness, asked resolutely that we consent to give over and to confirm with our royal charter a certain estate called Epfendorf, with all of its appurtenances situated in the places and villages of Bösingen, Mössingen, Zimmern, Harthausen, and Irslingen in the *pagus* of Baar and situated in the county of Count Hildebald, to the monastery of St. Gregory, which the aforementioned man, beloved Bishop Gebhard, dear to God and men, built from the ground up for the use of the monks serving God under the Rule of St. Benedict, with devout consideration for the remedy of his soul and the souls of his parents. For as we have learned from our faithful men, the above-named estate Epfendorf, with all of the things legally appertaining to it, belongs to the aforementioned monastery of St. Gregory through the gift of Duchess Hadwig of blessed memory. Whence we grant the following wishes and petitions of a good man who is dear to us and hand over the oft-mentioned estate Epfendorf with all of its appurtenances, in grounds, buildings, unfree laborers of both sexes, cultivated and uncultivated lands, fields, meadows, plains, pastures, vines and vineyards, forests, lakes and flowing rivers, fisheries, mills, roads and impassable areas, ingress and egress, acquired and to be acquired, and all other appurtenances that could yet be mentioned or named, to the aforementioned monastery built in honor of St. Gregory, and also to the monks soldiering for God there under the Rule of St. Benedict, and we transfer it in its entirety from our rule into theirs. Moreover, we confirm with all our royal authority those things that have been or will be given to the monastery by our beloved Bishop Gebhard or by whichever other person, great or small, so that they might remain secure, unshaken, and free from any disturbance, such that no trouble might be caused in that holy place by the insolence of malicious men. And so that this charter of our royal donation might endure constant from this hour forward, we ordered that this document be marked with the impression of our signet, and we corroborated this with our own hand, as is shown below. The signet of the most glorious King Otto. I, Hildebold, bishop and chancellor, in the place of Archbishop Willigis, confirmed it. Given on 4 November in the year of the Incarnation of the Lord 994, in the seventh indiction, in the eleventh year of the reign of Otto III. Happily transacted in Ingelheim."[99]

1.46. ON THE DECORATIONS OF THE CHURCH. Blessed Gebhard acquired many splendid and honorable decorations for his beloved monastery, the greater part of which was squandered by the wickedness of certain men. {For certain professed monks, in an act of sacrilege, tore apart silk dorsals[100] and made them into luxurious garments for themselves, and in this and other ways they destroyed the monastery's property by living luxuriously.}

1.47. ON THE TWO CHANDELIERS. Bishop Gebhard acquired two silver chandeliers, one of which he had suspended in the choir and the other before the cross in the vestibule. {But one of the monks, misled by ambition at some point, broke one of these apart and gave the silver to the bishop as a price for the abbacy. But after the bishop had acquired it, he refused to appoint him as abbot over the brothers. But increasing his sin, the wretched man broke apart the other chandelier and regained the favor of the bishop with this money.}[101]

1.48. ON THE CEILING PANELS. The bishop decorated the entire ceiling of the basilica with gilded bosses, spaced apart;[102] above the

---

99 See Krebs, "Quellenstudien," 488. This royal charter is also printed in MGH DD O III, 152. The CP is the only surviving witness to this charter; Ingelheim was the site of an imperial palace from the mid-eighth through the eleventh century.

100 A dorsal is a curtain-like textile, often ornately decorated, that hangs behind the altar.

101 Here the chronicler offers a remarkably candid accusation – that one abbot, who remains unnamed, was able to circumvent the proper procedure for election and to be granted the abbatial office through the sin of simony. It is unclear when this alleged simoniacal transaction between the would-be abbot and the bishop (also unnamed) took place. In fact, the story may serve more as a statement of the perils of simony and improper electoral process, from the perspective of a monk writing in the period after the reform of 1086, than as a factual account of events. Simony was one of the key abuses targeted by contemporary monastic and church reformers. On the problem of simoniac abbots in this period, see Joseph H. Lynch, *Simoniacal Entry into Religious Life from 1000 to 1260: A Social, Economic, and Legal Study* (Columbus, OH: Ohio State University Press, 1976). It should also be noted that during the medieval period, someone attempted to erase this account, as well as the account of the luxury-loving monks who pulled apart precious silk vestments in CP 1.46, from the manuscript. A later medieval hand attempted to recover the erased text in both CP 1.46 and 1.47 in the top and right margins of f. 49r. Our translation is based on that recovered text.

102 In his *Life of Gebhard* (1.12), the chronicler explains that this elaborate ceiling evoked the vault of Heaven.

choir he had an image of holy Mary, the Mother of God, painted on a single panel in gold and the best colors, and around it, images of the twelve apostles arranged in the shape of a cross. Today, due to their great age, all of these things have ceased to be what they were.

1.49. ABOUT A CERTAIN WOMAN. Another time, a certain lady came to the blessed priest Gebhard and told him how armed enemies of her husband had surrounded their household one night, wanting to capture the man himself, or cut him down and kill him. Although he opposed them with manly vigor before the doors and kept the enemy at bay, they finally wounded him so severely that he fell and lay half dead. The aforementioned woman, standing with her husband and seeing him collapse, took up arms and bravely fought against the enemy all night. She bloodied them with multiple wounds, and even killed some of them. These men, now very fatigued and totally exhausted, were by no means able to invade the house. They began to marvel and to ask one another what thing this was that could resist them so tenaciously and indefatigably all night long. After a light was brought so that they could see that an armed woman was standing against them, marveling exceedingly and driven by great shame, they dispersed. The woman, coming to the venerable Gebhard, as it was said, seeking his counsel and assistance, as well as his grace, asked how she ought to do penance for so many murders. But imbued with the grace of Christ, he said to her: "Daughter, do not be discouraged on account of this, but rather go and glorify God, who worked miraculously with you. Therefore, do not believe that you did these things with your own strength, but rather that the right hand of God threw down the enemy for you." And he imposed absolutely no penance on her, but consoled her with great grace and sent her away. Indeed, he showed grace to all people, which he himself found most abundantly before the Father of Mercies.

1.50. PERRIGER, THE FIRST ABBOT AFTER THE CONSECRATION OF THE MONASTERY. In the year of the Incarnation of the Lord 993, in the second year after the consecration of the monastery, Perriger was appointed as the first abbot.[103]

1.51. WHEN THE BLESSED GEBHARD FINISHED HIS LIFE. Afterwards, in the fourth year, that is in the Incarnation of the Lord 996, sixteen years after his ordination, the blessed and venerable Bishop

---

103 Perriger is also referred to in the Chronicle as Pezilin; cf. CP 1.13, *Life of Gebhard* 1.18.

Gebhard finished his temporal life and crossed over to eternal life in the twelfth year of Emperor Otto III, in the ninth indiction, and he was happily and gloriously buried in the church that he himself built, in the southern apse.[104]

1.52. CONCERNING HIS TOMB.[105] Indeed I saw his tomb, most gracefully adorned with illustrious decorations. For at his head he had an altar dedicated in honor of St. Benedict, where the first mass was sung every day. Across from this same altar was a panel that had an image of the Lord on the lower part, and on his right hand was the image of St. Gregory and on his left St. Gebhard, and in the upper part of this same panel were affixed copper plates, on which this epitaph was written in gold letters:

1.53. EPITAPH. The verse:

> *O fated plot of land, spurn the beguiling times*
> *And remember the journey that these ashes attest.*
> *Here lies the honor of our people, and also their sorrow.*
> *He was the prefect of the city, but the profit of the entire world,*
> *He founded a sanctuary and seat of the temple to God.*
> *Graciously forgiving this plot of land, O God,*
> *Justly reward this man, since he loved you.*[106]

1.54. ON THE OTHER EPITAPH. But I also found another epitaph written about this servant of God in an old book in the monastery of Stein, which goes like this:

> *Earnestly cast a pious glance here, traveler,*
> *Where this inscription shines; look down upon what lies hidden.*
> *Behold, Bishop Gebhard is entombed here,*
> *For whom there is nothing much left in the world,*
> *And happy mother Constance deserved such a father;*
> *Though overjoyed at his resurrection, she now laments his absence.*

---

104 For the chronicler's account of the dispute over the proper resting place for Gebhard II's remains, see the *Life of Gebhard* 1.22–1.23.

105 Gebhard's tomb was renovated by Abbot Conrad in 1134 (CP T.1). The chronicler, writing after 1134, thus has to describe Gebhard's original tomb from memory in this chapter. CP 3.15 places Gebhard's sepulcher near the well in the crypt he himself had constructed (CP 1.17), although the well was demolished by Bishop Gebhard III well before Conrad's renovations.

106 In Latin, this is a rhyming poem, switching the rhyming pattern halfway through the verse. The second epitaph (in CP 1.54) similarly begins rhyming only partway through the poem.

He lived as a bishop, and bore a noble pedigree.
He was a good and wise man, desirous of virtue,
Hungering and thirsting for God. While present he was away,
With Martha in body, and with Mary in spirit.
He erected that building to the merits of Gregory
The High Pontiff, and he gathered together monks.
Thus filled with merits, he departed the flesh on the sixth
Kalends of September, and rests in heaven.
Speak, and let young and old say alike:
"May the Omnipotent grant you eternal rest."

1.55. ON THE DECORATION OF THE SEPULCHER. There were five columns rendered in stucco on the wall surrounding the sepulcher, the capitals and arches of which were decorated with elegant sculpture and vines; winged creatures and quadrupeds were also richly fashioned above. Moreover, at his head was the image of the Cross, and on his right side was an image of him lying prostrate, and in the middle was an image of him in priestly vestments as if prepared for the office of the altar. Figures of his servants were assisting him on the upper right side, one holding a book, another a linen cloth, and this all was magnificently done in stucco relief. This tomb was next to the entrance to the crypt, raised off the ground on four square slabs and always covered by a cloth. Here, for the sake of demonstrating the magnitude of this man's merits and on account of his piety, the compassionate and merciful Lord has healed many sorrows up to the present day.

HERE ENDS THE FIRST BOOK

BOOK TWO

Introduction

Book Two covers the early years of the monastery, from the death of Bishop Gebhard II of Constance in 995 to the ascent of Bishop Gebhard III in 1084, and closes by setting the stage for the arrival at Petershausen of monks from Hirsau. Book Two does not present a coherent narrative account of the history of the monastery in these early years, which would probably have been beyond what the sources available to the chronicler could support. The first half of the book is rather an eclectic collection of privileges, anecdotes, and stories of patronage or conflict, which while somewhat haphazard in structure, broadly reflects a period of growth in land ownership and patronage, despite various external challenges. Although he does attempt to compile a catalog of Petershausen's abbots, the chronicler is unable to produce any detail for the earliest of these, saying little of them beyond what he can deduce from the privileges that some left behind.[1]

Of particular note in Book Two are the chronicler's efforts to illustrate the monks' commitment to the liberty of the monastery, rights that he documented carefully in Book One. He describes, for example, a struggle between the monastery and Gebhard II's successor, Bishop Lambert of Constance (r. 995–1018), over his demand for monastic goods to support the diocese of Bamberg, recently established by Henry II. Although Lambert's demands were in clear violation of the exemptions described in CP 1.37 and 1.38, he persisted in pressing his demands and finally resorted to taking by force treasure given to the monastery by Gebhard II himself. For his transgressions, the chronicler claims with some relish, Lambert was struck down by God.[2] The chronicler also offers a vivid account of Abbot Meinrad's (r. 1078, 1080–1081) bold stand against the over-reaching Bishop Otto I of Constance; when Otto ordered the monks to prepare for service to King Henry IV, the abbot objected vigorously, "saying that he had no right to anything from

1 CP 2.6–2.14.
2 CP 2.3–2.5.

that place." When the bishop continued to press his demand, Meinrad threw his crozier, saying that he would "absolutely never be willing to allow this sacred place to be forced to part with its liberty by violence."[3] Whether or not either of these dramatic encounters took place, their inclusion in the text, and the prominent contemporary addition of the "nota" that draws attention to the encounter between Meinrad and Otto in the margin of the manuscript, suggests that the liberty of the monastery was on the mind of the chronicler as he compiled his text.

In the second half of Book Two, the chronicler turns to the conflict over investiture.[4] While Book Three provides valuable insight into the experience of the controversy at the local level, in Constance and at Petershausen,[5] this section of Book Two engages the crisis at the level of the Empire. Here the chronicler recounts events at the highest levels, describing the character, career, and demise of such key figures as Emperors Henry IV and Henry V, Pope Gregory VII, anti-King Rudolph, and anti-Pope Clement III (referred to only as Wibert by the chronicler). His extraordinarily colorful and vitriolic characterization of Henry IV leaves no doubt as to the chronicler's own ecclesiopolitical stance or Petershausen's support for the papacy, along with other Hirsau-influenced monasteries.[6] The chronicler's coverage of the major events and military campaigns of the conflict is largely derivative of other chronicles, notably the Chronicle of Bernold of St. Blasien (particularly on the Battle of Pleichfeld in 1086) and the Annals of Lambert of Hersfeld (which he seems to follow nearly word-for-word in some places). There are also two cases in which the wording of the CP and the Chronicle of Berthold of Zwiefalten are quite close. As Berthold began his work c. 1137, just one year after this section of the CP was completed, it is possible that both drew on a common (unidentified) earlier source. In the notes that accompany the text, we have highlighted significant borrowings, as well as interesting alternative accounts and characterizations, from other chronicles and annals.

Some of the historical narrative in Book Two is confused or erroneous. Incorrect dates are provided, for example, for the excommunication of Henry IV, his invasion of Rome, his invasion of Saxony during the

---

3 CP 2.15.
4 On the investiture controversy, see Blumenthal, *Investiture Controversy*.
5 See CP 3.28–3.32, 3.35–3.36.
6 See esp. CP 2.26–2.31.

Saxon Rebellion of 1073–1075, and the death of Gregory VII (listed as 1081 in CP 2.41, although the chronicler describes his activity in 1085 in CP 2.47).[7] The chronicler also wrongly distinguishes the battle "on the Streu," which he calls the "second battle,"[8] from "the Battle of Mellrichstadt," which he identifies as the "third battle"[9] when they were one and the same, fought in August 1078. Perhaps this confusion may be explained in part by the fact that the Annals of Lambert of Hersfeld, on which the Petershausen chronicler seems to have relied for his account of some of the earlier battles, ends with 1077. For events in 1078 and later, then, he would have had to turn to other sources. In still other places, the narrative fails to maintain chronological order, and several stories are repeated with greater detail not long after their first telling, including the coronation of anti-King Rupert, Henry IV's invasion of Rome and imperial coronation by anti-Pope Clement III, and Gregory VII's expulsion and condemnation of Henry and Wibert.[10]

The closing chapters of Book Two introduce Hirsau and recount the election of Bishop Gebhard III of Constance, setting the stage for the arrival of the Hirsau reformers at Petershausen at the bidding of the newly elected bishop, an event that opens Book Three.[11] The chronicler situates the origins of the Hirsau reform in the context of the struggles between pope and emperor, metaphorically constructing Hirsau as a safe harbor from the "tempest" of the conflict over investiture. It must be partially for this reason that the controversy, so significant for Petershausen itself (as will be seen in Book Three) receives such extensive treatment at the imperial level in Book Two.[12]

Book Two

2.1. HOW DUSSNANG WAS ACQUIRED. After the blessed Bishop Gebhard crossed from this world to heaven, the monk Lambert succeeded him as bishop[13] and Abbot Perriger took

---

7 CP 2.28, 2.30, 2.32, 2.41.
8 CP 2.34.
9 CP 2.35.
10 Specifically, CP 2.29 is repeated in 2.33, 2.30 is repeated in 2.36–2.37, and 2.41 is repeated in 2.47.
11 CP 2.48–2.49.
12 CP 2.48. The investiture controversy is first characterized as a tempest in CP 2.28.
13 Bishop Lambert of Constance (r. 995–1018).

over the direction of the monastery of St. Gregory, called Petershausen.[14]

2.2. SIGGER. At that same time, a certain rich nobleman named Sigger sold his estates in Dussnang and Oberwangen with all of their appurtenances (churches, tithes, and everything else appertaining to those places) to the aforementioned monastery.[15] And when Sigger had received everything as agreed and had confirmed this transaction according to the law of the Alemanni, Bishop Lambert, with the aid of Emperor Otto III, acquired from Gregory V[16] (who was also called Bruno) this privilege over the same monastery as well as everything that was, is, and will yet be surrendered.

Privilege of Pope Gregory over the monastery and Dussnang: "In the name of the holy and indivisible Trinity. Gregory, also called Bruno, by the grace of God Bishop of the holy catholic and apostolic church of Rome and Servant of the Servants of God. A petition pertaining to the religious life and the security of sacred places should be executed with the help of God without delay, and whenever our approval and the customary protection of apostolic authority is requested for the benefit of the holy Church, we should willingly assist this proposal with favorable consideration and ensure its complete security, so that the veneration, health, and security of sacred places may thus be gained and also so that we may be rewarded with the foremost prize by the Creator of all things. Therefore, on account of the desires and requests of the august Emperor Otto III and Bishop Lambert of the holy church of Constance, we fortify with apostolic protection a certain monastery on the bank of the Rhine next to Constance in the village called Petershausen, which was built by Bishop Gebhard of blessed memory in honor of St. Gregory. And we honor it with the precepts of the Roman church, with the stipulation that this same monastery, over which Abbot Perriger now presides – with all the many estates appertaining to it, including cultivated and uncultivated lands, tenants, and dependents, and whatever Bishop Gebhard delivered to that monastery by right of inheritance or some other acquisition, and whatever he sold from his

---

14 Although the wording here implies that the abbacy of Perriger began only after the death of Gebhard, previous entries suggest otherwise; cf. CP 1.13, 1.50, *Life of Gebhard* 1.18.

15 Sigger is named as the donor of Dussnang and Oberwangen in Petershausen's twelfth-century necrology on 23 November. MGH Nec. Germ. 1, 677.

16 Pope Gregory V (r. 996–999).

episcopate or relinquished without sale, as well as whatever the aforementioned Bishop Lambert granted to that same monastery in any transaction, with the estates of Sigger called Dussnang and Wangen situated in the *pagus* of Thurgau under Count Berthold (one of which was acquired from the episcopal property by Bishop Gebhard and the other from his monastic property under Abbot Perriger),[17] or anything that will be granted by any God-fearing person to that same godly place or that has been granted already – shall remain and persist stable and undisturbed under the testimony of Christ, supported by the apostolic defense and protection of blessed Peter. Also, by this apostolic command, with the consent of the august Emperor Otto III and the aforementioned Bishop Lambert, who requested that these things be done, we wholly forbid that anyone be placed over that monastery except he whom the common accord of the brothers serving God there choose; this involves the bishop only so far as to establish the one who is thus elected. We decree this also for the election of an advocate. When an abbot or advocate of the monastery is elected, let it be his charge to administer the property of the monastery and resist those dispersing it. Meanwhile, if, contrary to our expectations, someone should be tempted in reckless audacity to defy these things, which have been rightly and firmly established by our authority in this privilege, or otherwise to oppose or in any way transgress these measures that have been instituted by us for the praise of God and for the stability of the aforementioned monastery, let him know that he, by the authority of blessed Peter, the Prince of the Apostles, whose humble successor we are, is bound with the chain of anathema and will be consumed by eternal fires with the devil and Judas, the betrayer of Christ. But let him who piously stands as guard of our saving precept be blessed with manifold grace by the just Lord of retribution and deserve to be made a partaker of eternal life forever. Amen."[18]

2.3. CONCERNING KING HENRY II AND BISHOP LAMBERT.

Later, when Emperor Otto III had died and Henry II became emperor and built the diocese of Bamberg,[19] he reclaimed as if by right of

---

17 cf. CP 1.36 for the previous transaction of these two estates.

18 JL #3897 (996). This papal privilege, like John XV's privilege of 989 (JL #3831, CP 1.27), is preserved only in the CP. For the hypothesis that JL #3831 was thoroughly modified by the chronicler and that JL #3897 was a complete forgery, see pp. 57–58, n. 74 above.

19 The diocese of Bamberg was established on 1 November 1007 at a synod held in Frankfurt.

inheritance everything that once belonged to Duke Burchard and his wife Hadwig from the mountain of Twiel and gave it to the church of Bamberg. And thus even the monastery of Stein came into the rule of this church.[20] But our monastery, Petershausen, still retained Epfendorf through a privilege of Emperor Otto, which the aforementioned Hadwig had long before given to the blessed man, Bishop Gebhard.[21] But since the aforementioned King Henry was eagerly collecting from other churches everywhere the necessary goods to enrich and decorate the place he had built, he plundered many places with his demands until he enriched his church beyond measure. Thus it happened that Henry also demanded of Bishop Lambert of Constance that he provide some contribution from his church, just like the other bishops. Whence it happened that this same Lambert, in order to satisfy the emperor's desire, forcibly took from the monastery, which blessed Gebhard had built, much of the treasure that the aforementioned blessed Gebhard had given to God and to St. Gregory.

2.4. ABOUT THE TREASURE OF THE BLESSED GEBHARD. This is the treasure that Bishop Gebhard of Constance of blessed memory gave to the place that he had built in honor of the blessed Pope Gregory, and that his successor, Bishop Lambert, took away: a cup adorned with gold, two silver combs, two silver cups, a silver dish, two silver spoons, two silver chandeliers – the amount of silver comes to the weight of 28 pounds – two dorsals, two combs, one ivory comb adorned with gold, seven altar cloths, one hand-towel, one tapestry, one silver chalice, one golden stole and a cloak of the same workmanship, the hanging piece of which one of the monks stole and concealed, and which is still considered to be very splendid.

2.5. THE REVENGE OF GOD UPON LAMBERT. But divine judgment in no way left unpunished that transgression that Lambert obstinately committed in that holy place. For when the end of his life drew near, he began to swarm with lice, which are called *pediculi*, such that he could be rescued from them by no means. He was washed frequently by servants both in the Rhine and in baths in order to lessen his terrible suffering a little. But in that same water, they came out of his ears like a swarm of bees, and from each limb

---

20 cf. CP 1.44.
21 cf. CP 1.45.

like a multitude of ants, until he breathed his last breath under this loathsome torment.[22]

2.6. Abbot Ellimbold,[23] who succeeded Perriger, left behind no monument of himself for us.

2.7. HOW AN ESTATE IN GAMS WAS ACQUIRED. In the second year of the reign of Emperor Henry II,[24] Abbot Walter[25] acquired for the monastery an estate [which was later exchanged for an estate in Schnetzenhausen] in the area of Gams, Eschen, and Grabs through an exchange with a certain Burchard for estates that the monastery owned in Beuren, in Berg, and in another Berg, and a church in Lienz. During the time of Emperor Otto, a certain priest by the name of Theiter had acquired that estate bit by bit. We hold many privileges over this estate, but they are not written in such a way that I would want to insert them here.

2.8. Sigfrid was first a canon in Constance, then a monk in the monastery of St. Meinrad,[26] and finally was made abbot at the monastery of St. Gregory.[27]

2.9. Abbot Erchimbold[28] {left behind nothing worth remembering.}

2.10. Abbot Folmar[29] acquired Riedlings and Wegesaza for the monastery, just as the following privilege testifies:

The privilege over the estate of Riedlings. "In the name of the holy and indivisible Trinity. Let it be known to all the faithful of Christ, both present and future, that I, Erimbreth, at the request of Eberhard, Bishop of

---

22 This account of the Lambert's death suggests the chronicler's animosity toward the bishop. No other source reports this terrible death. See, for example, the Chronicon of Theitmar of Merseburg 8.18 in *Ottonian Germany*, trans. David A. Warner (Manchester: Manchester University Press, 2001), 273, which simply states that Lambert died on 16 May. Herman of Reichenau notes only that Lambert died in 1018 and was succeeded by Rudhard. See *Eleventh-Century Germany*, trans. I. S. Robinson, 62. See also REC, 420, for a complete list of medieval reports of Lambert's death.

23 r. ?–1003.

24 That is, in the second year of his kingship, i.e., 1003.

25 r. 1003–1004.

26 That is, the monastery of Einsiedeln, from which the first monks came to Petershausen; cf. CP 1.15.

27 Abbot Sigfrid, who was abbot some time between 1003/1004 and 1043.

28 Abbot Erchimbold, who was abbot some time between 1003/1004 and 1043, after Abbot Sigfrid.

29 Abbot Folmar (r. 1043).

the church of Constance,[30] together with the hand of my wife, Irmingard, without any contradiction, legally give to God and St. Gregory in the monastery that is called Petershausen, as well as to the monks serving God there, the estate that I have in the *pagus* of Nibelgau, in Riedlings and Wegesaza – with farmsteads, fields, meadows, pastures, lakes and flowing rivers, cultivated and uncultivated land, and paths and entrances – and enough from my estate in the forest of Arnach to suffice for construction and lumber in the aforementioned places, with its pastures and ingress and egress. Moreover, I wish it to be known that Bishop Eberhard, together with the hand of Abbot Folmar of the same monastery and of advocate Herman, accepted this same estate in the aforementioned areas of Rieldings and Wegesaza, and gave in benefice fourteen manses in the area of Aichstetten to me and my wife until we depart this life. These things were done in the year of the Incarnation of the Lord 1043, in the eleventh indiction, in the seventh epact and the fifth concurrence, on 16 June, the fifth moon, with these witnesses present: Ulrich of Bregenz, Switker, Wezil, Swigger, Ernest, Gerald, Roger, Landold, Otgoz, Liutbert, Sigbert, Hartnid, Engelschalk, Enceli, Simpert, Hunald, Ebbo, Ello, and Alberich. Bishop Eberhard ordered this record to be made."[31]

2.11. Further, it is reported that the gold that had been on the little doors of the panel that stood opposite the main altar was removed at that time and given for the aforementioned estate, and gilded silver was affixed to the panel in its place.

2.12. UHLDINGEN. In the time of Abbot Albert,[32] Swigger gave an estate in Uhldingen, concerning which the following privilege is kept.

The privilege over Uhldingen: "Let all persons, present and future, know how I, Swigger, together with the hand of my wife, Adalheid, and my son, Gottschalk, surrender to the monastery of St. Gregory, situated on the bank of the Rhine, into the hand of Abbot Albert and his advocate, Count Eberhard, half of the estate that I am known to own lawfully in the village called Uhldingen, in the *pagus* of Linzgau, in the county of Count Otto,[33] with such consideration and with the

---

30 Bishop Eberhard I of Constance (r. 1034–1046).
31 Krebs, "Quellenstudien," 488; Petershausen's twelfth-century necrology (22 September) notes that Abbot Folmar acquired Riedlings. See MGH Nec. Germ. 1, 675.
32 Abbot Albert (r. c. 1044, 1058–1060).
33 Count Otto of Buchhorn (d. 1089), according to Feger (1956), 95, n. 4.

stipulation that as long as my aforementioned wife and I shall live, we should have mutual fraternal participation in the buildings and in every use of the brothers whenever it pleases us to be present, and after our death, that our memory might always be celebrated as if for one of the brothers, and that food service might be given to the brothers according to the decree of the aforementioned abbot of reverend character on the anniversary of both our deaths, or if that is impossible, of the one whose soul should depart the body first. Done in this same church of St. Gregory in the year of the Incarnation of the Lord 1058, with the men present whose names we have written below. Count Rudolf, Eberhard, Ulrich, Albert, Hezo, Hezil, Adalhold, Gerald, Herman, Alwich, Albert, Ratold, Hezil, Rudolf, Marquard I, Deacon Bernard, have written and signed this with young King Henry IV ruling, in the second year after the death of his father, in the seventh year after the ordination of Bishop Rumold[34] [of blessed memory], in the twelfth indiction."[35]

2.13. This Albert was noble of family and handsome of body. He died in the year of the Incarnation of the Lord 1060.[36]

2.14. Siggo[37] succeeded Albert {...} After his death, Arnold[38] succeeded him. Arnold was deposed, and Meinrad[39] was set in his place.

2.15. ABOUT ABBOT MEINRAD. After Meinrad had been abbot for some time,[40] when the bishop of Constance[41] had to prepare for service

---

34 Bishop Rumold of Constance (r. 1051–1069). Berthold of Reichenau refers to Bishop Rumold as "an extremely pious and humane man who was the most sagacious restorer of the cathedral, which fell down in his time..." CBR, 123. Both Frutolf of Michelsberg (CFM, 105) and Lambert of Hersfeld (ALH, 73 and n. 204 and 205) report that Bishop Rumold was entrusted ("whether through advice or cunning is unfortunately unknown," according to Frutolf) with the care of Matilda, minor daughter of Henry III and Agnes, sister of Henry IV, during her betrothal to Rudolf of Rheinfelden.

35 Krebs, "Quellenstudien," 489.

36 Abbot Albert is commemorated in Petershausen's twelfth-century necrology on 23 April. See MGH Nec. Germ. 1, 669.

37 Abbot Siggo (r. 1061–1062); seven lines of text have been thoroughly erased here. The chronicler reports in CP 4.27, however, that Siggo died from a broken back. One can imagine that the erased account of his abbacy and/or death was not a glorious one.

38 Abbot Arnold (deposed 1064).

39 Abbot Meinrad (r. 1079, 1080–1081). Meinrad, "who ruled our monastery for many years and later Bregenz," is commemorated in Petershausen's twelfth-century necrology on 3 July. See MGH Nec. Germ. 1, 672.

40 In 1079.

41 Bishop Otto I of Constance (r. 1071–1086).

to the king,[42] he began to seek provisions rudely from the aforementioned abbot, saying that he had a right to a gelding with a tabard from that monastery. When Abbot Meinrad resisted vehemently, saying that he had no right to anything at all from that place,[43] and when the bishop insisted that it should be given, the abbot threw the crozier from himself saying that he would absolutely never be willing to allow this sacred place to be forced to part with its liberty by violence. "And because," he said, "I am not able to resist, it is better that I renounce my abbacy." Thus he renounced the abbacy, and the bishop got nothing there. But on a certain day, after Meinrad was restored to his office,[44] when the bishop wanted to sing mass in that same monastery without the abbot's invitation, Meinrad threw his staff upon the altar and withdrew.[45]

2.16. ON THE CHAPEL OF ST. JOHN THE BAPTIST, OGGELSHAUSEN AND JUDETENBURG. Around this time, when Rumold was presiding over the church of Constance, the nobleman Wolfrad of Weiler and his wife Gotistiu built a chapel in the cemetery of the monastery in honor of St. John the Baptist, St. Nicholas, and other saints, and gave Oggelshausen and Judetenburg there as an endowment, and established that the chapel should have its own priest. And there he and his wife lie buried before the sanctuary in individual tombs, one on the right wall and the other on the left.[46]

2.17. BOOS, GEIßELMACHER, SCHWÄBLISHAUSEN, MAGENBUCH. In the time of Bishop Otto, Sigfrid, the son of the aforementioned Wolfrad, also added an oratory dedicated to St. Jacob the Apostle to this same chapel and gave Boos, Gießelmacher, and Schwäblishausen to endow it. He built a tomb for himself in this same oratory, but he died in Chiavenna while returning from Rome and was

42 Henry IV (r. 1053–1105; crowned emperor in 1084); on Henry IV, see Stefan Weinfurter, *The Salian Century: Main Currents in an Age of Transition* (Philadelphia: University of Pennsylvania Press, 1999), 112–158.

43 The monastery repeatedly asserted that it was exempt from any service to the bishop (cf. CP 1.37), even under the pressure generated by the king's demands on him; for an English-language study of monastic exemption, see Kriston Rennie, *Freedom and Protection: Monastic Exemption in France, c. 590–1100* (Manchester: Manchester University Press, 2018).

44 In 1080.

45 In 1081.

46 Wolfrad is listed in Petershausen's twelfth-century necrology on 4 January (MGH Nec. Germ. 1, 665) and Gotistiu on 7 January (MGH Nec. Germ. 1, 665).

buried there. This man loved our monastery beyond measure, and he frequently visited it and stayed there. And so it happened that on a certain night after Matins had been sung, he tried to leave the church, but in the darkness of night, he fell down the stairs that used to lead down from the door into the cloister (but were later moved a bit farther from the door by my uncle Gebino[47]). Immediately after this fall, Sigfrid donated an estate in Magenbuch with the condition that every night a light should burn continually before this same door after Matins.[48]

2.18. ABOUT THE ARM OF A MARTYR OF THEBES. And now let us return briefly to an earlier time. In the time of Emperor Conrad II,[49] Herman the Elder of Hirschegg[50] acquired an arm of one of the companions of St. Maurice in Agaunum.[51] He carried it back to his homeland with due veneration, enclosed it in a small but gilded sarcophagus, and gave it to the monastery.[52] This same Herman and his brother gave two estates in Allmannsweiler and Winnenden.

2.19. CONCERNING THE PRIEST URSUS. Around this time,[53] a certain venerable old foreign priest named Ursus, who had lost his eyesight to old age, lay ill in bed in the house of an old woman in the village of Petershausen. A certain lady of Constance was accustomed to minister to this man most diligently for the sake of God, but it took great effort because he teemed irredeemably with lice, such that

---

47 Gebino, active 1106–1129 (cf. CP 3.38, 3.45, 4.32–4.34, and 4.40–4.41).

48 Sigfrid, "a layman who expanded the chapel of St. John which his father had built, and who gave Boos, Gießelmacher, and Schwäblishausen," is listed in Petershausen's twelfth-century necrology on 15 April. See MGH Nec. Germ. 1, 669.

49 Emperor Conrad II (r. 1024–1039; crowned emperor in 1027); on Conrad II, see Herwig Wolfram, *Conrad II, 990–1039: Emperor of Three Kingdoms* (College Park, PA: Pennsylvania State University Press, 2006). Conrad II also features in CP 2.45.

50 Herman the Elder of Hirschegg, alive c. 990–1039. Herman's death is recorded for 1 March in Petershausen's twelfth-century necrology. He is credited there with donating this relic, as well as with donations of property, together with his brother. See MGH Nec. Germ. 1, 667.

51 As Eucherius of Lyon tells the story in the fifth century, this entire legion of 6,666 men, garrisoned in Thebes, was sent by Emperor Maximian (r. Caesar 285–286, Augustus 286–305) to Gaul to fight a group of rebels in Burgundy in 285. The entire legion, commanded by St. Maurice, is said to have converted to Christianity and subsequently refused to sacrifice to the emperor. The place of this legendary martyrdom, Agaunum, is now St. Moritz, Switzerland. For more on the legend of the Theban legion, see David Woods, "The Origin of the Legend of Maurice and the Theban Legion," *Journal of Ecclesiastical History* 4 (1994): 385–94.

52 cf. CP 6.2; Herman's burial epitaph recorded in CP 2.24.

53 Somewhat later, during the abbacy of Abbot Meinrad (r. 1079, 1080–1081).

whenever he had just been washed and a robe was placed around him, before one hour passed, the lice would gush forth again like a multitude of ants. Whenever the venerable Abbot Meinrad visited this man and sat before him, the man would say, "everything that was foretold to me by prophesiers and diviners has befallen me except this one thing: that I should be killed by iron. I really wonder how this should happen to me, decrepit and paralyzed as I am." Nevertheless, this priest was most learned in letters and handsome in body. When the already venerable lady could no longer sustain her labors, as she was so often required to cross the river, she moved him to Constance and there strove to minister to him in her house. And it came to pass during the Vigil of All Saints that a certain madman entered her house early in the morning, and paced about eating, agitated and out of his senses. When the venerable priest, lying in bed, heard this man eating, he said to him, "Sir, you shouldn't be eating at this hour." But as it is written that the foolish man abhors rebuke,[54] he responded indignantly, saying, "How is it that this man speaks like a bishop?" And he grabbed his shovel and bashed him in the head, thereby immediately ejecting his spirit. When certain men desired to hang the man who did this from a gibbet, other calmer men carried out a plan to lead him away and send him off unharmed.

2.20. ON GEBINO AND HIS LAND. There was also a certain nobleman named Gebino of Pfrungen who befriended the holy place and there gave his estates in Riggenweiler, Frimmenweiler, and Danketsweiler. He also made a small dwelling for himself at the monastery and lived there continuously for the sake of the divine service.

A CERTAIN WONDER. Moreover, it happened on a certain day that he began to burn with a great fury – I do not know why it came upon him – and he desired to leave the monastery. Raging with fury, he came to the altar of St. Gregory in order that he might there receive permission to leave. And when he descended from the altar on the stairs that at that time led down to the choir, he fell and broke his leg. He then exclaimed, "O St. Gregory, you struck me with such just judgment, since I wished to leave you ignominiously!" He was carried to the hospice in the hands of servants. His bone could never be healed with any medicine, so he was always carried by young servants to the church in a chair. Thus it happened that he who wished to leave enraged remained until his death confined and debilitated. He gave an excellent chasuble

---

54 cf. Proverbs 12:1: *but he that hateth reproof is foolish.*

the color of a crocus.[55] He was buried in the portico in front of the basilica.[56]

2.21. At a certain time, Bishop Conrad[57] {... often... to the brothers... before the tomb of the blessed Gebhard, saying: ...[58]} Thus for many years, no vegetables grew from the earth throughout the entire abbey.

2.22. After Abbot Meinrad abdicated, as I said above, Liutold replaced him.

2.23. HERDWANGEN, BIGENHAUSEN, ALBERWEILER. In these times, many nobles befriended the monastery and rejoiced to have themselves buried there.[59] Among these was Count Eberhard of Bodman, who gave an estate in Herdwangen and who rests before the Lord's Cross in the basilica. Also, Count Ulrich the Elder of Bregenz,[60] who gave Bigenhausen, rests in the cloister. Count Gero of Pfullendorf,[61] who gave a small estate in Alberweiler, also lies before the entrance to the church, about whom something remarkable was told by our forebears. When his mother carried him in the womb and his birth was near, some reason arose (I do not know what) that compelled her to cross the lake toward Constance. When they had come near the place called Eichhorn, she began to go into labor on the ship. Since this was unexpected and they could not get her to a house, her

---

55 Probably a shade of violet, a color associated with the liturgical season of Lent.
56 Gebino of Pfrungen is commemorated on 29 September in Petershausen's twelfth-century necrology: "This man gave Riggenweiler, Frimmenweiler, and Danketsweiler, and a very beautiful chasuble the color of a crocus." MGH Nec. Germ. 1, 675.
57 Bishop Conrad I of Constance (r. 934–975); Feger (1956) suggests that this is an error, and that the scribe should have written "Abbot Meinrad" here, but the text has been so thoroughly erased that it is impossible to determine the meaning and context of the entire passage.
58 This episode on f. 54v has been effaced, and a later hand (seventeenth-century?) has attempted to retrace the words of the original text. The partial translation here is based on the reconstructive transcriptions of Feger (1956) and Mone (1848).
59 On the human remains discovered during various excavations at the former site of the monastery, including in several of the areas in which the chronicler states that nobles were buried, see Carola Berszin, "Kloster, Dorf und Vorstadt Petershausen. Anthropologische Untersuchungen.," in *Kloster, Dorf und Vorstadt Petershausen. Archäologische, Historische und Anthropologische Untersuchungen,* ed. Ralph Röber (Stuttgart: Konrad Theiss Verlag, 2009), 117–190.
60 Count Ulrich IX (d. c. 1099). Ulrich's son, Ulrich the younger, would donate Bigenhausen a second time (cf. CP 3.26).
61 Count Gero of Pfullendorf (c. 1095/1116).

maidservants surrounded her there on the boat and hid her, and there she gave birth to a son [whom she called Gero]. After many years, in the time of Abbot Theodoric, when death began to wrestle with this Gero and he saw the end of his life drawing near, he pledged obedience to the aforementioned abbot and ordered that he be taken to the monastery by ship. And when they had arrived at the place where he was born as I related above, and as those who lived through both events can attest, he died in that place, and as I said, was buried in the monastery in front of the church.[62]

2.24. ON THE NOBLES BURIED IN THE MONASTERY. Ebbo of Heiligenberg and his wife Tuta lie entombed in the same church at the altar of St. Peter. Their images are painted on the wall above the altar. These verses are written over the image of the man:

> *Here lies the good patron, Ebbo of Heiligenberg.*
> *He died on the fifth Kalends of May.*

And these verses are written over the image of the woman:

> *There lies his companion, safe from evils.*
> *She was entombed on the sixth Kalends of December.*

Moreover, there is on that same side the following epitaph above Herman of Hirschegg and his wife Bertrada:

> *Bertrada and Herman, receive the eternal blessings of the*
> *Heavenly kingdom by the prayers of Peter and Gregory,*
> *You and your splendid offspring, after the owed Sabbath*
> *Await thence to approach the blessed octave.*

In another part of the church, at the altar of St. Stephen, lie four noblemen who were killed at the same time: Werner, Burchard, Herman, and Wolfarn.

2.25. ABOUT GERALD AND HIS BROTHER HERMAN. MIMMENHAUSEN, REUTE, ESCHERICHSWEILER, NEUFRACH. Also during this time, Gerald and his brother Herman gave property in Mimmenhausen, Reute, Escherichsweiler, and Neufrach. During the time of the most venerable Abbot Theodoric,

---

62 Gero of Pfullendorf is commemorated in Petershausen's twelfth-century necrology on 17 May. MGH Nec. Germ. 1, 671.

Gerald himself lived until his death in this same monastery, first in the habit of the bearded brothers, then in the habit of the monks.[63]

2.26. CONCERNING KING HENRY IV. In the year of the Incarnation of the Lord 1057,[64] Emperor Henry III died and his son Henry IV, still a boy of nine years, succeeded him[65] and bored through the eyes of the faithful like a smoking firebrand for forty-eight years. And although he had inherited an exceptionally serene and happy Roman Empire, he left it disgraceful and tumultuous in all respects, just as had been shown to his mother in a vision while he was still a little infant. For she saw in a dream the infant sitting at a most beautiful and spacious table, but he completely befouled it with an immense discharge of the stomach, such that nothing whatsoever appeared undefiled. For when he attained immature liberty, like a mule or horse without intellect, he surrendered himself and his admirers to lasciviousness so far beyond measure that, spurning the lawful marriage bed, he idled unceasingly in unheard of debaucheries. Moreover, he erupted into so much madness that, as it was rumored far and wide at that time, he even secretly worshiped an idol and sold all ecclesiastical offices through simony. When he found out that devout bishops were cursing his sins, he deprived them of their own sees and replaced them with others who supported his disgraces,[66] and he muddled all laws, both ecclesiastical and secular. This curse then

---

63 This internal *transitus* from the habit of the bearded brother to that of the monk highlights a significant distinction between Hirsau lay brothers and their Cistercian counterparts. In Hirsau communities this change of status was permitted, while the Cistercians forbade it. On Cistercian prohibitions against secondary conversions, see Idung, *Le moine Idung et ses deux ouvrages: "Argumentum super quatuor questionibus" et "Dialogus duorum monachorum,"* ed. R. B. C. Huygens (Spoleto: Centro italiano di studi sull'alto Medioevo, 1980), 463; Constable, *Reformation*, 79. On transfers from the status of lay brother to that of monk in Hirsau-affiliated communities, see Beach, *Trauma of Monastic Reform*, 66–67; Gerald and his donation of Mimmenhausen, Reute, Escherichsweiler, and Neufrach are commemorated in Petershausen's twelfth-century necrology on 14 January. MGH Nec. Germ. 1, 666.

64 The correct year is 1056.

65 On Henry III, see Weinfurter, *The Salian Century*, 85–111. Henry IV was actually just six or seven at the time of his father's death in 1056. Berthold of Reichenau reports Henry IV's accession to the throne in the first and second versions of his Chronicle (1056) more neutrally. See CBR, 101 and 114. Berthold, however, reckons the length of Henry IV's reign at twenty years, considering it to have ended with his excommunication and deposition by Pope Gregory IV in 1076. See CBR, 114, n. 62.

66 "When he found out... supported his disgraces" echoes, albeit in very slightly modified form, a sentence in the CBZ 7, 160–161. Berthold began his work in c. 1137, only one or two years after this section of the Petershausen chronicle was completed, suggesting that both drew on a common earlier source.

came over the Roman Empire, which is read from Solomon: *Woe to thee, O land, when thy king is a child* [Eccl. 10:16]. And in Job: *Who maketh a man that is a hypocrite to reign for the sins of the people?* [Job 34:30].[67]

2.27. In the year 1069, Bishop Rumold of Constance died, and a certain Carl was sent to this same church as bishop[68] by King Henry through simony. But having been discovered in this heresy, he was accused by a cleric of Constance in the presence of the king, and although Carl raged excessively, he was condemned. Then the king, deeply moved with wrath, said: "Since they rejected a suitable man, let them get a villainous one." And so he gave them a certain Otto of Saxon descent as bishop.[69]

2.28. HOW HENRY WAS EXCOMMUNICATED. King Henry lived tyrannically in every way and respected neither God nor the people and distributed the investitures of bishops and abbots according to his will, and refused to be corrected even though he was often admonished for this by the legates of Pope Gregory VII.[70] Because of this, the aforementioned Pope Gregory, also called Hildebrand, convened a synod in the year 1075[71] and excommunicated him and all of his followers, and he freed his sworn men and allies and removed them from him, and he forbad anyone to accept an ecclesiastical office or investiture from him. In addition to this, under the penalty of anathema, he forbade marriage for clerics. For this reason, such a great tempest struck the church that it overturned countless numbers. This goes on even into the present, and will continue to the end of time, as we believe the storm will not cease to strike and swamp the ship of God. Then what the Lord said in the Gospel was fulfilled: *Do not think that I came to send peace upon earth: I came not to send peace, but the sword. For I came to set a man at variance against his father, and the daughter against her mother, and the daughter in*

---

67 This remarkably negative depiction of Henry IV, later the great opponent of Pope Gregory VII in the contest over investiture, is another clear reflection of the chronicler's pro-papal stance. The chronicler Frutolf of Michelsberg, who supported the royal/imperial party, paints quite a different picture. He claims that "all bishops who had rebelled against the emperor were judged to be deposed and other were condemned with anathema," at the Synod of Mainz in 1085, in which Henry IV participated. See CFM, 123–124.
68 Bishop Carl of Constance (r. 1069–1071).
69 i.e., Bishop Otto I of Constance; cf. CP 2.15 for conflict with Abbot Meinrad; Bernold of St. Blasien also mentions Carl's condemnation in his Chronicle. See CBSB, 251.
70 Pope Gregory VII (r. 1073–1085).
71 The correct date is 22 February 1076.

law against her mother in law. And a man's enemies shall be they of his own household [Matt. 10:34–36].

2.29. In the year 1077, Duke Rudolf of Swabia[72] was made king by order of Pope Gregory and with the counsel of Duke Berthold[73] and Duke Welf of Bavaria[74] and many others of the catholic faith in the village of Forchheim.[75] Rudolf held the kingdom against Henry for three and a half years. These things marked the beginning, nay, rather the increase of tribulations, for thence came battles and riots and the shedding of much blood and, what is worse, the damnation of many souls.[76]

2.30. HOW HENRY BROUGHT DISORDER TO THE PRIESTHOOD. In the year 1080,[77] the anathematized King Henry, supported by a great army, reached Rome, took up arms, and besieged the city, which justly fought back. He impiously drove Pope Gregory, who had been forced from the apostolic seat, into exile, and he put in his place Archbishop Wibert of Ravenna,[78] who had been excommunicated seven years earlier on account of his evil deeds, and Henry had Wibert crown him emperor.[79] This most abominable heresiarch molested holy mother Church for more than nineteen years.[80] He was, however, highly

72 Rudolf of Swabia (c. 1025–1080), also known as Rudolf of Rheinfelden; papal antiking in 1077.

73 Duke Berthold II of Carinthia (r. 1061–1077), also Margrave of Verona, aka Berthold I of Zähringen (c. 1000–1078).

74 Duke Welf of Bavaria (d. 1101), duke 1070–1077 and 1096–1101. On Welf I and this powerful ducal family, see Bernd Schneidmüller, *Die Welfen. Herrschaft und Erinnerung (819–1252)* (Stuttgart: Kolhammar Verlag, 2000).

75 For differing accounts of the March 1077 gathering in Forchheim and the role played by both Berthold and Welf in the election of Rudolf of Swabia, see I. S. Robinson, "Pope Gregory VII, the Princes and the Pactum 1077–1080," *The English Historical Review* 373 (1979): 721–756. Berthold of Reichenau (CBR, 164–167) chronicles the election at Forchheim, identifying the key players in the election only as the "magnates of the kingdom," and Bernold of St. Blasien (CBSB, 258) refers to them only as "the princes of the kingdom." The Annals of Lambert of Hersfeld (ALH, 364) contain a fuller account that places Berthold right at the center of the action.

76 For the view of events of 1077–1080 and an account of Rudolf's deeds and motivations from the imperial perspective, see Frutolf's account: CFM 21–24 and 115–120.

77 The correct year is 1084.

78 Archbishop Wibert of Ravenna, made anti-Pope Clement III (r. 1080–1100).

79 "[W]ho had been excommunicated… crown him emperor" matches the language of the Chronicle of Berthold of Zwiefalten (CBZ 8, 162). See note 66 above for a discussion of a similar nearly word-for-word parallel between the two chronicles.

80 Petershausen's chronicler offers a description of Wibert similar to that of Berthold of Reichenau, who refers to him as one of the "simoniacal heretics and nicholaites

learned and most eloquent in speech, and if he had been just he would have been quite suitable for this office.

2.31. HOW HENRY THREW THE KINGDOM INTO DISORDER.

When King Henry was wrongly managing ecclesiastical offices, as I said, and grief and misfortune were already hanging over his path through divine justice, he began to disturb the way of peace, and neither did he have the fear of God before his eyes nor did he offer what was just to the people. To make a long story short, he took the duchy of Bavaria from Duke Otto[81] and gave it to Welf of Ravensberg. He also stripped Berthold of Zähringen[82] of his duchy and gave it to Liutold of Genoa.[83] And since he so often stayed in Saxony for these things (because this province is called the kitchen of the emperor), he began to defile both wives and daughters of princes and in this way had no limit to vile deeds. The Saxons, not tolerating these

---

who obstinately and disobediently persevered willingly in their insane error" (CBR, 204) and as not pope but "heresiarch... formerly bishop of Ravenna, but deposed without hope of restoration and excommunicated" (CBR, 265–266), here incorporating the text from his excommunication in the synodal protocol of the Lentan synod in Rome in 1078. See Robinson, trans., *Eleventh-Century Germany*, 265, n. 188. The imperially minded Frutolf of Michelsberg, by contrast, legitimizes Wibert's elevation to the papacy, noting that he was consecrated "by many bishops and, taking the name Clement, was reverently enthroned" (CFM, 123). The 1106 continuator of Frutolf's Chronicle notes his death in 1100, calling him "undoubtedly a man full of eloquence, and most distinctly eminent in nobility and person," adding a claim that he had heard Wibert/Clement himself state that he would have preferred never to have accepted the "apostolic title" (McCarthy, trans., *Chronicles of the Investiture Contest*, 161–162).

81 Otto of Nordheim, Duke of Bavaria from 1061 until 1070, and one of the leaders of the Saxon Rebellion of 1073–1075 and the Great Saxon Revolt of 1077–1088 against Henry IV.

82 Aka Duke Berthold II of Carinthia. Frutolf of Michelsberg claims that Berthold took refuge in a fortress in Limburg and seeing that "all could be devastated by the will of the king... was seized by sickness – it is said the sickness of the mind that physicians call lunacy – and surviving after that for seven days, uttering many crazed words as if delirious, he ended his life." See CFM, 116–117. The pro-papal chronicler Bernold of St. Blasien, by contrast, painted a more positive picture of Berthold, claiming that he "burned with such zeal to do justice in the duchy of Swabia that he surpassed almost all his predecessors in his revenge for justice and he filled the mouths of all men with pious reports of his doings." See CBSB, 318.

83 Aka Liutold of Eppenstein (d. 1090), made Duke of Carinthia by Henry IV at the Imperial Diet at Ulm in 1077. Liutold held the title until his death in 1090; Berthold of Reichenau gives an account of Henry's stripping of offices and benefices from Rudolf and his supporters, including Berthold and Otto, at Ulm. See CBR, 173–174.

disgraces, were incited to revolt and thereafter endured harsh battles and insurrections.[84]

2.32. ABOUT THE BATTLE ON THE UNSTRUT.[85] **[THE FIRST BATTLE]** Let us now briefly return to an earlier time. In the year of the Incarnation of the Lord 1074,[86] King Henry gathered an army and entered Saxony, which was in hostile rebellion against him.[87] He fought the Saxons at the river Unstrut and defeated them. Many were killed, many put to flight, and some even surrendered themselves to him unconditionally. He attained victory, not through his merit, but, as we believe, because God was honoring the happy Roman republic. In this battle, the dukes of Swabia – Rudolf (who was later king), Welf, and Berthold – were with the king, although they were suspect to him. Ernest from the Eastern March[88] was killed there on the side of the king, as were two sons of Count Eberhard of Nellenburg,[89] who founded the monastery of Schaffhausen.[90]

2.33. HOW THE SWABIANS REBELLED AND MADE RUDOLF KING.[91] Immediately after this battle, the aforementioned dukes of Alemannia began to rebel against the king, and after they consulted with one another at length, finally, with the consent of Pope Gregory VII, also called Hildebrand, they gathered in a town called Forchheim with the Saxons and made Duke Rudolf of Swabia king, because Henry,

---

84 The Great Saxon Revolt of 1077–1088. The Chronicle of Lambert of Hersfeld provides an extensive account of this revolt. See ALH, 273–287 and *passim*.

85 Also known as the Battle of Langensalza, or the Battle of Homburg on the Unstrut (1075). The account given here seems to be drawing on the account of Lambert of Hersfeld, or at least includes a number of the same details. See ALH, 260–266; on the battle on the Unstrut, including references to accounts in various medieval chronicles, see also I. S. Robinson, *Henry IV of Germany 1056–1106* (Cambridge: Cambridge University Press, 2000), 101.

86 The correct date is 9 June 1075.

87 During the Saxon Rebellion of 1073–1075 (not to be confused with the Great Saxon Revolt of 1077–1088).

88 Ernest of Austria ("the Brave"), Margrave of Austria from 1055 until his death in 1075.

89 Count Eberhard of Nellenburg (d. 1078/1080).

90 Monastery of All Saints, Schaffhausen, founded 1049. Count Eberhard's role as founder of Schaffhausen, well-known to Petershausen, is not noted in the Annals of Lambert of Hersfeld.

91 The content of this chapter is partially repeated from CP 2.29, but with added detail. CP 2.30 is similarly elaborated in CP 2.36 and CP 2.37.

although he still lived, had been excommunicated.⁹² [Rudolf was the son-in-law of King Henry III, as he had married Henry's daughter.⁹³] This took place in the year of the Incarnation of the Lord 1077, in the month of March. [Pilate, the crucifier of the Lord, is said to be from Forchheim, with a father called Ato and a mother called Pila, from which "Pilate" is composed. And the earth on which he was born bears no crops. Whence the common folk then sang of Rudolf, that another Pilate had arisen.] Rudolf spent the next Easter in Augsburg, but Embrico, the bishop of this city,⁹⁴ refused to see or greet him, although he sent him abundant provisions. When he left, King Rudolf laid siege to castle of Sigmaringen. But when he learned of the arrival of King Henry, who had come with an army through a pass in the Alps to liberate the fortification, he fled and pressed on into Saxony. King Henry then gave the duchy of Swabia to Frederick of Staufen⁹⁵ and joined him in marriage to his daughter, who later bore him Frederick⁹⁶ and Conrad, who was later king.⁹⁷

92 Here the CP clearly suggests that the dukes who supported the deposition of Henry IV worked in concert with Pope Gregory VII to elect Rudolf in his place. This contrasts with royalist accounts, which generally present Gregory VII as the primary agent of Rudolf's election. See Robinson, *Henry IV of Germany*, 169 and n. 128.

93 This isn't quite accurate, although the two were related by marriage. Rudolf had first married Henry's sister Matilda in 1059 (demanding the right to do so after kidnapping her). When Matilda died in 1060, Rudolf then married Adelaide of Savoy (d. 1079), a daughter of Count Otto of Savoy (d. c. 1057), in 1066. In the same year, Adelaide's sister Bertha of Savoy (d. 1087), aka Bertha of Turin, married Henry, making Rudolf brother-in-law to the king twice over.

94 Bishop Embrico of Augsburg (r. 1063–1077); Berthold of Reichenau claims that Embrico had allied himself, "most firmly, though unwillingly," with Rudolf the previous Easter, but he switched his alliance to King Henry and followed him to the imperial Diet in Ulm where he publicly defended Henry's kingship. See Robinson, *Henry IV of Germany*, 174, n. 20; according to Berthold of Reichenau, to demonstrate his allegiance to Henry, Bishop Embrico offered to receive the holy Eucharist, "as a trial and as a judgment of the fact that the cause of his lord King Henry was just, while that of Rudolf was utterly unjust." Soon after, as Berthold recounts, Embrico was "seized by a deadly affliction," and a few days later, "was overtaken by a most bitter death and breathed his last." (CBR, 175). Lambert of Hersfeld, on the other hand, refers to Embrico as, "a man of the discretion and dignity befitting a bishop" (ALH, 97).

95 Frederick I, Duke of Swabia from 1079 until his death in 1105. Frederick was the first ruler of the Hohenstaufen line.

96 Frederick II, Duke of Swabia from 1105 until his death in 1147 and the father of Emperor Frederick Barbarossa (r. 1152–1190; crowned emperor in 1155). On Frederick Barbarossa, see John B. Freed, *Frederick Barbarossa: The Prince and the Myth* (New Haven, CT: Yale University Press, 2016).

97 King Conrad III of Germany (r. 1138–1152).

2.34. ABOUT THE BATTLE ON THE STREU.[98] **THE SECOND BATTLE.** After this same Henry gathered an army against the Saxons, he made haste to capture Rudolf. But those gathered against him rushed upon him in the province of Bavaria on the River Streu, saying that they were no longer willing simply to harry the king. After a most violent battle, King Henry fled with his men, and there he lost Margrave Diepold of Giengen[99] with many others. The victory won, the Saxons hastily gathered their injured and dead and departed. King Henry, however, after the Duke of Bohemia[100] arrived on that same day with a strong force, returned to the battlefield after his retreat and sought the Saxons, hoping to fight with them again. But since he found only very few of them, he gathered his dead and wounded men and departed, and he devastated all of the surrounding property with fire and sword.

[**2.35. ABOUT THE BATTLE OF MELLRICHSTADT.** There was also a third battle at Mellrichstadt, in which King Rudolf again stood forth victorious and Henry fled.]

2.36. HOW THE KING TOOK ROME.[101] After this, King Henry proceeded to Italy, arrived at Rome with an army, and seized the city, which was rebelling against him. After Henry's followers imposed many unjust acts upon Pope Gregory, the king cast him out. For when he celebrated Mass on the holy night of the Nativity of the Lord in Rome at cockcrow, as is the custom, a certain Crescentius, a Roman citizen and follower of the king, sought Gregory out and dealt him a powerful blow to the head with a sword, knocking him to the ground. And then, to add to his insanity, he drove Gregory into captivity and forced him into his tower. But on the same day, this tower was stormed by the faithful, and before Vespers the pope was piously returned to

---

98 7 August 1078. This is the Battle of Mellrichstadt on the River Streu. The chronicler seems to have been confused about this battle, presenting it as two distinct events in consecutive entries. The second account (CP 2.35), however, was inserted in the right margin of f. 57r, perhaps not in confusion but rather in an attempt to press the argument that it was Henry IV's men alone who fled; on the Battle of Mellrichstadt, including accounts from medieval chronicles, cf. Robinson, *Henry IV of Germany*, 181–182.

99 Margrave Diepold II of Vohburg, lord of Diengen (d. 1078).

100 Duke Vratislaus II (r. 1061–1092).

101 The content of this chapter is partially repeated from CP 2.30, but with more detail, much as the content of CP 2.29 is elaborated in CP 2.33; the wording here is very close to that in the CBZ 7, 162, again suggesting a common earlier source for Berthold's chronicle and the CP. See notes 66 and 79 above.

the altar from which he had been impiously dragged. At Vespers, the pope completed the mass that he had begun to sing at cockcrow, still fasting and supported by others, for earlier he had sung the mass up to the Communion.

2.37. ABOUT WIBERT. After the catholic Pope Gregory was expelled and impiously driven into exile, King Henry appointed a certain schismatic by the name of Wibert – formerly the bishop of Ravenna but excommunicated by the pope for his wicked deeds seven years earlier – undeservedly to the apostolic see, and Henry received an imperial coronation from him that was well suited to his wickedness. For this should not be called a consecration, but rather a great execration. I have already spoken about this above.[102]

2.38. THE BATTLE OF THE ELSTER.[103] THE FOURTH BATTLE.[104] In the meantime, King Rudolf, having gathered an army, wanted to enter Bohemia and lay waste to it. But the duke of Bohemia, together with the Slavs and other allies of King Henry who were bound to him, met him at the River Elster and there joined a mighty battle and many men fell on both sides.[105] King Rudolf himself, moreover, was gravely wounded by a lance in this river and fell from his horse into the water, but raised up by his men and taken to the field, he made confession and accepted Last Rites from the arriving bishops.[106] While he was still dying, he lifted his head, as it is told, and asked: "Who has the victory?" When the men standing around said, "You, Lord," he lowered his head and said: "I now have no care for my death, if I receive it in honor with triumph." Thus King Rudolf died on that same day at Elster and was carried by his men to Merseburg.[107] There he was buried with

---

102 cf. CP 2.30.

103 15 October 1080; cf. Robinson, *King Henry IV of Germany*, 202–205.

104 The CP omits the important intervening Battle of Flarchheim on 27 January 1080, which resulted in Henry's withdrawal to Franconia; cf. Robinson, *King Henry IV of Germany*, 193–194.

105 According to I. S. Robinson, Henry had failed to make contact with the Bohemians, and as a result, there were no Bohemians among the king's army. See Robinson, *King Henry IV of Germany*, 203.

106 In pro-Henrician accounts of Rudolf's death, he was found mortally wounded, his right hand cut off. Henry IV's anonymous biographer saw in this wound a just punishment for his failing to keep the oath he had sworn to his king. See Robinson, *King Henry IV of Germany*, 204–205.

107 It was after the defeat of Rudolf that Henry would march on Rome and install Wibert of Ravenna as anti-Pope Clement III, as reported in CP 2.30 and again in 2.36–2.37.

honor in the choir of the basilica, and his image, cast in bronze and gilded, was installed above his tomb.[108] His victory in this battle was dubious, since men on both sides had fled, although the Slavs had defended their region from the invasion of the Saxons. This happened in the year of the Incarnation of the Lord 1080, on 15 October.

2.39. ABOUT KING HERMAN. Next, in the following year, the princes of Saxony and Swabia convened in a place called Ochsenfurt, and they made Herman king.[109] He was a Frank of Glücksburg by descent, a noble man, handsome, vigorous, and capable, and he ruled for seven years from the year of the Incarnation of the Lord 1081.

2.40. ABOUT THE BATTLE OF HÖCHSTÄDT.[110] **THE FIFTH BATTLE.** After this, Duke Frederick of Swabia and Count Palatine Cuno of Vohburg,[111] together with other followers of King Henry, captured certain fortifications in Bavaria, and they went up to the fortification called Donauwörth and captured it. When they departed from that place, King Herman arrived with an army of Swabians and overtook them in the place called Höchstädt. After the battle started, they were fighting fiercely on both sides. And when they were fighting boldly and neither side was willing to withdraw, one man on the side of the Alemanni is said to have exclaimed with a great clamor: "Come then, Swabians, fight valiantly! Look! See the fleeing Bavarians! Let none of them get away!" Hearing this voice and reckoning the situation to be just as the malicious voice had said, the Bavarians all turned their backs at the same time, and each one wanted to outrun the others in flight. Many, however, died there. Count Palatine Cuno died there along with many others.

2.41. HOW THE POPE WAS SENT INTO EXILE IN SALERNO AND HOW HENRY WAS AGAIN ANATHEMATIZED. King Henry again charmed Pope Gregory with many flattering words, so that they might reconcile. But the pope, holding fast to justice, was in no way able to be swayed unless the king should come to his senses with

---

108 The inscription on Rudolf's bronze memorial plate in Merseburg's presents him, not as a treacherous oath-breaker, but as a martyr and a "lawful king who died defending the Church." Robinson, *Henry IV of Germany*, 204.

109 Herman of Salm (c. 1035–1088), aka Herman of Luxembourg, papal anti-king from 1081.

110 27 March 1086.

111 Cuno I of Rott, Count of Vohburg (d. 1086).

regard to his impiety. Because of this, Gregory was expelled from his native land and repaired to Salerno, and there he convened a synod and again wielded the sword of excommunication against Wibert, Henry, and all of their supporters and those who agreed with their errors, with the exception of simple people, children, and women, who had helped them neither with weapons nor with advice.[112]

ABOUT THE DEATH OF THE POPE. Gregory came to the end of his life in this city, and he is reported to have uttered these words before his death: "I die in exile because I loved justice and hated iniquity." He died in the year of the Incarnation of the Lord 1081.[113]

2.42. While King Henry was returning from Italy to German lands, he came upon Duke Welf besieging Augsburg out of hatred for Bishop Siegfried[114] and frightened him off.

2.43. ABOUT THE BATTLE OF WÜRZBURG.[115] **THE SIXTH BATTLE.** In the year of the Incarnation of the Lord 1086, those faithful to St. Peter called for a general assembly near Würzburg after the Feast of the Apostles. King Henry arrived with an army hoping to disrupt this gathering, but he surrendered the place after a great force of Swabians arrived at the same time with their princes. After their Saxon allies surrounded Würzburg, however, King Henry gathered an army of twenty thousand men and arrayed his troops to liberate the city. The people of the city, however, raised up a cross and processed toward him for two miles, trusting in the mercy of God rather than in arms. Very many were killed on the side of the king, but the Swabians and Saxons stood forth victorious and lost no more than three men from their ranks. Not only did they carry off chests with royal vestments, but they also took away the ornaments of the bishops who were with Henry in battle. They made camp that night on the battlefield among the bodies of the dead. From there they returned to the city to lay siege and took the city without bloodshed.

---

112 This is repeated in CP 2.47.

113 Gregory actually died on 25 May 1085. It is likely that 1081 is a simple scribal error, since Gregory is mentioned in the year 1085 in CP 2.47.

114 Bishop Siegfried II of Augsburg (r. 1088–1096).

115 The Battle of Pleichfeld (11 August 1086). The account in the CP incorporates a number of details (including the size of the king's army, the procession with the cross, and the seizing of the chests of royal vestments) given in Bernold of St. Blasien's eyewitness account of the battle. See CBSB, 285–287; on the Battle of Pleichfeld, cf. Robinson, *Henry IV of Germany*, 260–261.

2.44. ON THE DEATH OF KING HERMAN. While King Herman was staying in Alemannia, he did not have the royal means to live with regal dignity, and because no bishop wanted to be subject to him, he went to the city of Constance and remained there for a few days. From there, he crossed the Rhine and spent nearly a week at the monastery of Petershausen, and then proceeded to Saxony. One day, when the king was passing by a certain castle, someone by chance threw a rock from above and dealt him an unexpected blow to the head, and he died from this not long after.[116]

2.45. ABOUT KING CONRAD, THE SON OF KING HENRY. Not quite six years later,[117] Conrad,[118] the son of King Henry, went to Italy, fleeing – so he said – the wickedness of his father. He reigned there for a short time, died by poison,[119] and was buried in the city of Florence.

2.46. HOW KING HENRY OBTAINED SOLE RULE. After these various grievous things, many calamities, great bloodsheds, and the loss of many souls, Henry at last obtained sole rule, and almost all the princes were reconciled to him and acknowledged him as legitimate emperor. He always had all the cities along the Rhine and other powerful and metropolitan cities as allies, and many bishops were united to him in such a way that they could not be torn away from him by any argument.

ABOUT BISHOP OTTO. Among these men was Bishop Otto of Constance.[120] Since Otto was unwilling, even under papal order and authority, to break the oaths that he had sworn to the king, he was rejected by right-thinking catholics.

2.47. THE REPEATED DAMNATION OF WIBERT AND HENRY.[121] In the year of the Incarnation of the Lord 1085, Pope

---

116 (Anti-)King Herman died on 28 September 1088, according to several contemporary chronicles while laying siege to a castle in his native Lotharingia. See Robinson, *Henry IV of Germany*, 268–269.

117 In 1093.

118 Conrad II of Italy (King of Germany 1087–1098, King of Italy 1093–1098). Conrad swore fealty to Pope Urban II (r. 1088–1099) in 1095, but was deposed by Henry IV in 1098 and replaced by Henry V.

119 In 1101.

120 cf. CP 2.27 and 2.15.

121 This condemnation was previously reported in CP 2.41, where Gregory's death was also recorded; the content of this chapter largely follows Bernold of St. Blasien (CBSB, 278).

Gregory, also called Hildebrand, convened a synod while he was an exile in Salerno and again pronounced a sentence of anathema on the schismatic Wibert and the so-called King Henry and on their supporters. This sentence was made known throughout the land of the Germans by the legates of the Apostolic See, that is Bishop Peter of Albano in France and Bishop Otto of Ostia (who was later pope).[122]

2.48. ABOUT HIRSAU. During this storm,[123] the flame of spiritual discipline burned most brightly at the monastery of Hirsau, and many men, both noble and non-noble, clerical and lay, and also monks from other monasteries, flowed together and, as if emerging from a great shipwreck, took refuge there as if in a harbor from the tempest of anathema then dashing violently against the ship of the church, rejoicing that they had found the quiet of the safety they desired.[124] Among them was Gebhard, a most noble man, the brother of Duke Berthold II of Zähringen and prior of Xanten. Leaving the things of the world, Gebhard joined the aforementioned monastery, and just as he exchanged his secular garb for the monastic habit, so too he took on excellence of conduct.

2.49. HOW BISHOP GEBHARD III WAS PLACED AT THE HEAD OF THE CHURCH OF CONSTANCE. When Bishop Otto of Ostia from the papal legation came to Constance and found that church devoid of a pastor because of the condemnation of Otto [I of Constance] (who had been bishop there), he consulted the venerable fathers and right-thinking catholics about how he might provide for the governance of that same church.

ABBOT WILLIAM. Just by chance, Abbot William of Hirsau[125] was there – a man, I say, who was pleasing both to God and men because he was extremely learned and most zealous in regular discipline, humble, gentle, a despiser of the world, and a most diligent lover of monks and of all virtue. Since he was present at this gathering and had the aforementioned Gebhard with him, he began to talk about electing a catholic bishop, because there was no hope for the condemned Otto.

---

122 i.e., Pope Urban II.
123 i.e., the struggles between pope and emperor.
124 This is not the chronicler's first use of the image of a storm. His first use of this metaphor is in CP 2.28, where he has Henry IV initiate the tempest. There the chronicler asserts that the storm still rages in his own day and will continue until the end of time.
125 Abbot William of Hirsau (r. 1069–1091).

In the middle of this conversation, the venerable monk Gebhard withdrew behind the altar of St. Mary and there privately devoted himself to prayers. What else is there to say? They elected Gebhard Bishop of Constance, and after it was unanimous, since he was utterly unaware of what had just taken place, they went to him and said: "By the grace of God, this church has elected you today to be its bishop." After he heard this, his spirit left him and he fell to the ground and lay there as if he were dead. Once his spirit returned to him, on that very same day (that is, on the Feast of St. Thomas), Otto made him a priest against his will, and on the next day he ordained him bishop. After he was expelled, the deposed Otto went to a property of this church in a place called Colmar and died there after barely a year.[126]

HERE ENDS THE SECOND BOOK

---

[126] Colmar (in Alsace) was among the earliest properties belonging to Constance's cathedral chapter. See Feger (1956), 122, n. 1.

BOOK THREE

Introduction

Book Three begins with the arrival at Petershausen of the Hirsau reformers in the year 1086. The anchor of the reform at Petershausen, from the chronicler's perspective, was the charismatic Theodoric, whose thirty-year abbacy (1086–1116) represents a golden age for the monastery. After the monks reject Otto as abbot in the first rocky days of the reform,[1] it is Theodoric who restores a certain amount of stability to the community. Quickly reversing the decline of monastic discipline that the chronicler laments, Theodoric, a "truly venerable" monk from Hirsau, reinvigorates religious life at Petershausen, and enhances the monastery's spiritual and social standing with numerous building projects and land acquisitions. The chronicler writes extensively about Theodoric's expansion of the choir,[2] improvements to the monastic buildings,[3] construction of chapels dedicated to saints Mary and Michael and the apostle Andrew,[4] and the purchase of land for building and maintaining more monasteries.[5]

It should be kept in mind that the chronicler had completed Book Three by 1136. He thus details a course of events that had taken place between fifty and twenty years earlier. As with many second-generation reformers, the chronicler (who was too young to have lived through the initial period of reform himself) spins a narrative of decline, heroically halted and reversed by the agents of reform. This is a constructed narrative, which like many other medieval monastic chronicles, serves to legitimize the present woven from the "messy memories" of the community.[6]

1 CP 3.1 and 3.3.
2 CP 3.7.
3 CP 3.8.
4 CP 3.9–3.13.
5 CP 3.24–3.27, 3.41–3.42.
6 Steven Vanderputten, *Monastic Reform as Process: Realities and Representations in Medieval Flanders* (Ithaca, NY: Cornell University Press, 2013), 29.

Book Three also offers an interesting local perspective on the great ecclesio-political crises of the eleventh century. As a monastery affiliated with Hirsau, Petershausen became entangled with the struggle over investiture, a conflict that swept with particular fury through Swabia in the 1090s.[7] Theodoric found himself caught up in this ecclesio-political crisis, and because he remained loyal to Bishop Gebhard III,[8] Theodoric was thus deposed and exiled with Gebhard when King Henry IV appointed Arnold of Heiligenberg (r. 1092–1112) as bishop of Constance in his stead.[9] During this period of exile, Werner (r. 1103/1104) was set in the office of abbot at Petershausen.[10] The political winds shifted just over a year later, and both Gebhard III and Theodoric were returned to their respective posts.[11]

Theodoric's involvement with the investiture controversy continued even after the death of Gebhard III. The newly appointed Bishop Ulrich I (r. 1111–1127) had been invested by the king, and thus was refused ordination by the Pope Paschal II (r. 1099–1118). Ulrich dispatched Theodoric on two separate trips to Rome to attempt to persuade Pascal to allow the ordination, without success.[12] It was during a heatwave on the way home from the second failed mission that Theodoric and his companions fell ill and died.[13] At the close of the book, the chronicler laments the passing of this beloved abbot, who had embodied so many of the ideals of the reform.[14] The chronicler does nothing to disguise his dislike of Ulrich I, clearly holding him to blame for Theodoric's death, "alone in a foreign land, deprived of all of his possessions and companions",[15] and complaining further that the bishop "always proved to be ungracious to [his] monastery."[16]

Book Three also includes detailed accounts of several visions experienced by Petershausen's monks. The longest of these is

---

7 On the course of the conflict in Swabia, see Hermann Tüchle, *Kirchengeschichte Schwabens*, 2 vols. (Stuttgart: Schwabenverlag, 1950), Vol. 1, 207–237.
8 See Robinson, *Henry IV of Germany*, 298–300.
9 CP 3.29–3.31.
10 CP 3.32–3.34.
11 CP 3.36.
12 CP 3.45.
13 CP 3.45.
14 CP 3.46–3.50.
15 CP 3.45.
16 CP 3.48.

recounted in the words of the schoolmaster Bernard, whose detailed account of his elaborate purgatorial dream-vision is given in full,[17] accompanied by a sketch depicting souls flying through the heavens to receive judgment, the only illustration in the Chronicle (see Figure 1, p. 110). Other visions suggest continued division, unrest, and even anxiety within the community. After Bernard's death, two of the monks are shown disturbing visions of him being tortured and wandering the monastery halls as a penitent.[18] Another priest in the monastery has a vision of the Apostle Peter pointing to a number of individuals at Petershausen, all of whom died shortly thereafter.[19] The chronicler's accounts of these visions reflect prescribed Hirsau custom, as the *Constitutiones* required that members of the community report any vision that they receive to the abbot in secret, in order to provide intercessory prayer, if deemed appropriate, for any brother(s) in need.[20]

Book Three

3.1. HOW MONKS FROM HIRSAU CAME TO PETERSHAUSEN.

When Gebhard III became Bishop of Constance, lamenting that a monastery near his church was neglecting the Divine Office, since the vigor of religious life at the monastery of Pope St. Gregory, which is called Petershausen, had faded by that time and was not existing to any benefit, he appealed to the venerable Abbot William of Hirsau that he might send monks from his monastery to Petershausen, through whom monastic order in that place might be revitalized.[21] And, since he was eager to accomplish every good work, William sent excellent and very pious men, including a certain Otto,[22] who was to be their abbot if his life and customs should be pleasing to them after a trial period. But when this same Otto displeased his brothers after a short time, they

---

17 CP 3.18.
18 CP 3.19–3.21.
19 CP 3.22.
20 William of Hirsau, *Willehelmi abbatis Constitutiones Hirsaugienses*, ed. Pius Engelbert O.S.B., *Corpus Consuetudinum Monasticarum* 15 (Siegburg: Schmitt, 2010), 344–345.
21 Bishop Gebhard was himself a former monk of Hirsau (CP 2.49), which no doubt contributed to his selection of monks from Hirsau to correct religious life at Petershausen.
22 Abbot Otto (r. 1085–1086).

absolutely refused to be placed under his authority, and he was ordered to return to his own monastery.

3.2. HOW THE PREVIOUS BROTHERS HANDED THE MONASTERY OVER TO THE NEWCOMERS.
Liutold, abbot of the same monastery, the teacher Rupert, and certain other of the previous brothers, handed over the monastery to the arriving men from Hirsau and joined the monastery of Reichenau; some of them even transferred to the clerical habit. The aforementioned Rupert was an excellent teacher in all the liberal arts, and the monk Bernard[23] of the same monastery was similarly a man of the highest wisdom and learning. At that time they both looked after a great number of students because they were in charge of the school, and they brought many to the highest level of education. This Bernard and a certain Werner (who was almost his equal in erudition), fleeing anathema, had already joined the monastery of Hirsau long before.

3.3. HOW THEODORIC CAME; AND CONCERNING HIS DESCENT AND WAY OF LIFE.
After the truly pious monks of Hirsau sent by Abbot William reached Petershausen, they offered spiritual service, soldiering vigorously, just as they had been appointed to do. When they caught their appointed master Otto acting reprehensibly in certain matters, to put it briefly, they immediately sent him back to his monastery, and with Bishop Gebhard's blessing they asked that another man be sent who was worthy to be placed over them. Abbot William thus followed the best counsel and sent the truly venerable man Theodoric, who was filled to the highest degree with all secular and monastic learning and was quite suitable for this office.

His father, Count Cuno,[24] kept a servile concubine named Bertha, who was most dear to him, and he took no other wife besides her.[25] She bore him three sons – Liutold, Marquard, and Theodoric – who were very handsome in body and no less sharp in mind. After the death of their

---

23 This is the Bernard discussed in CP 3.14 and CP 3.17–3.19. His death date (15 March) also appears in the necrology under the name Bernard *sapiens*.

24 Count Cuno of Achalm (d. 1092), also count of Wülflingen from 1086.

25 The chronicler here appears to find the degree of commitment between Cuno and his servile concubine noteworthy. Evidence from contemporary Bavarian cartularies detailing the donation of illegitimate children had by servile concubines to monasteries as *censuales* demonstrates that concubinage in the eleventh and twelfth centuries most often retained its casual, non-permanent or non-exclusive quality despite the nascent attempts of canonists to redefine it as a kind of quasi-marriage. See Sutherland, "Mancipia Dei," 119–135.

father, Liutold and Marquard fell to the ownership of Count Hartman of Dillingen, since they had been born from his maidservant. They nevertheless became exceedingly keen and courageous in every art of war to such a degree that because he was strong and very swift among men and distinguished in all military activity, Liutold was selected by King Henry IV to be among the twelve men whom he always kept with him as supporters and accomplices of his wicked deeds. Because of this, Liutold earned a privilege of liberty from this same king, both for himself and for all of his posterity.

3.4. In the early flower of youth, Theodoric indulged in enticements of the flesh to his heart's desire. But when he was more mature, he restrained his spirit from this inclination. Indeed, he was instructed in letters to the highest degree, and was of the best character, elegant in speech, and had a physique to be revered. He went to the monastery of St. Ulrich in Augsburg, and there he first became a monk. But because the poison of anathema at the time infected not only clerics and the laity, but even many monastics, the venerable Theodoric removed himself from this peril and made haste for and joined the monastery of Hirsau. He placed himself under the guidance of Abbot William, worthy before God, and within a short time under him he distinguished himself so much in every discipline of the regular life that it was more fitting for him to be in charge than to be a subordinate. At that time he was first placed in charge of a certain monastery called Hasungen,[26] and when he was called back to the monastery and made the prior of the entire community, he led vigorously for a time.

3.5. HOW THEODORIC WAS ORDAINED. In the year of the Incarnation of the Lord 1086, with insistent requests, the reverend Bishop Gebhard of Constance – the third of the same name – persuaded Abbot William of Hirsau of blessed memory to send the venerable Theodoric to the monastery of St. Gregory called Petershausen, where he would preside and establish the regular life according to the example of his monastery. After he had accomplished this and Theodoric had arrived, the aforementioned bishop ordained him abbot of this same monastery with the common consent of all the brothers on the feast of

---

26 Hasungen, founded in 1074 as a house of canons, was converted to a Benedictine monastery following the customs of Hirsau in 1080/1081. See REC, 534 and Feger (1956), 126, n. 4.1. The years of Theodoric's tenure as abbot of Hasungen are not recorded.

the Holy Apostle Barnabus. The bishop loved and favored Theodoric, and was always a comfort to him in every way possible.

3.6. CONCERNING HIS DILIGENCE. After he was ordained, Theodoric set to work with all piety, and he attended to the souls and bodies of his subordinates with great care. He educated them in the highest discipline and increased the number of his disciples so greatly that he soon had more than forty monks and more than fifty bearded brothers.²⁷ He gave them abundant food and clothing, and he corrected their way of life with great strictness.

3.7. ON THE CHOIR. Because the choir was short (since the steps leading up to the altar occupied the space²⁸), he removed some of the stone steps and increased the number of singers, thus taking away stones and putting men in their place. Indeed, he made the choir almost level with the altar, now higher by only one step, and he thus enlarged the space for those standing in the choir. It was thus fulfilled in this place that which scripture said in the person of Israel to the Lord of the Church: "Because this place is too straight for me and the Lord has blessed me, give me a larger place to dwell" [Isa. 49:20, loosely].

3.8. ON THE BUILDINGS THAT HE BUILT. He then adorned other buildings with the steps that he removed from the choir. He built a washroom, where he put some of these stairs, as well as a chapter house, and he renovated the whole cloister, all the way around. He surrounded the perimeter of the monastery with a wall, and he built a portico over the graves of the previous abbots. He made all of these improvements, and more that will yet be mentioned, not from the income or savings of the monastery, but from the donations of the faithful. For everyone praised and loved him, and many gave their possessions to him on account of the novelty of pure life that had recently come to the region through him. Bishop Gebhard of Constance also helped him as much as possible by giving and committing to him any cleric or layman who was subjected to him on account of his crimes,²⁹ and also by giving him

---

27 Bearded brothers, also called lay brothers, were a distinctive feature of monasteries associated with the Hirsau Reform. See Joachim Wollasch, "A propos des fratres barbati de Hirsau," in *Histoire et société. mélanges offerts à Georges Duby*, Vol. 3 (Aix-en-Provence: Université de Provence, 1992), 37–48.

28 cf. CP 1.21.

29 The precise meaning of the bishop "giving and committing" to the abbot "any cleric or layman who was subject to him on account of his crimes" is uncertain. That these subjects could be given to the abbot suggests that they may have been in some way

a favorable hearing in all things, since this same father was eloquent in speech. Theodoric was also very generous to everyone, but sparing with himself; for while he would weaken his body with extreme fasting, he would give all abundance to everyone who stayed with him or even approached him. This always put him in great difficulty, since he was constantly constrained by large debts, but since he trusted in the Lord, he would still give away everything with easy generosity.

3.9. ON THE CHAPELS HE BUILT. In the year of the Incarnation of the Lord 1092, the venerable Abbot Theodoric built a chapel in the southern aisle of the basilica next to the area of the high altar, which he had dedicated on 26 June in honor of Bishop St. Ulrich, St. Nicholas, St. Afra, and Sts. John and Paul. There he collected the relics of St. Simon the Apostle, Stephen the Protomartyr, Hippolytus, Sebastian, Pelagius, Alexander the son of Felicity, Bishop Paulinus of Nola, Bishop Maximin, Gall and Magnus, the martyrs Felicity, Agatha, Fortunata, and Eutropia.

3.10. ON THE CHAPEL OF SAINT MARY. Then, in the following year (that is, in the year of the Incarnation of the Lord 1093) in the first indiction, Theodoric built a chapel in the northern side of the sacristy and had it dedicated on 9 September in honor of St. Mary the Mother of God and all the other saints whose relics he had there – that is, the holy apostles Peter, Paul, Andrew, Bartholomew, and Simon; and the blessed martyrs Stephen the Protomartyr, Pope Stephen the martyr, Blaise, Lawrence, Vincent, Cyriacus, Hippolytus, Sebastian, George, Christopher, Alexander the son of Felicity, Cosmas and Damian, Pelagius, Pancras, and Maurice; and the confessors Nicholas, Paulinus of Nola, Maximin, Gall and Magnus; and the virgin martyrs Agatha, Cecilia, Barbara, Hilaria, Eunomia, and the Eutropia; and the virgin Verena.

3.11. Every day after Vespers and Matins, the community solemnly processes to this chapel in honor of St. Mary and there after the hymn, antiphon, and prayer of this Vespers or Matins, they sing the Vespers or the Matins for all the saints and for the dead.

---

reduced to servile status as a penal measure, at least temporarily. Although unlikely to be related to this instance given how far removed it is chronologically, there was, interestingly, legal precedent for punishment by loss of freedom for certain religious crimes in southern Germany, as attested in the eighth-century *Lex Baiuvariorum*, according to which, for example, a free man who performed labor on Sundays multiple times could be reduced to slavery (7.3a). T. J. Rivers, trans., *Laws of the Alamans and Bavarians* (Philadelphia: University of Pennsylvania Press, 1977), 137.

3.12. ON THE CHAPEL OF SAINT MARY AND SAINT MICHAEL. Likewise, in the year of the Incarnation of the Lord 1094, in the second indiction, Abbot Theodoric renovated and expanded the chapel of St. Michael, for it was so small that it could scarcely fit twelve men. It is next to the infirmary, between which and the aforementioned chapel there was a small room in which many sick men also used to rest. Destroying this, the aforementioned abbot added on to the chapel and made a new altar, and he had this dedicated by the venerable Bishop Gebhard III on 5 June in honor of the Lord and the Holy Cross, and especially in honor of St. Mary the Mother of the Lord and St. Michael the Archangel and all the saints. Contained in this altar are the relics of the apostles Peter, Paul, Andrew, Bartholomew, and Simon; and the martyrs Felix, Maurice, George, Pelagius, Wenceslaus, Pantaleon, Anastasius; and the confessors Martin, Nicholas, Maximin, Paulinus of Nola, Benedict, Gall, Magnus; and of the virgin martyrs Agatha, Cecilia, Barbara, Afra, Hilaria, Eunomia, and Eutropia.

3.13. ON THE CHAPEL OF SAINT ANDREW THE APOSTLE. He also expanded the chapel of St. Andrew and assigned the bearded brothers to the houses attached to it, which were originally the dwellings of the abbots of this monastery. This chapel had been very small, and a grille ran in front of it, giving a view into the cloister. He blocked up this grille and added it to the chapel wall, usefully extending it.

3.14. WHAT SORT OF DISCIPLES HE HAD. At this time, the venerable father had very extraordinary and pious men of the best form and learning under his care, among whom were Meinrad, formerly abbot (about whom I spoke above[30]); Bernard the teacher;[31] Cuno and Werner of Altshausen, who was blind;[32] Gotzhalm, Eberhard; and Henry the scribe. All of these men were among the former brothers, as were Sigger the teacher, Ebbo, and Gebhard, who was my forefather.

3.15. A MIRACLE OF GEBHARD. This Gebhard, when he was still a young cleric, dwelled in that place. One night after Matins, he went out from the choir to the well in the crypt to draw up and drink some water because he was thirsty, but he carelessly dropped the water bucket into the well, which is deep and narrow, and he himself fell in head-first after it. What hope of life was there for him then? He had no

---

30 cf. CP 2.14, 2.15, and 2.22.
31 cf. CP 3.2 and 3.17–3.19.
32 cf. CP 3.21, 3.40, and 4.1.

way of getting out, no space to lift his head, no voice to shout, and no one to hear him. In this moment of death, he needed a suitable helper. When he was thus suddenly in these straits, the blessed Gebhard, the founder of the monastery, whose sepulcher was then nearby, aided him by pulling him out of the water by his feet and bringing him back up unharmed. When he entered the choir soaking wet, Werner, whom I have already mentioned, was surprised and asked him whence he had come and what had happened to him. He related the event as it had happened, and everyone who was there was moved in wonder.

3.16. ABOUT GERALD AND GEBHARD. One day when he was still young, this Gebhard, along with another young man of the same age, a cleric and sub-deacon by the name of Gerald, confidently entered the Rhine to bathe because it was summer, and they happily began to swim in the middle of the river. Suddenly, with shouts of terror, Gerald began to call out to Gebhard to hasten to his aid, for his strength had failed and he had already begun to sink. Shaken, Gebhard quickly swam to him and saw him already underwater. As soon as he drew near, however, Gerald forcefully grabbed him around the neck and they both began to sink. Since he saw that he could not sustain him and feared that he too would perish, Gebhard pulled himself away from Gerald with difficulty and quickly swam to the shore. When those who were there saw Gerald drowning and were shouting along with Gebhard, behold, Gerald suddenly emerged in the middle of the river and with his arms raised up exclaimed, "Help, Lord!" But he immediately sank again and died on 14 June.[33]

3.17. ON BERNARD. Bernard, whom I also mentioned above,[34] was an excellent teacher and shined forth as a most diligent guardian of monastic discipline. One night he saw a vision, which he himself recorded in writing:

3.18. BERNARD'S VISION. "After midnight and before the bell for Matins was sounded – when fatigue strikes and dreams are their most true – I seemed to be standing in the open air with four others. When I looked up, a great mass of embers suddenly burst forth from an opening in the sky. Instead of falling straight down, the embers glided transversely to the ground in an endless stream. I saw what looked like a ladder extending toward these embers from the earth to the sky, and

---

33 Gerald's death is not noted in Petershausen's twelfth-century necrology for 14 June.
34 cf. CP 3.2 and 3.14.

the top of the ladder touched heaven, or rather the edge of the opening in the sky. By divine decree, all men, and also the dead who rose at the end of the world, had to climb this ladder to heaven so that they might be incinerated by the fire in the sky, and the damned and the elect alike might be sent down to the earth as embers.

Seeing this, I said to the people around me: 'Behold, here we have already at hand what we have always heard concerning the end of the world. Do you see the flying embers, white and black?' For I saw flying embers, most of which appeared white, but some were black. 'The white ones,' I said, 'are the souls of the saints, made pure by the testing fire.'[35] And I added: 'Why do we delay here so long? Why are we not rendered into embers like the others ascending the ladder, since we will not be spared?' We thus approached the ladder and eagerly began to climb it.

It was decreed that after flying through the air, the embers should return through the same opening in the sky to receive flesh again and be judged according to their merit. A guard was stationed above the opening, and he separated the embers from one another after their return. He allowed the good to enter a court in the presence of the Judge, but enclosed the bad in a nearby room soon after they had entered with the elect, so that scripture might be fulfilled: *it will come to pass that the wicked shall not see the glory of God* [Isa. 26:10, loosely]. The guard who stood before the opening revealed all of this to me while I was standing at the top of the ladder.

The mouth of the opening appeared to be so narrow that a single man could scarcely enter. While I stood there at the top of the ladder blocking the opening, the flame, which was burning the bodies above and sending their embers down from heaven, died down (as happens when one blocks the opening of a hearth), thus decreasing the density of the smoke inside. This comparison was also shown to me in the dream. After the dampened fire in the sky ceased to emit embers, I gathered all my strength, and climbing on my hands, feet, and elbows, I barely made it through the opening. The guard did not stop me, and I entered, fearing greatly lest I, conscious of my sins, should be deprived of the glory of God. The returning embers were animated

---

35 This is clearly a reference to the developing concept of Purgatory as an intermediate station between Heaven and Hell in which souls undergo purification from sins by fire. On the development of the medieval doctrine of Purgatory, see Jacques Le Goff, *The Birth of Purgatory* (Chicago: University of Chicago Press, 1984); Isabel Moreira, *Heaven's Purge: Purgatory in Late Antiquity* (Oxford: Oxford University Press, 2010).

in the same opening, just as it was shown to me while I was standing on the ladder before I entered. Then the guard, as I said, separated the elect and allowed them to walk freely in the presence of the Judge. But he closed the reprobate off in a separate room as soon as they entered and did not allow them much space so that they could see the face of the Judge, who was present, with even the smallest movement of the eyes.

A great disagreement broke out among the multitude of the elect in their shining white robes regarding the order in which they were to be seated at the feast of the Lamb.[36] Desiring to be hidden among those fighting, lest the Judge see me and order that I be cast into the room of the damned, I repeatedly begged the saints among whom I was hiding to repay me with their help if I had served any of them while on earth. It seemed to me that the Judge had not yet noticed me hidden among them. Finally, after the uproar died down, they arranged themselves in a single line extending from the end of the court all the way to the entrance. First came the holy patriarchs and prophets, then the other ranks of saints who had passed from the world throughout the ages since the beginning of time, and finally the twelve apostles at the end of the line, just as they were called in the last age of the world. This row was placed along the length of the court, and the other part along its breadth, such that the apostles were positioned before the throne of the Lord. There was very little space left at the end of the row beyond the apostles – hardly enough for two men. But, because I was not able to take a seat in the row of saints, I furtively took the empty space that I had seen at the end of the row of apostles along with one of my companions, hoping to be hidden there at the end. But fearing the Judge under whose gaze I stole my place, I dared not sit upright like the others, but rather remained prostrate, and with my companion I began to hide like a snake in the grass.

While we stayed there, the guard of the opening came forward and carried with him innumerable loaves of the whitest bread, and beginning from the first in the court – that is, the patriarchs and prophets – he distributed a loaf to each one in the row, continuing in this way up to the end of the apostles, who were seated at the very end of the row. Then two loaves remained, one of spelt and the other of wheat, which the server angrily threw to us as if indignant, since we, still untouched by the fire, now joined the purged community of the saints. The wheat

---

36 An oblique reference to Apoc. 19:6–7.

loaf happened to fall to me, since I was behind my companion at the very end of the hall.

Then the Judge looked at the two of us and saw the way the bread had been distributed and gave a sort of cheerful nod to me. Sensing what he wanted, I stood up – for I had lay prostrate – and jumped forward into the place of my companion who was in front of me and snatched his bread along with his place, and I pushed him, not unwilling, down to the place where I had lain before. Then like the others, I hungrily ate the bread that I had seized. I rightly rejoiced in these events, for I remembered the verse of the Gospel in which it is said to the guest in the last place: *Friend, go up higher!* [Luke 14:10]. After I had eaten half of my bread, weighed down with grief in my soul, I said to my companion, who was sitting next to me: 'I cannot stand this bread, although it is very sweet, since I know that I will pay for my sins according to my merit later'. My companion answered: 'Keep silent, most foolish man! Have you not read in scripture: *Blessed is he that shall eat bread in the kingdom of God?*' [Luke 14:15]. Comforted by these words, I again began to eat as before.

Meanwhile, the server offered a measure of wine to each, starting anew with the first. When he reached us, he cast a grim eye on us as though still moved by his earlier anger, and he gave us none of the drink that he had given to the others. When the Judge saw that we had no cup, he rebuked the server for not giving us a drink. But looking for an excuse, the server said that he did not have a vessel. At last, compelled by the Judge, he offered us a cup of wine, which he brought to me first. In his anger, he turned too little so that he spilled some of it onto the ground. To my companion, however, he gave nothing at all. As these things were happening, it seemed to me that only the Judge abstained from the food. He then ordered the server to give food to the reprobates who were closed off under separate guard, saying that he could not bear to have them suffer a double loss: cut off both from his glory and from food. The server did this immediately and willingly.

After the meal was finished, however, a burning furnace suddenly opened behind our backs in that same court. As it was then said, the Judge was obliged to send the sinners into this furnace. Standing before it, I looked at the flames and was stricken with exceedingly great sadness, for I knew that I would not escape the penalty for the misdeeds that I had committed on earth, even though the Judge had not condemned me for any sins. When he came to send the guilty into the fire, I humbly begged that he might release me for the briefest hour to descend to earth to purge myself somewhat with lashes, for I said that this type of penance is most quickly effective. But the Judge said: 'You may no longer be purged in this way. You needed to consider this before, while you were freely on earth. This penance, put off for so long with excuses, is now too late. Even now you try vainly to defer it, when indeed you neglected to atone with good works before'. My time to be given to the fire was already near, but he indulged me – I have no idea why – and delayed the last day for a few months, not years. I awoke and rejoiced that this was not real." Bernard himself described the appearance of the court, which had been shown in this manner [see Figure 1, p. 110].

3.19. A VISION. After he died a blessed death in holy intention, this same Bernard was seen by a certain brother in a vision in the night in which he saw him being tortured, prostrate over burning coals. When he reported this to the brothers, Gebhard of blessed memory, then bishop of Constance, responded: "Don't worry about this vision, because those who were known to hate him when he was living are now also the ones who seem to be dreaming cruel things regarding his death. For Blessed Bernard soldiered for the Lord without reproach in this life, and therefore it must truly be believed that he has already entered blessed rest to reign eternally."

3.20. A VISION. Not long after, it seemed to another brother as he was walking about in the monastery as if this same Bernard came up to him. Because he knew that Bernard had been buried, this vision caused him to tremble, but he nevertheless questioned him, saying: "Why do you walk here? How is this possible?" And Bernard replied: "I walk because it pleases the Lord, for in his judgment he assigned me the penalty of walking through the halls of this monastery and watching for as long as it pleases his mercy." This brother was a sub-deacon, with graying hair, and particularly learned. He walked with a limp and was always supported by a walking stick, and because of this he was considered unfit for the priesthood.

3.21. ABOUT CUNO. There was another priest in this same monastery, a handsome man called Cuno, whom I mentioned before.[37] One of the prior monks, he won the leadership of the monastery of Rheinau and there became abbot.[38] But one day, provoked by anger against a

---

37 Cuno of Altshausen, one of the monks who remained at Petershausen after the arrival of the reformers from Hirsau. cf. CP 3.14.
38 Cuno would serve as abbot of Rheinau from an unknown year after 1085 until 1098.

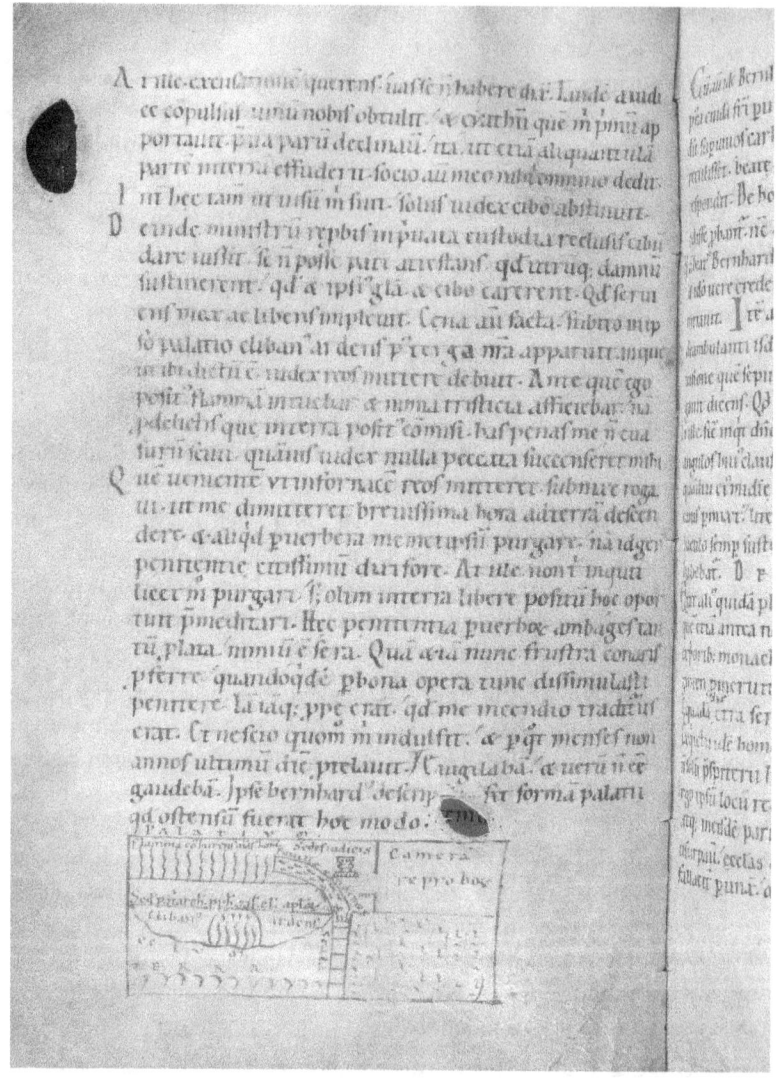

Figure 1 The Dream-Vision of Bernard (University of Heidelberg, *Codex Salemitani* IX 42a, f.64v.)

servant, he recklessly struck him with a door-bolt, from which blow the man became ill and died. Cuno was stripped not only of the honor of the priesthood, but also of the dignity of his leadership for this crime. He thus left the monastery and went to the province called Ries, and there he deceitfully usurped the office of the bishop, dedicated churches, falsely anointed men with the oil of confirmation, and carried out other priestly duties, and moreover collected no small sum of money for himself. When he had fully satisfied his desires, he laid down the badges of his foolishness and returned to his former monastery (that is Petershausen), and he placed himself under the leadership of the venerable Abbot Theodoric. And although Cuno rightly abstained from the office of the altar, Abbot Theodoric obtained permission by determined requests to Bishop Gebhard III for him to administer the Mass because he was a most capable man. Foolishness crept upon him again, such that if he ever celebrated the Mass in private, he chose the larger chalice for himself and filled it to the brim with wine, and thus he pursued such avarice in the sacred mysteries. One night he saw a vision in which the blessed Bishop Gebhard II, founder of the monastery, and the former Abbot Albert, about whom I spoke extensively above,[39] led him by the hand into the basilica before the image of the Holy Cross and stripped him of his garments, and afflicted him with the harshest blows. After they had done this, St. Gebhard said to him: "Behold this thing was done to you as punishment for your crimes, which you perpetrated in my monastery, and still more will befall you."

Not long after, late in the evening when the brothers wanted to walk to the dormitory after Compline, this same Cuno made for the lavatory and suddenly fell backwards! He lost his senses, and he began to wheeze and gasp excessively. When the venerable Priest Sigger, who was next to him, heard this, he rose and looked to see what might be the cause of this commotion, and he saw Cuno lying and gasping flat on his back in the privy. He first suspected him to be sleeping and snoring. He waited for a time, but once Cuno was not breathing at all, he finally drew near and removed him from the privy and laid him on the floor, and he at last called the brothers together. When they came, they saw that he was voiceless and out of his senses and completely debilitated, so they lifted him up half-alive and brought him to the infirmary. Gravely ill, he was kept there for quite some time. Although he recovered little by little, he nevertheless remained mute until his death.

39 cf. CP 2.12–2.13.

3.22. ROUTHARD'S VISION. There was another venerable priest in this same monastery called Routhard, to whom Peter, the Prince of the Apostles, appeared in a vision one night, standing above the cloister near the image of our Savior in the presence of the entire congregation, and with a gesture of his finger he called forth from among the brothers those whom he wanted. And when all had come to his signal, he sent them immediately to heaven. Finally, St. Peter summoned this same Routhard who was seeing these things. But before Routhard could arrive, Peter suddenly vanished, ascending into heaven. When Routhard arrived at the spot where the apostle had been, he quite justly began to grieve that he had been left behind and forsaken by the apostle, who had sent the others to heaven. As he stood overcome by great anguish, a golden cord suddenly dropped down from heaven and circled him under his arms, and he was thus conveyed up to heaven. On the following day, however, when this same priest reported this vision to Abbot Theodoric, he forbade Routhard in the name of God to recount these things to any of the men he had seen in the vision. After a few days, those who had been called began to die in the same order in which they had been called by holy Peter. Finally, Routhard himself – the one who saw this vision – died.

3.23. ABOUT ULRICH OF BREGENZ. Around this time, many enjoyed close friendship with the venerable Theodoric, since he was a pious, prudent, and helpful man in act and counsel. Noble and wealthy men, and all those who visited him from all over, wanted to profit from his example and counsel. Among these was Count Ulrich of Bregenz,[40] a most noble and handsome man, who enjoyed the greatest friendship and familiarity with Theodoric.

3.24. ABOUT ANDELSBUCH. There was a certain solitary named Diedo who built himself an oratory and dwelling in a forest called Andelsbuch. He plowed a field around himself, and it seemed to be a suitable place for serving the Lord. After the aforementioned solitary died in the Lord,[41] Count Ulrich asked the venerable Theodoric if he might build a monastery in that very place and institute the regular life there. Theodoric absolutely refused to build it unless Ulrich handed ownership of the place over to Petershausen, so that if he did the work, he might receive some fruit from it. After a while spent in deliberation,

---

40 Count Ulrich X of Bregenz (d. 1097).
41 In 1080.

the count finally agreed and sent the monastery of St. Gregory the relics of the saints that the aforementioned servant of God had kept in his solitary oratory. And afterwards, in the presence of proper witnesses and without any objection, he delivered Andelsbuch and another property called Hasenau to the monastery of Petershausen in perpetual ownership and ministry of the brothers who there serve God and St. Gregory continuously and forever, so that a monastery might be built there and that monks might forever live in that place.

With this donation complete, Abbot Theodoric began to inhabit this place, and with much effort and expense he built an oratory and enclosure there out of wood.[42] He had it dedicated in honor of the holy apostle Peter, and after suitable brothers were sent, he placed Meinrad (about whom I spoke above) in charge over them.[43] After they dwelled there for some time and the number of brothers began to increase, they were not able to acquire sufficient provisions and other necessities due to the long and difficult journey, since the monastery was situated deep in the forest. They formed a plan to relocate the monastery to Bregenz, where the brothers would more easily and readily be able to have what they needed.[44]

3.25. ON BREGENZ. Abbot Theodoric therefore came to the place called Bregenz and brought with him Bishop Gebhard, Meinrad, and Count Ulrich, as well as the others who were necessary for this business, in order that they might consider where a monastery should be built, since they desired it to be transferred from the forest. After much deliberation concerning these matters, all agreed that it should be next to the church, if Count Louis would agree to relinquish his half of it for this purpose.[45] For there was a baptistery there, half the proceeds of which along with half of the forest and of all the proceeds from these regions, belonged to the nobles of Pfullendorf, and the other half to the nobles of Bregenz. But the original plan was abandoned because Count Louis would by no means agree to hand over his half, and they turned their attention elsewhere. Since the monastery already possessed a certain small house nearby, they went there and looked around in the thickets for an opportune place, and with the Lord showing the

---

42 In 1086.
43 cf. CP 2.14, 2.15, 2.22, and 3.14.
44 In 1092.
45 Count Louis of Pfullendorf (c. 1067–1116).

way, they found one. For the venerable Gebhard, while he wandered in prayer looking around and exploring places, suddenly stopped in one spot and decided that the monastery should be built there. When everyone agreed on this same place, Theodoric began to build a monastery there at the expense of and with the proceeds of his own monastery, to which this place had earlier been donated. He built an oratory and then an enclosure, both entirely of wood, and he had it dedicated in honor of St. Peter.[46] He established Meinrad as the abbot there, just as he had once been at Petershausen.[47] Still, Theodoric frequently visited this place and provided for its needs. For nearly five years, he spent whatever was supposed to come to Petershausen from Aichstetten[48] for the construction of both of these monasteries, and he provided sacred vestments, books, and saints' relics – those that were originally sent from Andelsbuch as well as many other magnificent things.[49]

3.26. MORE ON THE ABOVE. When that place began to prosper and grow wealthy, they began to consider how it might be given its liberty. After much consideration, they determined that it could by no means be improved unless Count Ulrich give Petershausen the estate called Bigenhausen, which his father had already donated long ago,[50] and receive Bregenz from the monastery in return.[51] Indeed, the same count had betrothed himself as a young man to the daughter of Count Werner of Habsburg[52] and had confirmed that betrothal with an oath. But before he married, he came with Duke Welf to Kelmünz and secretly had sex with Bertha, the daughter of King Rudolf.[53] He wished to hide this, but the girl made it known, and thus it happened that he was compelled by her relatives to take her as his wife and make amends for the broken oath that he had sworn to Werner's daughter, and he handed over from his property everything that he had promised to them. And

46 In 1092.
47 On Meinrad, cf. CP 2.15.
48 For acquisitions in Aichstetten, see CP 1.41, 1.42, and 2.10.
49 On the founding of Mehrerau, see REC, 585.
50 cf. CP 2.23.
51 In order for Mehrerau to be independent of Petershausen, it would need to own the land on which it stood in Bregenz, which Petershausen owned. Petershausen thus arranged to trade the land with Count Ulrich of Bregenz, acting as advocate of Mehrerau, in exchange for Bigenhausen (which Ulrich's father had already given to Petershausen, but which had since fallen back into the use of the comital family).
52 Count Werner of Habsburg (d. 1096).
53 Anti-King Rudolf of Rheinfelden.

so upon his return he gave them some of his ministerials' income and benefices, and he gave these ministerials other benefices, thus transferring some of them to Bigenhausen, where their descendants still live.[54] It was on this pretext, I believe, that this same estate was taken from the monastery.

Thus, as was said above, in order to receive our land in Bregenz, Count Ulrich restored Bigenhausen to the monastery of Petershausen. Nothing was done concerning Andelsbuch and Hasenau, but that which had originally been established remained in effect. Through the neglect of our men, however, Bigenhausen had earlier fallen to the use of the counts of Bregenz, and its exchange for our land in Bregenz was not legitimate because it had already belonged to the monastery. Therefore, [that which had fraudulently been taken away] was legally restored, but without compensation. Thirty talents were given so that the decorations and accoutrements from the monastery in Andelsbuch – the sacred vestments, metal objects and books, and the saints' relics that had been sent there from Petershausen – might remain in Bregenz. After these things were done, they began to build a church out of stone.

At the same time, Count Ulrich arrived at Brettingen and stayed there for several days with many of his men. On a certain day after lunch, young men climbed almost to the top of a tall mountain and began to roll stones down into the valley for fun. And behold, one named Opert rolled a stone and shouted to those who were in the valley below so that they might see it. It happened, however, that Count Ulrich was walking in the path of the stone and refused to dodge it, intending to leap over it instead. But the stone hit him in the calf and broke his leg, and not long after, a bad inflammation developed and quickly killed him. He was therefore carried to Bregenz and left unburied until the bishop was summoned to dedicate the oratory, since the church had not yet been dedicated. But Abbot Theodoric, hearing the count's family murmur that they wished to take Bigenhausen yet again, did not allow the bishop to dedicate the church until Ulrich's widow Bertha, with the hands of her sons Rudolf and Ulrich and in the presence of many freedmen[55] and servile men, confirmed that property in perpetual ownership to St. Gregory. Thus the monastery in Bregenz was given

---

54 On Bigenhausen, cf. CP 2.23.

55 The witnesses are specified as *libertis et servilibus* – both probably drawn from among the monastic *familia*, which included servile members of various types alongside semi-free *censuales*, called elsewhere in the Chronicle *liberti tributarii* (CP 5.13).

its liberty with the condition that the inhabitants there always have respect for Petershausen, and receive counsel, aid, oversight, and their abbot from there, and always be one with them. And so the oratory was finally dedicated and the body of Ulrich was buried there.⁵⁶

3.27. ABOUT WAGENHAUSEN. There was a certain nobleman called Tuto, who gave his estate in Wagenhausen, everything else that he owned, and himself to Schaffhausen, and he lived a holy life there for some time. Later, removing himself and all the things that he had given there, he afflicted them with such great troubles that they finally renounced him and gave three estates back to him, namely Wagenhausen, where they had already built a monastery, Kappel and Honstetten, so that they might at least have the others in peace. After this was accomplished, this same Tuto gave the aforementioned monastery of Wagenhausen with all of its appurtenances to the church of Constance, with Abbot Albert of Schaffhausen⁵⁷ present, and with his advocate Count Albert of Mörsberg and many of the brothers, with nobody contradicting. This took place in public at the Synod of Constance before many appropriate witnesses. Bishop Gebhard entrusted Wagenhausen to Abbot Theodoric, who led suitable brothers there, through whom he tended that same place for many years. After this, the monks of Schaffhausen and Tuto's heirs began to claim this same place, both asserting that it belonged to them by law, and because of this there was a great impediment to the monastery's development, which continues to the present day.⁵⁸

3.28. ABOUT THE MARTYRDOM OF ARCHBISHOP THIEMO. Around this time there was a great schism in the church on account of the excommunication of King Henry IV and of his pretender, with some favoring these men and others favoring the church, and because of this, certain bishops were driven from their sees and wandered abroad.⁵⁹

---

56 Bernold of St. Blasien notes the death of Count Ulrich X of Bregenz with less drama: "The most celebrated Count Udalric... suffered a very untimely death, alas! but ended his days after a good confession. He received honorable burial on 27 October in Bregenz, where he himself had established the monastic life." CBSB, 332. Ulrich (identified only as Uodalricus l[aicus]) is commemorated in Petershausen's twelfth-century necrology on 27 October (MGH Nec. Germ. 1, 676).

57 Abbot Albert of Schaffhausen (r. 1099–1132).

58 On the protracted struggles between Tuto and Schaffhausen and the ensuing problems with the oversight and development of Wagenhausen, see Beach, *Trauma of Monastic Reform*, 93–101.

59 A later excommunication than that enacted by Gregory VII, noted in CP 2.47.

Among these was Archbishop Thiemo of Salzburg,[60] who stayed in exile for many days with Bishop Gebhard III of Constance at the monastery of Petershausen and afterwards departed for Jerusalem.[61] On this journey, Thiemo was captured by heathens and taken to the city of Chorazin, put in prison, and was finally crowned with martyrdom.

3.29. ABOUT PATRIARCH ULRICH. King Henry installed Ulrich,[62] the patriarch of Aquileia, as the abbot of the monastery of St. Gall, allowing him to hold both offices because Ulrich was always eager to aid and abet him in his errors. Ordained by Wibert, he tyrannized catholic Christians. On this account, Ulrich prompted the king to depose the venerable Bishop Gebhard and replace him with another, since Gebhard was unwilling to communicate either with Ulrich or with any of his supporters on any account, for Gebhard was legate and apostolic vicar in German lands at that time.[63] The aforementioned Ulrich, who for a long time had conspired with Henry, thus at last presented the king with one of his monks of St. Gall by the name of Arnold, from the family of Heiligenberg,[64] promising that if Henry should give Arnold the episcopate, Ulrich himself would impose Arnold without the king's help. And thus, when the king fulfilled his wish, Ulrich returned home with a large band of soldiers and led Arnold to Constance. But because the citizens took up arms and resisted them with great tenacity, they left empty-handed.[65]

60 Archbishop Thiemo of Salzburg (r. 1090–1101/1102); on the hagiographical tradition regarding Thiemo, see David Thomas and Alex Mallett, eds., *Christian–Muslim Relations: A Bibliographical History* (Leiden: Brill Publishers, 2011), 555–556.
61 Thiemo participated in the crusade of 1101 under Duke William IX of Aquitaine (r. 1088–1127).
62 Abbot Ulrich of Eppenstein (r. 1077–1121), whose abbacy was contested first by Liutold of Eppenstein and then by Werner (1083–1086); Patriarch of Aquileia from 1086.
63 Bishop Gebhard III served as a papal legate for Pope Urban II from 1089.
64 Bishop Arnold of Heiligenberg was the imperial rival of Bishop Gebhard III from 1092 until 1105. Bernold of St. Blasien states that Abbot Ulrich of Eppenstein "who had obtained the abbey of St Gallen and the bishopric of Aquileia, *not entering through the door* [John 10:1], attempted to supplant Bishop Gebhard of Constance with a certain monk of his monastery and obtained for him the investiture of that bishopric from Henry." CBSB, 310.
65 Bernold of St. Blasien similarly reports that Arnold was, "not received by the people of Constance but instead he met with insults and was forced to turn back" when he attempted to enter the city for his investiture. See CBSB, 311. Bernold reports similar popular resistance against Henry's picks for the bishoprics of Augsburg and Metz. CBSB, 312–313.

3.30. Moreover, Arnold's brother Henry of Heiligenberg, the advocate of Constance and of Petershausen, came with a multitude of men and tyrannized the monastery of St. Gregory. He seized the provisions of the brothers with a rash hand, tested his men's swords on their animals, and committed many disgraces. Amidst these various and manifold struggles, Bishop Gebhard built a fortification for himself on an island at the head of the Rhine River so that he might remain protected within it. At last, his brother, Duke Berthold, and almost all the others were corrupted with bribes, and they did abominable things to Gebhard, and there was no one who supported him, except for one – Theodoric – who remained faithful through all of these tribulations.[66]

3.31. ABOUT THE EXILE OF BISHOP GEBHARD. Thus surrendering that place to their perfidy, Gebhard departed and labored with great renown on behalf of the pope throughout the kingdom, although an exile.

ON THE PRETENDER ARNOLD.[67] After that, as if unbridled, they led Arnold in with a great uproar and placed him in the seat of the church of Constance on the Feast of the Purification of Holy Mary in the year of the Incarnation of the Lord 1103. This feud, which had dragged on for almost twelve years, finally came to a bad end. After Arnold seized the episcopate, he immediately contacted the congregation of Petershausen and strongly urged them to remain quietly and peacefully in their monastery and serve the Lord, and he promised them that absolutely no harm would be inflicted upon them. He himself went to Rome and was consecrated by Wibert.

3.32. ABOUT THE EXILE OF ABBOT THEODORIC AND HIS BROTHERS. But Abbot Theodoric had no peace after the departure of Bishop Gebhard, because he loved him as his own soul. Rather, in that same year (that is, in 1103), he left his monastery and dispersed his monks and bearded brothers and commended them to other monasteries. He took with him twelve whom he chose and led them to the

---

66 As papal legate and regional leader of the pro-papal party, Gebhard III was totally isolated after the German dukes (including his brother Berthold II) made peace with Henry IV in 1098. With Henry's authority over Germany thus reestablished, Gebhard III was forced to withdraw from political life and direct his attention to his diocese and to monastic reform there. See Robinson, *Henry IV of Germany*, 298–300.

67 It took Henry IV eleven years to expel Bishop Gebhard III and install Arnold as Bishop of Constance. See Robinson, *Henry IV of Germany*, 284. Gebhard III was returned to his see in 1103.

monastery of Wessobrunn in Bavaria,[68] where he was received with honor and love by the venerable Albert, the abbot of that place,[69] and he lived there for some months with his men.

3.33 ABOUT THE MONASTERY IN KASTL. After this, a certain noble and devout man [called Frederick] brought them from that place and entrusted the monastery that he had begun on his land at the top of the mountain of Kastl to them,[70] and he showed respect for all of them and supported them with kindness. This same lord Frederick of blessed memory had a son called Otto, a man of the greatest nobility and splendor, who together with his father and other nobles of this region – his relatives, neighbors, and friends – greatly honored the venerable Theodoric and his brothers. These men enhanced the place with such great riches that Theodoric quickly gathered many brothers and arranged the monastic life there most honorably.

3.34. ABOUT ABBOT WERNER. After Theodoric left Petershausen, those who remained there made a certain Werner of Epfindorf their abbot,[71] and they forgot the monastic discipline that they had learned and began to live a more relaxed life. The pretender Bishop Arnold began to grant benefices to his followers from the monastery's property – something that had never been permitted for any of the bishops. After Werner with his supporters, and Arnold with his, led the monastery into utter poverty and destitution, however, the former set aside the title of abbot and went to Abbot Theodoric in Bavaria and subjected himself to him. Theodoric received him kindly and restored him to the office of the altar against the will of Bishop Gebhard. But he did not remain long in the *horn of the sinner* [Ps. 74:11, 1 Macc. 2:48].

3.35. HOW KING HENRY V[72] WITHDREW FROM HIS FATHER. Then in the year 1105 Henry, the son of King Henry IV, withdrew from

---

68 The monastery of Wessobrunn was founded c. 753, according to legend by Duke Tassilo III of Bavaria (r. 748–788).
69 Abbot Albert of Wessobrunn (r. 1064–1110).
70 The monastery of Kastl was founded in 1103 by Count Berengar II of Sulzbach (d. 1125) together with Frederick and his son Otto, counts of Kastl-Habsburg.
71 Anti-Abbot Werner (1103/1104).
72 Henry V appears as *Heinricus quartus* in the manuscript, and Henry IV appears as *Heinricus tertius* in the following line. Although the chronicler uses the title "king," he seems to have based his numbering in this passage on their imperial rank, as Henry I was not crowned emperor. In any case, the chronicler provides the more common numbering for these same figures in CP 2.26. We have adjusted the regnal numbering for clarity and consistency.

his excommunicated father, and with the consent of the princes, seized royal power against him.[73] Thence the greatest violence arose; for his father Henry, since he was not able to call his son back to him, gathered an army and attacked all of his supporters with the greatest pillaging and burning, but he never provided an opportunity for pitched battle.

3.36. ABOUT THE RETURN OF BISHOP GEBHARD AND ABBOT THEODORIC FROM EXILE. After Henry V became king,[74] he immediately banished Arnold and restored Gebhard to his bishopric with the greatest honor, and he chose Abbot Theodoric as his confessor and restored him to his monastery. Henry also sent Theodoric thirty marks of silver, with which the abbot opportunely and profitably restored the dispersed property of the monastery.

Then the elder Henry and the younger Henry held a general meeting in Mainz, where the father gave his son the scepter and crown of the kingdom with the other regalia.[75] Henry IV then lay prostrate before Gebhard, since he was the legate of the Apostolic See, and weeping greatly, he begged to be released from excommunication. Gebhard refused him because he feared that, if he should absolve him, the kingship might return to him again, and his next error might be graver than his previous. Nevertheless, when Henry IV died shortly thereafter in Speyer,[76] his son entreated Pope Paschal II and he was granted a church burial on account of the satisfaction that he had not been ashamed to make publicly, prostrate before the clergy and the people.[77]

3.37. ON THE MONASTERY OF KASTL. After the venerable Theodoric had founded the monastery of Kastl,[78] built a church, and gathered a community of brothers, he appointed the venerable man Altman as their abbot,[79] and he returned with his brothers to Petershausen.

3.38. ABOUT NERESHEIM. After this, Count Hartman the Elder of Dillingen asked Theodoric to send monks to institute monastic life on the mountain of Neresheim, where he had established a house of

---

73 In 1104.
74 Emperor Henry V (r. 1099–1125; crowned emperor in 1111).
75 In 1105 (actually in Ingelheim).
76 In 1106 (actually in Lüttich).
77 Henry IV was buried in the Speyer cathedral in August 1111.
78 cf. CP 3.33.
79 Abbot Altman of Kastl (r. c. 1108–1128).

regular canons.[80] Agreeing to this petition, Theodoric led suitable men there: Bernold, whom he made prior, my uncle Gebino, Werner as their superior,[81] and a sufficient number of other men for this monastery. And if I might speak briefly about the aforementioned Werner: when he was in charge of the workings of this monastery, he freely did whatever he wished, and he was undeservedly honored by everyone. Although he was already old, he withdrew and put off the monastic habit and put on the secular, and he died while he was building a tower for someone.

3.39. ABOUT THE INVESTITURE OF BISHOP ULRICH I. In the year 1110, the great King Henry V marched to Rome most gloriously with a great army in order to be made emperor by the pope. But Henry became enraged when the pope demanded that he give back the symbols of investiture, which up to that point the kings had freely assigned according to their will, so that free election might be carried out, and he drove Pope Paschal II into captivity, injured the cardinals, and inflicted endless plunder and slaughter on the Romans.[82] The Romans then made war on him, but the king emerged as the victor and inflicted indescribable slaughter.

Meanwhile, Bishop Gebhard III of Constance of blessed memory departed from this world,[83] and while the king held the pope in custody, a messenger came and reported the death of Bishop Gebhard to the king, delivering the pastoral scepter and signet to him. Henry immediately offered them to Ulrich, son of Count Hartman of Dillingen, and he appointed him bishop of Constance. The pope and king afterwards reconciled with each other, and after Henry was consecrated as emperor, he left.[84] Ulrich, however, considered this same pope most troublesome, since Ulrich had been invested by the king while Paschal was held captive, and he was not able to receive the consecration while the pope still lived. He thus held the bishopric without consecration during the eight years that remained to Pope Paschal.

3.40. ABOUT NERESHEIM. When the monastery of Neresheim had developed to the point that an abbot was needed, Abbot Theodoric sent

---

80 In 1106. Neresheim was founded in 1095 as a house of Augustinian canons.
81 Werner of Epfindorf, anti-abbot of Petershausen (cf. CP 3.34).
82 This was Henry V's first Italian expedition (1110–1111).
83 In 1110. Gebhard III is commemorated (*depositio Gebehardi III epi(scopi)*) in Petershausen's twelfth-century necrology on 12 November (MGH Nec. Germ. 1, 676).
84 In 1111.

a certain old man named Sigbod from Hirsau and appointed him abbot. When Sigbod had been in charge for some time without consecration and was not able to endure the work, he left this place and returned to his monastery. Because of this, Theodoric was once again consulted, and he appointed Werner of Altshausen abbot,[85] his veteran monk who had weak eyes, and he was in charge without consecration for quite some time.

3.41. ABOUT RÖTSEE. It happened at a certain time that Ulrich, the Bishop-elect of Constance, was in dire need of money. Abbot Theodoric sold a certain estate called Dotternhausen for ten marks, because Lambert of Birchtlingen, who gave this estate to the monastery, could not reclaim it from those to whom he had previously granted it in benefice. Therefore, when the opportunity arose, the abbot gave the elected Ulrich eight marks for a certain island called Rötsee.[86] There a certain pious monk devoted to God named Ratpero had once built a large church, and God had made his tomb famous with numerous displays of miracles.[87] On account of his devotion, the blessed Ratpero had received ownership of this same place from the nobles then flourishing in Arnach, and he gave it to the church of Constance in the hope that it might thus be elevated, but this hope was in vain. After the venerable Theodoric bought this place, the following privilege was written for it.

3.42. THE PRIVILEGE OF GEILONOWA AND RÖTSEE. "Let it be known to everyone how the noble man Lambert of Birchtlingen gave two estates – one in Geilonowa and the other in Dotternhausen, which were his by right from the inheritance of his parents – without any objection into the hand of Henry of Heiligenberg, advocate of the monastery of Pope St. Gregory, called Petershausen, in the presence of proper witnesses, for the service of the brothers who serve God there day and night. But when Lambert was not able to reclaim Dotternhausen from those to whom he had given it in benefice, Theodoric, abbot of that same monastery, decided to sell the aforementioned estate called Dotternhausen for ten marks. When the occasion

---

85 This is not the same person as Werner of Epfindorf, who was anti-Abbot of Petershausen in 1103/04 and then a monk at Neresheim beginning in 1106. Cf. CP 3.34 and 3.38.

86 As explained more clearly in the following privilege, Abbot Theodoric bought Rötsee from Ulrich with funds made available by the sale of Dotternhausen.

87 cf. CP A.5–A.11, which comprises a Life of Ratpero.

arose, he gave eight marks from the proceeds of this sale for a certain island called Rötsee in the *pagus* of Nibelgau, which belonged to the church of Constance. After receiving the aforementioned price of eight marks, Bishop Ulrich of Constance gave the island with its oratory and all of its appurtenances – fields, meadows, lakes, forests, acquired and to be acquired – to the monastery of Pope St. Gregory, called Petershausen, for the use of the brothers of this same monastery, with his advocate Henry of Heiligenberg assenting to and conducting the transaction. The aforementioned bishop transferred the island with all of its appurtenances from the rule of his church into the rule of the monastery by lawful surrender, and he confirmed this surrender in the presence of the canons of the church of Constance and other proper witnesses."[88]

3.43. ON THE WAR THAT WAS CONDUCTED UNDER EMPEROR HENRY V.

At this time,[89] Bishop-elect Albert of Mainz,[90] who was said to have helped and counselled the king in all those evils that he committed in Rome, rebelled against him and now attempted to deprive him of the kingdom as if to avenge the pope, but really more for his own ambition than for justice.[91] The emperor captured and imprisoned Albert and afflicted him severely for many days. In the end, he was freed and reconciled to the emperor at the petition of the people of Mainz, but soon afterwards he lit the spark that set the whole

---

88 cf. Krebs, "Quellenstudien," 489.

89 In 1112.

90 Archbishop Albert I of Mainz (r. 1111–1137), a member of the comital family of Saarbrücken, staunch supporters of Henry V in the struggle against his father. On Albert I and his changing loyalties during the reign of Henry V, see Weinfurter, *The Salian Century*, 174–179; cf. CP 4.6.

91 Albert served as Henry V's chancellor, exerting considerable influence over the king and accompanying him, as noted here, on his expedition to Italy in 1110/1111. He was invested as Archbishop of Mainz in 1111 after his return from Rome. In the following summer, however, the king had Albert arrested on suspicion of conspiracy with some of the German princes and, "enriching himself at the expense of imperial estates and castles." See Weinfurter, *The Salian Century*, 170–174 (quotation at 174). There are accounts of the conflict between Henry V and Albert of Mainz in the Anonymous Imperial Chronicle (McCarthy, trans., *Chronicles of the Investiture Contest*, 215–216) and the Chronicle of Ekkehard of Aura (McCarthy, trans., *Chronicles of the Investiture Contest*, 243); the Petershausen chronicler's skepticism regarding the motivations of Albert, despite his putative allegiance to the papal party, likely anticipates the showdown between Albert and Bishop Ulrich I of Constance. In 1121, Albert demanded that the body of Petershausen's patron Henry of Hirschegg be expelled from the monastery's cemetery and Ulrich I refused to allow it, as detailed in CP 4.6.

kingdom aflame. For he and Archbishop Frederick of Cologne[92] placed the emperor under anathema because he had imprisoned the pope, and thus within a short time the whole kingdom turned away from the emperor such that he could not remain in the German kingdom.[93] He turned over governance to Duke Frederick of Swabia, the son of his sister, and withdrew to Italy.[94]

3.44. ON AMILHARD. At that time, there was a certain old monk called Amilhard at the monastery of Petershausen. When he died, the voices of singing angels and howling demons were heard, as Abbot Theodoric himself publicly announced in the chapter.

3.45. ON BISHOP ULRICH I. In the year of the Incarnation of the Lord 1116, Bishop-elect Ulrich of Constance, because he was afflicted by great tedium on account of the long delay of his ordination, sent Abbot Theodoric, whom he persuaded with many requests, across to Rome, hoping that he would procure permission from the pope to consecrate him, given the familiarity that Theodoric had once had with the pope, and given the many favors that he had received from the pope's legates. Theodoric therefore set out for Rome and pleaded with Pope Paschal II on Ulrich's behalf, but didn't achieve anything. My uncle Gebino went with him on this journey. Ulrich sent Theodoric a second time for the same purpose; although in the first departure he had attended to himself and the monastery carefully enough, in the second he barely bid farewell to his brothers and left them overwhelmed with many debts. He wandered through Italy for the whole summer, sometimes heading for the pope, sometimes for the emperor.[95] But after he delayed there for a long time, Ulrich followed him into Italy and remained with the emperor, whom the pope and the others detested as an excommunicate. When Abbot Theodoric and his companions rather incautiously found themselves in Rome in the unusual heat of summer around the end of July, some among them began to die. Seeing the impending danger, those who were still alive left Rome and went to Sutri. They all left there equally ill, until only one man remained. Whoever wishes can

---

92 Archbishop Frederick of Cologne (r. 1100–1131).

93 Cologne rose against the emperor in 1114. After failing to take Cologne and suffering defeat at the Battle of Welfesholz on 11 February 1115, Henry would depart for Italy to address concerns there, crossing the Alps in 1116.

94 Frederick II of Hohenstaufen, Duke of Swabia (r. 1105–1147) and brother of the later King Conrad III.

95 Henry V was at this time involved in his second Italian expedition (1116–1118).

see what anguish, I say, what desserts, what a bitter death Theodoric tasted, when he saw that none of his companions remained and that he himself was about to die alone in a foreign land, deprived of his possessions and companions. From the moment of his conversion, he always avoided cohabitation with women like the plague, and no one was allowed to touch or even see his body unclothed, since he was modest and extremely chaste. But then he came to this misery, that he was kept in the care of women, who would lay him down, situate him, lift him, bathe him, and carry out all the other care that was necessary.

3.46. ON THE DEATH OF ABBOT THEODORIC. With suitable penance he thus crossed from the valley of tears to the joys of the heavenly city. He was raised to heaven, as we believe, on 2 August.[96] He was honorably buried in a certain church in the same city, and afterwards moved to the sanctuary within this same church and placed in a stone sarcophagus in the western side opposite the altar. I do not know the dates of the deaths of the others who traveled with him, that is of the priest Sigfrid, of the bearded brother Opert, and of three laymen, Eberhard, Reinbald, and Gozold.

3.47. A LETTER CONCERNING THE DEATH OF ABBOT THEODORIC. The bishop of the city of Piacenza[97] described his death in a letter in this way:

"A(ldo), by the grace of God Bishop of the church of Piacenza, brotherly love in Christ to the canons and all the faithful of the holy church of Constance. We give thanks to the Lord, the knower of the heart and reins [Wisd. of Sol. 1:6, loosely],[98] because you, happily formed in the womb of Mother Church, nobly begotten, gladly fattened by her milk, and strengthened by her hearty bread, have matured to manly strength, and through this you have learned to rejoice fully with those rejoicing, weep with those weeping, and conduct yourself with dignity in the middle of prosperities or adversities. Therefore, concerning the death of our brother, the abbot of Petershausen, I say a beloved man in God, let your heart not be disturbed, but powerfully rejoice because he has passed on happily and exchanged the uncertain for the certain

---

96 Abbot Theodoric is commemorated in Petershausen's twelfth-century necrology on 2 August (MGH Nec. Germ. 1, 673).

97 Bishop Aldo of Piacenza (r. 1098–1119/1121).

98 The kidneys (sometimes translated as reins), were seen as symbolic of the human conscience, and only God has knowledge of this innermost being. For example, see Jer. 20:12.

and the earthly for the heavenly. And because he multiplied the talents entrusted to him,[99] he entered rejoicing as a wise and faithful steward into the joy of his Lord. Truly, it must be believed that he has entered into the community of the living, because we know and testify that he consummated his death in pure confession and worthy penance through us. For this reason, we diligently commend him to your prayers and those of the whole church. As for the rest, we assure you that we and all of our fellow bishops unanimously support our brother in Christ, your Bishop-elect Lord Ulrich (may he be well), and the completion of his and his church's cause. Pray for us. On the death of our remembered brother abbot. 2 August."

3.48. When this letter was delivered to Constance, the canons went together to the monastery and read it to the whole congregation. An intolerable grief arose from all, and they lamented greatly for him and for those equally good men who accompanied him. The emperor ordered that the goods that Theodoric left be rendered to Bishop-elect Ulrich intact, and Ulrich expended these without giving any to the brothers, and in other matters he always proved to be ungracious to this monastery.

3.49. The venerable Abbot Theodoric was ordained in the year of the Incarnation of the Lord 1086, one hundred and three years after the founding of the monastery. He presided for thirty years, and so died peacefully at a good old age in the year of the Incarnation of the Lord 1116, one hundred and thirty-three years after the founding of the monastery. He left the library splendidly enhanced, and he ordered that the books he acquired be recorded: five Missals, two of which with Graduals and three containing Masses of the saints and for other required purposes; one book of the Gospels decorated in silver and ivory; two Lectionaries; one *Liber officialis*; one Benedictional; one Gradual; one Antiphonary; a Breviary for the Divine Office; a customary; Gregory's Commentary on Ezekiel; book three, part of book five, and all of book six of the *Morals on Job*; one copy of the *Dialogues*; Augustine's Commentary on John; Augustine's *On the Harmony of the Gospels*; Augustine's Commentary on the first part of the Psalms; Augustine's Commentary on the Epistle of John; Augustine's treatises on the work of monks, good marriage, virginity, widowhood, praying to God, and the suffering of Christ all in one volume; Augustine's

---

99 Matt. 25:14–30.

Enchiridion; a florilegium of works by Augustine; Augustine On Faith; Augustine on the Five Levels; Origen on the Old Testament; the Rule of St. Benedict; the Pentateuch; the Acts of the Apostles; the Hexameron of Ambrose; the Life of St. Ulrich; two Matutinals; and a book of winter homilies. Abbot Theodoric had these books copied; some of them were sold, but the majority remain.[100]

3.50. ON THE STATURE AND HABITS OF ABBOT THEODORIC. Moreover, this same father was tall in stature and most noble in habits. He had lowered eyebrows and respectable graying hair. He had a subdued voice because of his restraint, but he was avid in prayers and tears. He was friendly to good men and terrifying to sinful men, saying that a master ought to be a lion in the chapter, a father in the community, and a mother at the table. He was a most diligent guardian of monastic discipline and habits and also roused his subjects to this same diligence, and he was exceptionally learned. He wore down his body with frequent fasting and he often struck himself with rods, mostly in secret in the silence of night. He led no Divine Office publicly, neither singing nor reading, and although he was not able to do that, he nevertheless led others to do the divine work eagerly and honestly. He delighted in unison singing so much that he was often moved to tears, and he prohibited men from singing in the upper register altogether.

HERE ENDS THE THIRD BOOK

---

100 The listing of books produced by and for Theodoric adds weight to the argument that the chronicler was Petershausen's cantor, whose duties included managing the monasteries book collections, as noted above on p. 4, and highlights again the emphasis within Hirsau communities on liturgy, devotional reading, and biblical study.

BOOK FOUR

Introduction

Book Four opens with the election in 1116 of a successor for Abbot Theodoric. Here the chronicler offers a view of the perils of such moments of transition in the life of a religious community. The process of selecting a new superior could expose and exacerbate existing internal divisions and tensions, and could sometimes lead to bitter discontent and schism. Abbatial elections could also invite attempts, in this case by Bishop-elect Ulrich I, to pressure, influence, and increase control. The chronicler's account of the process, and particularly of the monks' refusal to be pushed into a hasty choice by the canons of Constance who had brought word of Theodoric's death, works as a kind of demonstration of proper procedure.[1] The monks successfully rebuff the canons' attempt to be present at the election, send away all visitors, and – thus free of any outside interference – deliberate and select Berthold, a venerable monk of the community, as their next abbot. This is an election that conforms both to the process set forth in Chapter 64 of the Rule of St. Benedict and to the principles of *libertas* championed by the Hirsau reformers.

A decade later, when the monks find it necessary to pressure Abbot Berthold to step down, they cautiously enlist Ulrich I's support, and the bishop convinces the faltering old abbot to abdicate.[2] The chronicler represents the abdication itself as an impressive triumph of *libertas*; when the bishop shrewdly tries to have Berthold complete the process by handing him the staff that represented the abbatial office – clearly a potent symbol in the context of the ongoing struggles over investiture – the monks shout him down. A self-abdication ensues: without reference to the bishop, Berthold approaches the altar, sets down his staff, returns to his seat, and casts the first vote for his successor. The exclusion of the bishop from the relinquishing of the abbatial staff is a vivid illustration of the monks' right to complete freedom in the election

---

1 CP 4.1.
2 CP 4.23.

THE CHRONICLE OF PETERSHAUSEN: BOOK FOUR

and investiture of their abbot. As their episcopal proprietor, the bishop is appropriately consulted about how to get Berthold to resign. His assistance in the matter is gratefully accepted, but his intervention in the delicate process of transition is not. The chronicler's assertion that Ulrich I died a miserable death, his eyes ejected from his head, may have been intended as a powerful warning about what happens to bishops who repeatedly threaten the monastery's rights.[3]

Book Four also offers further witness to the struggles over investiture that continued to lead to division and violent conflict in the broader region, and particularly to their impact at the local level. When Archbishop Albert of Mainz, who first appears in CP 3.43, demands the expulsion from Petershausen's cemetery of an enemy who happened to be a patron of the monastery, Ulrich I's refusal to force the monks to comply leads to a liturgical disaster in the form of a ban on the celebration of the Divine Office and the Mass during the Holy Week of Easter.[4]

It is also in Book Four that we find the chronicler's first revelations of profound trouble within the community in the generations following the reform. First, a group of bearded brothers beats the cellarer nearly to death for rudely refusing to give them the supplies that they had repeatedly requested.[5] Not long after, one of the monks steals the community's precious thurible (a liturgical implement for diffusing incense).[6] There are also clear signs of economic mismanagement. The monks manage to spend forty marks of silver given to them by a patron to buy land and are then forced to conceal their misuse from him,[7] and an incompetent *custos* runs the community into deep debt.[8] Further, a series of failed attempts to found and reform other communities results in the overextension of the monastery's economic and human resources.[9] There is a certain anxiety suggested by the chronicler's assertion that God will never allow the community to burn following a series of miraculously extinguished fires,[10] an anxiety even more

---

3 CP 4.25; for a similar account of a miserable fate that befalls an over-stepping bishop of Constance (Lambert), see CP 2.5.
4 CP 4.6.
5 CP 4.11.
6 CP 4.13.
7 CP 4.36.
8 CP 4.15.
9 CP 4.18–4.20.
10 CP 4.14, 4.16, and 4.17.

urgently expressed in a passage in which the chronicler remarks on the unnatural death of each of the community's previous seven abbots. "Who would believe," he comments, "that this occurred without harsh divine judgment?"[11] That this passage was deleted from the manuscript suggests that a subsequent reader thought it best to erase these messy memories in a later act of "social forgetting."[12]

Book Four

4.1. ON THE ELECTION OF ABBOT BERTHOLD. After the death of the venerable Abbot Theodoric was made known, the canons of Constance gathered and went to the monastery of Petershausen. They entered the chapter of brothers, and after they read the letter concerning both the death of the abbot and the exhortation of Bishop-elect Ulrich in which he instructed the brothers to elect an abbot, as the canons thought that the monks should hold a free election, they urged them to do this right away. The senior monks then modestly and humbly responded that this business could not be completed so hastily, but rather that the brothers ought to deliberate among themselves with careful counsel through prayers to God, and thoughtfully discuss whom they should select for this office, so that they might entrust to him the monastery's spirit, body, and property, as well as the place itself. They said that no one ought to be present at this election except he who wished to live under the person elected. The venerable Abbot Cuno of Altdorf,[13] who had always been a friend of this same monastery, happened to be present. When the canons argued that they ought to be present at the election, the entire congregation of monks began to contradict them with one voice and made them leave. After they discussed among themselves, they elected venerable old Berthold,

---

11 CP 4.27.

12 University of Heidelberg, *Codex Salemitani* IX 42a, f. 78v and 79r. This erasure, which another (undatable) hand has attempted to retrace, is visible in the digitized manuscript: https://doi.org/10.11588/diglit.605#0170. (Date of last access: 22 December 2019); on the concept of social forgetting – "the rejection of certain memories in order to make others intelligible and to allow for the construction of a coherent narrative of the past" – see Vanderputten, *Monastic Reform as Process*, 15–16.

13 Abbot Cuno of Altdorf (r. 1109–1132). Altdorf was a Benedictine community founded by Welf IV in 1056. After 1123, the name Weingarten was more commonly associated with the community. It is unclear why the chronicler, writing well after 1123, uses the obsolete "Altdorf" here.

who had long held the office of prior in this same monastery, and absolutely no outsider took part in this election. Indeed, Werner, who had been made abbot of Neresheim, then appeared and occupied the principal seat.[14] Berthold was ordained by Bishop Wido of Chur[15] in the year 1116.

In the year 1119, Pope Paschal II died and Gelasius II[16] succeeded him. Bishop Ulrich was then ordained by the archbishop of Milan,[17] and thereafter he was a friend of the Romans. After the emperor heard about the death of Paschal, he hastened to Rome, hoping that he might conduct the papal election by his own hand. But when the newly ordained Gelasius heard about the unexpected arrival of the emperor, he fled during the night and refused to greet or see the emperor at all. Since the emperor was unable to call Gelasius back to him, he appointed another by the name of Burdinus and named him Gregory, but Gelasius excommunicated them both.[18] Burdinus received Rome through the power of the emperor, while Gelasius held the entirety of the Church.

4.2. ABOUT AN EARTHQUAKE. Earlier, in the year of the Incarnation of the Lord 1117, on 3 January, around the third vigil of the night, and again on the same day at about the eleventh hour, there was a mighty earthquake that struck far and wide across the earth, such that many churches and certain cities were damaged from the immense shaking.[19]

4.3. ON WOLFRAD'S VISION. During this same time, a certain brother and priest named Wolfrad fell ill. One day after lunch he became

---

14 Werner of Altshausen (introduced in CP 3.40), to be distinguished from the Werner who briefly held the abbacy in Petershausen (cf. CP 3.34 and 3.38); as Abbot of Neresheim, one of the communities for which Petershausen had spiritual oversight at the time, Werner may have been called, in the absence of an abbot at Petershausen itself, to oversee the election.
15 Bishop Wido of Chur (r. 1096–1122).
16 Pope Gelasius II (r. 1118–1119).
17 Archbishop Giordano da Clivio of Milan (r. 1112–1120).
18 Mauritius Burdinus, Antipope Gregory VIII (r. 1118–1121).
19 The seismic activity on 3 January 1117 was actually two earthquakes, a smaller one in lower Germany followed some twelve hours later by a more massive one in the area of Verona. These earthquakes were recorded in some ninety-four, mainly monastic, sources. See Emanuela Guidoboni and Alberto Comastri, "The 'Exceptional' Earthquake of 3 January 1117 in the Verona Area (Northern Italy): A Critical Time Review and Detection of Two Lost Earthquakes (Lower Germany and Tuscany)," *Journal of Geophysical Research* 110 (2005): 1–20.

so unresponsive that the brothers who came to him thought that he had just died. After a short while, however, he opened his eyes, and when the abbot and the others asked him how he was, he said that he had died and been brought to heaven and saw its brightness; there he also saw Theodoric in great glory, and his chaplain Sigfrid, and Opert from among the bearded brothers, and certain others who are unknown to me.[20] One night he again became lifeless as if dead, and after the bells were sounded and his body was stripped bare for washing, he turned over and said to those standing around him: "Is it possible that you wish to bury me alive?" He nevertheless died not long after this.

4.4. ON AZALA AND PFRUNGEN. During this same time, a certain noble woman named Azala gave the estate that she held in a village called Pfrungen to the monastery of Pope St. Gregory, and she herself remained in this same monastery in the spiritual habit until the end of her life.[21] Nevertheless, Abbot Berthold was only able to redeem the estate with a large sum of money from her daughters and sisters.

{4.5.[22] There was a certain nobleman in the *pagus* of Linzgau called Cuno.[23] He owned a certain village called Pfrungen, which he had inherited in its entirety from his parents. He begat two sons, one called Meginzo and the other Cuno. After the death of their father, they divided the aforementioned village of Pfrungen between them. After this, the one who was called Meginzo gave his part to the holy church of Constance with the condition that he himself, as long as he should live, and after that his heirs, would hold both the right of investiture and advocacy of the church without any contradiction. His brother Cuno, however, took a wife and begat from her two sons, one called Wezil and the other Gebino. After the death of his father, Wezil added

---

20 Sigfrid and Opert were among those who traveled to Italy with Abbot Theodoric and died along with him, cf. CP 3.46.

21 Azala of Pfrungen is the first woman whose entry into the community (1117) was recorded. She is commemorated in Petershausen's twelfth-century necrology on 31 January: *Azala sor(or), haec dedit Pfruwangin* (sister Azala, who gave Pfrungen). MGH Nec. Germ. 1, 666. The village of Pfrungen stands in modern-day Switzerland, in the area of Winterthur in the Canton of Zurich. The counts of Pfrungen were long-time patrons of Petershausen, and one, Gebino (d. pre-1086), even lived within the monastery precinct in a small dwelling (*habitaculum*). See CP 2.20.

22 This chapter is a marginal addition made by a different hand in the manuscript on f. 74r–v.

23 This Cuno is the ancestor of Azala from the previous chapter, four generations prior, as laid out in this chapter (Cuno → Cuno → Wezil → Cuno → Azala).

a chapel to the church at Pfrungen using his own property, and had it dedicated in honor of the holy martyr Nazarius. He then gave the chapel one of his own servants,[24] Giselmar, as an endowment, marrying him to the freeborn Azala.[25] All of their descendants, as can still be seen today, are the property of this same chapel.[26] His brother Gebino gave his estate in Ringgenweiler to the monastery of Pope St. Gregory, which is called Petershausen, and furnished those living there with many other possessions, and remained there until his death. Gebino's brother Wezil, whom I mentioned above, took a wife, who bore him a son called Cuno. But Bishop Rumold gave the estate that the aforementioned Meginzo had given to the holy church of Constance to the advocate Henry of Heiligenberg as a benefice, who in turn gave it to Benno of Spaichingen. Benno at first began to dispute the advocacy of Pfrungen with Cuno, which all of Cuno's descendants had held without any opposition. This struggle between them continued until it was resolved at a synod called to address the issue in the time of Bishop Gebhard III of Constance.[27] The bishop sought an opinion from the synod and different people offered different views. At last, Count Liutolf of Achalm was asked for his opinion on this matter, since he was the oldest and steadfast in matters of virtue and truth.[28] Liutolf replied that it seemed to him entirely just that the privilege of advocacy and of investiture should never be taken away from the descendants

24 Giselmar, here called a *proprius servus*. Although his exact status is ambiguous, he was likely a *servus cottidianus* because he could be freely donated to the church along with his descendants as movable property.

25 This is a different Azala from the previously mentioned noble Azala who would later give her estate in Pfrungen (as reported in CP 4.4).

26 Cases of intermarriage between servile members of society – even the lowest class of *servi cottidiani* – and free people are attested frequently in the eleventh and twelfth centuries in the Bavarian *libri traditionum*. As evident in these cases, children produced by such unions would inherit their servile condition from the parent of inferior status, rather than by patrilineal or matrilineal patterns. This passage suggests that the same principle for the inheritance of servile status extended to Swabia, as Giselmar's descendants remained the property of the church despite his wife Azala's freeborn status.

27 This may refer to the synod convened in Constance in 1094 by Bishop Gebhard III, who was also Urban II's permanent legate in Germany. According to Bernold of St. Blasien (CBSB, 318–319), this synod addressed, among other matters, the problem of clerical unchastity and simony. Cf. Robinson, *Henry IV of Germany*, 278.

28 The seat of the comital family of Achalm was a castle built around 1030 on a hill overlooking the river Ach, between the towns of Reutlingen and Pfullingen, in the area known as the Swabian Alb. The family died out not long after the construction of the castle, but not before Count Liutolf rose to local importance.

of those who are known to have given the church this same estate. This decision was accepted on the same day that the synod ended. The aforementioned Cuno, retaining the right of investiture and advocacy, then took a wife and begat a son called Conrad and five daughters. One of these daughters, Azala, gave the monastery everything that she owned in Pfrungen.[29] Her advocate was her brother Conrad, who lived in Frickingen.[30]}

4.6. ABOUT ETTISHOFEN AND HENRY. After this, Henry of Hirschegg, a highly noble and prudent man, nearing the end of his life, gave the monastery half of his small estate in Ettishofen.[31] When his wife Richinza was dying, she gave the other half with the condition that, on the anniversary of each of their deaths, the brothers receive bread, wine, and fish from it.

When Archbishop Albert of Mainz heard that Henry of Hirschegg was dead, he sent a letter in which he ordered that Bishop Ulrich expel his body from the cemetery or stop the Divine Office in that same monastery until he was removed. For when Emperor Henry was in Italy and Duke Frederick of Swabia was laying waste to the church in Mainz on account of Archbishop Albert's rebellion against the emperor, Henry of Hirschegg had helped the duke, and for this crime the archbishop wanted him ejected from the cemetery.[32] But Ulrich had buried Henry with his own hands, and during his burial rites Ulrich had offered full evidence of the man's penance. Nevertheless, the archbishop prohibited the Divine Office in that same church on Maundy Thursday. The monks tearfully beseeched Albert that they might at least be permitted to sing the Easter feasts for the sake of the soul of Abbot Theodoric who had died for his obedience. The archbishop, however, swore on his own soul, and on all souls, that he would not permit this at all and attested firmly under seal that he would not permit them to offer any private prayers whether in the church or the connected chapels. But after further pleas, he reluctantly conceded that they could celebrate the Divine Office at the altar of St. Mary in the chapel next to the

---

29 cf. CP 4.4.

30 Conrad of Frickingen is commemorated in Petershausen's twelfth-century necrology on 8 December. MGH Nec. Germ. 1, 677.

31 Henry of Hirschegg is commemorated as the donor of Ettishofen in Petershausen's twelfth-century necrology on 19 December. MGH Nec. Germ. 1, 677; the seat of this noble family was a castle near Eichstegen.

32 cf. CP 3.43.

infirmary. This took place in the year of the Incarnation of the Lord 1121. Then, first Walter and then Wiserich, both monks of this same place, approached the archbishop with deprecatory letters, and in the end, moved deeply by compassion, he allowed them to serve God and let the dead rest in peace.

4.7. ABOUT EMPEROR HENRY V. In that same year, the emperor went to Reichenau and presided over the feast of St. Mark, and from there he and the queen,[33] the daughter of the King of England, went to Constance. But none of the clerics remained there because the bishop had departed and forbidden the others to stay, since Pope Callixtus II[34] had already condemned the emperor. The emperor was not moved to anger on account of this, nor did he go to the monastery of Petershausen. Neither the emperor nor any of his men made any trouble.[35]

4.8. ABOUT PFRUNGEN. The aforementioned worthy Azala of blessed memory again confirmed this estate to the monastery in the presence of the princes, as the following privilege shows:

4.9. THE PRIVILEGE OF PFRUNGEN. "Let it be known to all the faithful of Christ, both present and future, that a certain religious woman named Azala, with the hand of her advocate Berthold, and without any contradiction, gave to the monastery of Pope St. Gregory situated near the Rhine River, then under the direction of Abbot Berthold, a certain estate in the *pagus* of Linzgau in the county of Count Hartman.[36] She gave half of the village called Pfrungen, as well as an associated small estate called Tafern, and everything pertaining to them: open spaces, buildings, unfree laborers of both sexes, cultivated and uncultivated lands, fields, meadows, plains, pastures, forests, lakes, fisheries, mills, roads and impassable areas, ingress and egress, acquired and to be acquired, and all other useful things that can yet be mentioned or named. Azala legitimately transferred all of these wholly from her rule to that of the aforementioned monastery built in honor of St. Gregory, and also to the monks soldiering for God there under the Rule of St. Benedict. This transaction was conducted in Constance in the year of the Incarnation of the Lord 1121, in the fourteenth indiction, on

---

33 Empress Matilda of England (c. 1102–1167; m. 1114–1125), daughter of King Henry I of England (r. 1100–1135).
34 Pope Callixtus II (r. 1119–1124).
35 Henry V celebrated Easter at Reichenau on 25 April 1121.
36 Count Hartman of Dillingen, according to Feger (1956), 180, n. 9.2.

29 April, on a Friday, during the reign of King Henry the Younger, son of Henry the Elder, who at that time was with the queen in Constance. These things were carried out in their presence and in the presence of many witnesses." At this time Callixtus, also known as Guido, held the church of Rome, while Ulrich held that of Constance.[37]

4.10. ON THE DEATH OF BISHOP WIDO. In the year 1122, Bishop Wido of Chur[38] died at the monastery of Petershausen. He always showed much kindness and friendship toward this monastery, and he supplied many good things to the brothers. After he died, Berthold and the brothers clothed Wido in the things of the monastery, as was the custom, in episcopal garments. They placed him in a casket and brought him to Chur with great honor, but also with much effort. His successor Conrad[39] gave the monastery a silver chalice, which the abbot gilded, and a purple cloak, and he honored both the abbot and each brother in attendance with little gifts. In particular he gave to Conrad – who was then the chaplain and later became abbot – a piece of silk, out of which the abbot made a cloak, and a measure of silver, to which he and the rest of the brothers added, and they adorned the arm of the Apostle St. Philip[40] with gold and silver, precious stones, and the most attractive pearls.

4.11.[41] **ABOUT WOLFRAD.** {There was in that same monastery a certain cellarer named Wolfrad, who, when the brothers sought clothing from him, offered harsh replies and did not give them the things they needed. One day, therefore, the bearded brothers, incited to anger, beat him nearly to death with cudgels and dumped a cauldron full of water on him… thinking it… There was a great scandal on account of this incident… but nevertheless, those who had done this, publicly before the bishop and abbot, with the clergy and people of Constance looking on… to declare their guilt openly. After they did this, they sought

---

37 See Krebs, "Quellenstudien," 489.
38 Bishop Wido of Chur is commemorated as a benefactor – *iste benignus nobis fuit* – in Petershausen's twelfth-century necrology on 18 May: MGH Nec. Germ. 1, 671.
39 Bishop Conrad I of Chur (r. 1123–1144), commemorated in Petershausen's twelfth-century necrology on 1 March, with the same wording as for his predecessor, Wido. MGH Nec. Germ. 1, 667.
40 cf. CP 1.29.
41 This chapter is almost entirely erased in the manuscript, but the story is repeated in CP 5.7. In the second telling of this story, penned in the 1160s, Countess Bertha of Bregenz (d. post-1128) has disappeared from the narrative, perhaps because the family had, by that time, died out.

grace and reconciliation, but they were by no means able to bring this about – even with the intervention of the bishop – until after many days Countess Bertha of Bregenz came with many imprecations and saw to it that they were received back into the monastery.}

4.12. ON THE PRIEST OPERT. There was a certain old priest named Opert in that same monastery, who was particularly devoted to psalmody. He spent night and day in this labor, except for those hours that were taken by necessity for his body. When he died, there were certain travelers on the banks of the Rhine wanting to cross the river under the open sky in the silence of the night. In the very hour of his passing, these travelers saw a great light arise from the highest part of the basilica and rise up to pierce the heavens. Then, while standing astonished and amazed, they suddenly heard all of the bells ringing for his death and they knew that this sign was given on his account. Deeply inspired by this, they waited there and attended his funeral on the following day with great devotion.

4.13. ON THE THURIBLE THAT WAS STOLEN AND DESTROYED. There was in that same monastery a very beautiful censer made out of the most exquisite silver and brass, in which incense was placed on the major feast days. During these times, it happened that a certain monk, enticed by diabolical greed, stole this thurible after Vespers during the feast of St. Michael and hid it that same night. Later, once he got the chance, he broke it into pieces. When the thurible was sought at Matins to cense the altar as usual and could not be found, Herbert, the *custos* of the church, was deeply perturbed and looked everywhere he could but did not find it. A certain man from Constance named Wolfrad was then accused of this theft because he was seen walking near the sacristy late at night. Denying this, he carried a hot iron and appeared innocent, although his hand was badly burned.[42] Therefore, after deliberation it was proclaimed to the entire

---

42 Trial by ordeal, ultimately seen as a form of divine judgment, was used to determine guilt in the Middle Ages. Ordeals had been in use since the pre-Christian era and remained popular in the medieval period before the church condemned the practice during the Fourth Lateran Council in 1215 (canon 18). The most common method for ordeal was trial by hot iron, as depicted here. The accused person would hold a hot iron, then the wounded hand would be wrapped, generally for a period of three days, after which the hand would be inspected. A festering wound was an indication of guilt. Other methods for ordeal involved grabbing a stone out of a pot of boiling water, immersion in cold water, or trial by combat. Charles A. Radding, "Superstition to Science: Nature, Fortune, and the Passing of the Medieval Ordeal," *The American Historical Review* 84 (1979): 945–69; Robert Bartlett, *Trial by Fire and Water: The Medieval Judicial Ordeal* (New York: Clarendon Press, 1986).

congregation that they should prepare to clear themselves of this theft by an ordeal. All gathered in great fear and prepared themselves for undergoing the ordeal. And since the theft was committed during the festival of St. Michael, in whose octave the birth of the martyr and virgin St. Fides is celebrated,[43] the whole congregation of brothers vowed that they would celebrate her feast with the full office until eventually God should reveal the author of this theft on account of their intercessions. They thus conducted the Mass for seven days, full of the Holy Spirit, just as on Pentecost. With little delay, God quickly liberated his servants, contrite of heart. One day after lunch, a certain priest named Herman sat down to warm himself by the fire in the small room where the brothers let blood, and behold, he suddenly saw a piece of this same censer catching the light on the ground next to him, so he took this and showed it to all of the brothers. This Herman had been the first to offer the suggestion of celebrating the feast of St. Fides – what more is there to say? The author of this crime was then caught and examined. Such iniquity infected his heart that, even after he had confessed his guilt, he removed a piece of metal again and showed it off until finally he returned it, having been barely persuaded to do so by one brother as well as by others. The silver was kept for some time so that it could be returned to its prior condition, but Abbot Conrad spent it later, at a time of pressing necessity. And since I have come to the topic of the church, let me speak a little about its caretakers.

4.14. Sigfrid, who died with Abbot Theodoric in Italy, had been the *custos* of the church for a long time, and he managed its affairs wisely and excellently.

ABOUT THE FIRES. One day, the sacristy was set on fire through carelessness and it burned for some time, almost as though reluctant, until people who were walking along the bank across the Rhine in Constance saw the fire and pointed it out with shouts. It was quickly and easily extinguished.

---

43 The feast of St. Michael is celebrated on 29 September and its Octave ends on 6 October, which is also the day of the feast of St. Fides. While there is no clear connection between the ordeal by hot iron and St. Fides' martyrdom, she is said to have been burned to death on a hot iron brazier. The monks may thus have seen Fides as a fitting intercessor, and specially honoring her perhaps as a substitute for undergoing the ordeal themselves. Coincidentally, Conrad dedicated a new chapel to Fides and Mary Magdalene in 1134 (CP 4.31); because this chapel was not damaged in the great fire of 1159, this chapel was used for the celebration of the Divine Office just after the disaster (A.39).

On another occasion, during a storm in the dead of night while all were sleeping, a candle that was burning at St. Ulrich's altar fell over and everything that was laid out caught on fire. Waking to the sounds of crackling flames, Sigfrid arose and saw the fire. In his haste, he did not awaken anyone to help, but rather rushed out alone and discovered the chapel full of fire. He ran into the chapel and put out the flames. The fire destroyed a rush and straw mat, but astonishingly did not touch the wood or anything else at all.

4.15. ABOUT AMIZO. After Sigfrid died, Abbot Berthold appointed Amizo, who suffered terribly from falling sickness,[44] and who, rashly driving the monastery into the greatest poverty, squandered the things entrusted to him and gave many of the holy vestments to be held against chirographs.[45] When he had reduced to nothing nearly everything that pertained to the support of the monastery and had burdened himself with his many debts, one day after lunch he withdrew to a room where candles were stored, and he stayed there past noon, since he knew silverware and other such items were stored there; and, behold, he had a sudden attack of falling sickness that immediately killed him. After he was found dead and was buried, through subsequent investigation, the magnitude of the loss was discovered. The abbot then distributed the chirographs that needed to be paid off to the obedientiaries,[46] but he barely managed to track down where some of these individuals were.

---

44 The chronicler here uses the term *caducus morbus*, a form of epilepsy; see Owsei Temkin, *The Falling Sickness: A History of Epilepsy from the Greeks to the Beginnings of Modern Neurology*, 2nd ed. (Baltimore: Johns Hopkins University Press, 1994).

45 A chirograph was a document that recorded in duplicate an agreement made between two parties. The document, once drafted, was cut in half, dividing the word *Chirographum* or a similar inscription spanning both sides of the document, creating a record of the agreement for both parties as well as a means of verification of authenticity. On chirographs, see Brigitte Bedos-Rezak, "Cutting Edge. The Economy of Mediality in Twelfth-Century Chirographic Writing," *Das Mittelalter* 15 (2010): 134–161.

46 The term *obedientiarius* generally refers to an individual who holds a lesser office (e.g., *custos*, cantor, or novice master), so it is unclear to whom the chronicler refers. It is clear, however, that he is claiming that the monastery made an effort to find the individuals who held the property of the monastery (i.e., precious liturgical vestments or vessels) against a chirograph. These individuals had apparently loaned the monastery money and were holding monastery property as a form of collateral. By redeeming a chirograph, the monks would repay the loan and receive their property back. It was not uncommon, as was the case here, to have difficulty finding the parties to whom money was owed, and the property held by the creditor was thus lost to the debtor. See Bedos-Rezak, "Cutting Edge," 136.

4.16. A MIRACULOUSLY EXTINGUISHED FIRE.[47] One evening after Compline, this same Amizo lit a candle and sat for some time reading I know not what. When he wanted to go to bed, he set the burning candle down on the wooden railings of the choir, and forgetting to extinguish it, went off to sleep. Once the flame had consumed the candle, it reached the candleholder itself and ignited the whole thing all at once. A great fire burned on the wooden stand, which had been built out of two discs in the usual way. The fire touched neither the wall nor the wax-coated stand, except for only a very small part of its surface as if to point out the danger. Does it not seem extraordinary to you that, with the candleholder burning so intensely and the wax flowing down from the flame, that the fire destroyed so little of the wood over which it burned?

4.17. ADDITIONALLY. Moreover, a certain blind man named Eberhard was staying in the hospice for the poor at this time. He stated openly that he often set fire to thatch, but he was never able to set fire to our roof tiles. With so many mercies of this kind, this place is known to have been protected often from fire down to the present. For as our elders have often confirmed, this place can never be destroyed by a fire so long as it holds the body of blessed Gebhard.

4.18. ABOUT THE BLIND WERNER.[48] At this same time, Werner the Elder, who had become abbot at Neresheim, was enticed with promises from Bishop Ulrich to leave that monastery and he returned to Petershausen. When Abbot Berthold refused to replace him with another, the bishop brought Henry of Zwiefalten to the monastery and made him abbot. Thus Petershausen's supervision of the monastery, which it had exercised for many years, was lost.[49]

4.19. ABOUT HIS VISION AND DEATH. Since the bishop had delivered on none of his promises to him, this same Werner withdrew

---

47 The theme of fire – first in the context of the monastery's divine protection from it, and later as a sign of God's righteous anger at the community for its failure to protect the body and patrimony of its founder and for the moral failings of its monks – runs throughout the Chronicle. See Beach, *Trauma of Monastic Reform*, 10, 32–35, and 50.

48 Werner of Altshausen; cf. CP 3.40 and CP 4.1.

49 On this transfer of oversight of Neresheim from Petershausen to Zwiefalten from the perspective of Zwiefalten, cf. the chronicler Ortlieb's account: COZ, 84. See also Beach, *Trauma of Monastic Reform*, 110–112.

to the monastery of Erlach[50] and remained there for several days. One night, he was led in a vision to a certain dwelling where he saw Peter, Prince of the Apostles, sitting with many other most illustrious men. This same Prince of the Apostles held a huge book written with gold letters in his hand. Werner was ordered to sit at Peter's feet, and when the Apostle showed his name in the book, Werner saw it clearly in gold letters. He cleverly asked if the book held the names of Abbot Theodoric and the names of his father and mother, and the Apostle pointed out all of these names in the same way. On account of his love of this vision, Werner shut himself up in a certain oratory dedicated to St. Peter and remained there in service to God until his death. He died and was buried in this same place, and it was said that wondrous cures were exhibited there; since I did not learn these things from a reliable source, I shall refrain from speaking further about this.

4.20. ABOUT WAGENHAUSEN. During this time, the monastery of Wagenhausen was under the religious guidance and direction of our monastery, but because it has been impeded by the fight with Schaffhausen, it has made little progress even to the present day. A certain old priest named Folchnand was sent there and placed in charge, and I was a monk under him there at that time. Although we were united by a pact of confraternity with the monks of Schaffhausen and of Stein,[51] who like Schaffhausen asserted that monastery was theirs, they had both frequently laid waste to Wagenhausen, and continue to lay waste to it to this day. But although the divine and secular affairs of the time were then conducted there in a rather orderly fashion, Bishop Ulrich, believing that he could quickly accomplish something of great importance, dismissed us and made a certain Uto the abbot there, and he helped him in any way he could. But he was only successful for a short time, as perhaps my pen has shown elsewhere.[52]

---

50 The monastery of Erlach, in the modern Swiss Canton of Bern, was founded between 1093 and 1103 and colonized with monks from the monastery of St. Blasien in the Black Forest, an important center of the Hirsau Reform.

51 A pact of confraternity promising reciprocal prayer for the dead was established between Petershausen and Schaffhausen in 1092. For the text of this agreement, see Francis Baumann, Gerold Meyer von Knonau, and Martin Kiem, eds., *Die ältesten Urkunden von Allerheiligen in Schaffhausen, Rheinau und Muri*, Quellen zur Schweizer Geschichte 3 (Basel: Verlag von Felix Schneider, 1883), 27–28 (#12).

52 cf. CP 3.27.

4.21. ABOUT THE SILVER PANEL. In the year of the Incarnation of the Lord 1126, there was a great famine, and oppressed by scarcity, many people perished. There was a panel on the western side of the main altar in the basilica of St. Gregory that was covered with beautiful gold and silver, and this was displayed only for the greatest feasts. Abbot Berthold had this broken up on account of pressing necessity, and got one talent and 1/16 of a mark of gold, and of silver {...} and all of this, both gold and silver, was most pure and of the best quality. A beautiful rendering of the Holy Mother of God with an image of a dove on her breast was removed from the gold in the middle of the panel, and beautifully crafted images of the apostles and other saints from the silver on the side {...}[53]

4.22. ABOUT BOOS.[54] An estate in Boos was then consigned to a certain Bernard for a loan of twelve pounds of silver against a chirograph. Later, during another famine, Abbot Conrad sold this estate to Rupert of Otterswang, who still owns it today.

4.23. HOW ABBOT BERTHOLD WAS DEPOSED. In the year of the Incarnation of the Lord 1127, Abbot Berthold was already burdened with old age and so overbearing in his manner that he neither himself provided, nor allowed others to provide, the things necessary for the monastery. At this very time, everything seemed to fall into disarray all at once, and certain of the senior monks began to plead in secret with Bishop Ulrich that he might persuade Berthold to abdicate the abbacy, permit another to be set in his place, and spend the rest of his life as a private man, for he was excessively harsh. Because the bishop was eloquent and clever, he persuaded Berthold, although he resisted for a long time. On the appointed day, Bishop Ulrich and Abbot Ulrich of Zwiefalten,[55] after long consultation, went to the chapter house and announced the abdication to the congregation. And when Berthold consented freely to live as a private man, certain people said that he had at that moment completed the abdication, and others said that he ought to proceed to the altar to abdicate. The bishop said: "This is not necessary. He should return the staff of rule to me." Then all cried out in protest, saying that it in no way belonged to him. Berthold thus went up to the altar and placed the staff on it saying: "Behold I set down what

---

53 The text has been erased and is illegible here.
54 cf. CP 2.17.
55 Abbot Ulrich I of Zwiefalten (r. 1095–1139).

I held by your grace and God's, and I absolve all of you from obedience to me." After he said this, he returned to his seat and cast the first vote for Conrad, the chaplain.

4.24. HOW ABBOT CONRAD WAS ELECTED. The community then returned once again to the chapter house. The bishop left, and the entire congregation chose Conrad in a free election. Conrad had left, because up to that point he had been living at the monastery as a guest. After the election was carried out, however, he was sought out and found. Brought back by force – crying out and protesting – he was finally, with great effort, subdued and set in the abbot's chair.

4.25. ABOUT THE DEATH OF BISHOP ULRICH. Four months later, while at the monastery of St. Mary in Breisgau,[56] which was distinguished for its way of life, Bishop Ulrich was afflicted with a royal illness,[57] and after his eyes were violently ejected from his head, he died an arduous death – a man who would have been very well-suited to the episcopal office if his spirit had not been so very bitter. He established the house of canons dedicated to St. Ulrich in Constance.[58] His body was carried to Constance and buried with honor in the choir of the basilica of St. Mary.

4.26. ABOUT THE LAST DAYS AND DEATH OF ABBOT BERTHOLD. Earlier, when Abbot Berthold had first abdicated his office, he was attended to for some time with faithful care, but later he was treated with much neglect. After a few years he was nearly out of his senses and he babbled like a child. His clothing and bedding stank from his urine, and he often went about the cloister without his cowl, and he did and said many other senseless things. He who in his days was accustomed to have mercy on no one on account of old age or

---

[56] St. Märgen in the Black Forest, a house of Augustinian canons founded between 1115 and 1118.

[57] The chronicler is probably referring to what would later be called gout, long called "the disease of kings" and (wrongly) associated with the overconsumption of wine and rich food – an informal diagnosis perhaps intended to suggest that Ulrich was given to gluttony. For the history of gout, see W. S. C. (William Sydney Charles) Copeman, *A Short History of the Gout and the Rheumatic Diseases* (Berkeley: University of California Press, 1964).

[58] This refers to Kreuzlingen, a community of regular canons attached to a hospice originally founded by Bishop Conrad I in the tenth century. In 1123, Ulrich I refounded and relocated the by-then defunct hospice to the area just south of the walls of the city and attached a new community of regular canons, dedicated to both St. Ulrich and St. Afra.

infirmity, he, I say, came to this – that unaware of the times or hours, he ate and drank and excreted without order, and he was unable to fast on important fasting days. And thus covered with his own filth, he gave off no small stench. At the end of his life, he had barely enough sense remaining to seek and accept the viaticum. Nevertheless, after he died, out of the benevolence of the brothers, he was dressed in priestly garments, as is customarily done for abbots, and buried with honor at the head of the tombs of the abbots – but in the absence of Abbot Conrad.[59]

4.27. NOTE: SOMETHING STRANGE. {May he who wishes ponder the strange thing about which I shall now speak. For almost seventy years – that is, from the time of Abbot Albert to the time of Abbot Berthold[60] – not one of the abbots of Petershausen left this world in the usual way. Some of them died abroad and others died seized by infirmity. Albert died suddenly in Buchau. Siggo died from a broken back in the second year after his ordination.[61] Arnold, Meinrad, and Liutold were deposed. Theodoric died far from home. Berthold, who was deposed, died out of his senses. Who would believe that this occurred without harsh divine judgment?}[62]

4.28. ABOUT THE ANTS. When Abbot Theodoric expanded the chapel of St. Mary near the infirmary,[63] a small room was added to the chapel, but the posts and lintels of the doorway were built into the wall, and from their rotting wood an innumerable multitude of ants was born, which would march out and climb onto the altar, and no Mass could be sung there undisturbed. One day, a certain priest was singing there and had no peace. He finished the Mass and ordered the ants in the name of the Lord, all the saints of God, and every virtue that

---

59 Abbot Berthold is commemorated in Petershausen's twelfth-century necrology on 25 September: "Abbot Berthold, who ruled after Theodoric for 10 years, a most doltish man who broke up the silver panel of St. Gregory" (*iste post Theod. prefuit annos 10, homo pinguissimus, et ipse comminuit argenteam tabulam s. Gregorii*). MGH Nec. Germ. 1, 675. The harsher language used to describe Berthold in the necrology may reflect that fact that it was written after the great fire of 1159, when scapegoats were sought for the disaster.

60 i.e., from 1061 to 1127.

61 The chronicler's discussion of the abbacy of Siggo and its (apparent) bad end has been completely erased from the manuscript. See CP 2.14.

62 This ominous observation has been effaced and retraced by a later hand (date unknown).

63 cf. CP 3.12.

he could think to name, to leave and thereafter offer no disturbance to those serving God. Who could believe that such virtue was honored in such a small matter? From that day to the present, ants are absent from that place so completely that no ant appears anywhere on the altar, the wall, or on the ground, even though before this they could not be expelled by any means. On another day, when that same priest was conducting Mass there, as he often did, he found some winged ants there that did not appear to be like the multitude of others. "And you," he said, "go away and leave this place free forever." From this hour forward, they were completely gone and offered no more disturbance at all.

4.29. ABOUT ABBOT CONRAD. At the beginning of his abbacy, Abbot Conrad began to build a new residence for himself and his successors, and after long arduous work, he finally finished it beautifully.[64] At the same time, Ulrich, the second bishop of this name, out of fear of Count Rudolf of Bregenz, destroyed his fortification at Castell, which his predecessor Ulrich I had built with great effort and cost. He gave Abbot Conrad the paneling from the two chapels, and Conrad had one of the panels installed in his own chapel, and the other in the chapel of St. John the Baptist. For he built two chapels, one above the other.

4.30. ABOUT THE CHAPEL OF ST. MARTIN. In the year of the Incarnation of the Lord 1129, on 29 October, the upper chapel was dedicated. Conrad had built this chapel in honor of St. Martin and St. Oswald the martyr and of the other saints whose relics were kept there: the Cross and purple cloth of the Lord, and of the apostles Peter, Andrew, Philip, Bartholomew, the Evangelist Luke, the holy martyrs Stephen the Protomartyr, Sixtus, Fabian, Blaise, Cyril, Erasmus, Sulpitius, Servilian, Cyriacus, Pelagius, Maurice, Hippolytus, Gervasius, and Protasius, Alexander, Son of Felicity, and of Valentinus; the blood of Boniface (who laughed at death), Anastasius, Sigismund, Valens, Candidus, Innocent, and the holy confessors Nicholas, Augustine, Conrad, Ambrose, Leonard, Hylarion, Arsenius, and the holy virgins Cecilia, Agatha (with a piece of her veil), Regula, Margaret, the Eleven Thousand Virgins, Mary Magdalene, Afra, Hilaria, Eutrophia. Bishop Ulrich II dedicated it.

---

64 A continuator returns years later to Conrad's decision to construct a new residence for himself in CP 5.11, offering a notably more negative assessment of the project.

4.31. ON THE CHAPEL OF ST. FIDES. In the year of the Incarnation of the Lord 1134, in the twelfth indiction, on 22 November, the lower chapel was consecrated by the venerable Bishop Ulrich II in honor of St. Fides and St. Mary Magdalene, and the other saints whose relics were kept there. That is, of the holy apostles Paul, Jacob, Thomas, Matthew, and of the holy martyrs Alexander, Cornelius, Callixtus, Stephen, Vigilius, John and Paul, Sebastian, George, Pancras, Tiburtius, Primus and Felicity, Sergius, Gorgonius, Christopher, Victor, Ursus, Exuperius, Gereon, Metellus, Quiriacus, Sisinnius, Felix, and of the holy confessors Martin, Maximin, Valerius, Gebhard, Benedict, Gall, and the holy virgins Regula, Verena, Walburga, Basilla, Digna, Emerita, Cantianilla, Hostia, Leonida, Numia, the Eleven Thousand Virgins, Mary Magdalene and other saints.

4.32. ON THE CHAPEL OF ST. JOHN THE BAPTIST. In the year of the Incarnation of the Lord 1129, in the seventh indiction, the chapel of St. John the Baptist was renovated by my uncle Gebino. Originally, an oratory dedicated to St. Jacob the Apostle with its own altar was attached to it, but he demolished this and usefully combined two oratories into one. He obtained the ceiling panels depicting St. John the Baptist from Abbot Conrad and hung them there. Bishop Ulrich II dedicated this chapel on 24 August in honor of St. John the Baptist, John the Evangelist, his brother Jacob, Philip, and Nicholas, who are the patrons there. Also kept there are the relics of the apostle Bartholomew, Stephen the Protomartyr, Pope Callixtus, Pope Marcellus, Apollinaris, Blaise, Cyril, Desiderius, Basil, Vincent, Cyriacus, Sebastian, George, Pancras, Vitus, Hippolytus, Christopher, Saturninus, Valentinus, Antony, Cosmas and Damian, Maurice, Exuperius, Candidus, Victor, Innocent, and Vitalis the martyr, and the holy confessors Paulinus of Nola, Nicetius and Agricius, Ulrich, and the holy virgins Cecilia, Barbara, Gundelinde.

4.33. HOW THE CLOISTER WAS PARTIALLY RESTORED. This same Gebino had just recently restored the cloister, adding new columns with square stone bases on two sides.

4.34. GEBINO MADE A CHALICE. Gebino had a silver chalice made and decorated with gold and gemstones with exquisite workmanship. But when the goldsmith was supposed to make the paten and wanted to set many precious stones in it, he could not set the crystals and rubies all the way into the body of the paten. As often as he began anew, it always ended in failure, and the work was thus set aside for a long time. {In the meantime, when necessity arose, Abbot Conrad sold it. He also took the silver that had once been part of the censer mentioned above.[65]}

4.35. HOW BOOS AND AILINGEN WERE SOLD. At that time, an estate in Boos was sold for seventeen marks. Ailingen was also sold for forty marks.

4.36. ABOUT THE PRIEST WITIGO.[66] A certain priest named Witigo, born in Allensbach, was long chaplain to the archbishop of Trier and Cologne. He gave about forty marks of pure silver to Petershausen to enable them to buy fields, which he was to use as long as he lived, and leave to the monastery after his death. But all of the silver was spent and nothing was bought with it. When Witigo came to see what had been arranged, not knowing what the abbot and his brothers had done, they showed him some of the monastery's property in Frickingen, which they had recently bought with some of the money which they had received for Ailingen. This land was extended and they gave it to him for his money, which had been spent. He accepted this gratefully, and with the consent of and at the bidding of the abbot, had the following chirograph written:

4.37. THE PRIVILEGE OF WITIGO. "Let it be known to all, present and future, that I Witigo, priest by the grace of God, inspired by divine providence, purchased an *allodium*[67] in the village of Frickingen in the *pagus* of Linzgau, in the territory of Count Henry, for twenty-two marks. In addition to this, I sought what I believe to be the sound counsel of Abbot Conrad and all the brothers of the monastery of Petershausen, and they granted to me as a lawful benefice the farmstead that the monastery owns in that same village, and in return, I gave an additional twenty marks of silver for that same benefice, with the condition that as long as I live, I shall possess as a benefice both parts of the aforementioned estate, both the newly purchased and the previously owned, without any contradiction, and put its produce to my use, wherever I may be. Further, I will hand over this same farmstead to one of the brothers of this same monastery, whomever I shall

---

65 cf. CP 4.13 and CP 5.12.
66 cf. CP 5.10; Witigo and his donation of Frickingen are commemorated in Petershausen's twelfth-century necrology on 7 October. MGH Nec. Germ. 1, 675.
67 i.e., land freely held; allodial land tenure carried no obligation of service to a lord.

choose, whom I shall entrust to care faithfully for all I shall acquire for myself there. When I depart from this life, I desire that this same monastery have this same *allodium* forever, with the condition that, on the anniversary of my death every year thereafter, all the brothers should have a pittance, that is three measures of spelt, one measure of which especially for the abbot, and three jugs of wine, with half of one for the abbot and two and a half for the brothers, and twelve *solidi* for buying fish. I also wish twelve paupers to be fed on that day, and that each of them be given a loaf of bread, a cup of wine, and a portion of meat. Also, on the anniversary of my father Opert, that is, on 12 March, I desire that one measure of wheat and two jugs of wine be given to the entire congregation. Further, I desire that the same thing be done from the same property on the anniversary of my mother, Pechilda, that is, on 18 August. So that all of these things be kept inviolate just as written, I adjure all who shall inhabit the monastery for all time, through the reward of all the faithful and through every virtue that serves God in heaven or on earth, that absolutely no one, whether abbot or anyone else, dare violate them. If, God forbid, any should do so, may he be condemned in the company of the traitor Judas on the day of the Last Judgment. Done and confirmed in the year of the Incarnation of the Lord 1135 on the feast of Pope St. Gregory before all the brothers, and witnesses Henry, Herman, Eberhard, Liutfrid, Arnulf, Burchard, Albert, and many others." This same Witigo died on 7 October.[68]

4.38. ABOUT GISILFRID AND TEURINGEN. Gisilfrid of Teuringen[69] came with great devotion and with many tears handed over his only son, Rupert, to God and St. Gregory in the presence of the entire congregation. And he gave all of the estates that he legally owned in Swabia, both in Teuringen and Jettenhausen, in their entirety into the perpetual ownership of the brothers serving God there, with the exception of the portion of his brother Gerald. He also bought a vineyard in Allensbach for twenty-two marks of silver, and established with a most firm agreement, in the presence of and with the consent of the abbot and the entire congregation, that in the future a weekly Mass be sung on behalf of all of his deceased relatives, and that on this day all the monks might receive wine from the aforementioned vineyard, and that when this Mass was sung, it should be announced with

---

68 Krebs, "Quellenstudien," 489.
69 Gisilfrid and his donations are commemorated in Petershausen's twelfth-century necrology on 6 May: MGH Nec. Germ. 1, 670.

a single toll of the bells. And so that the vineyard might be cultivated without burden to the monastery, when a certain lady called Trutlind[70] desired at that same time to convert and to offer her field in Fischbach, and the abbot had refused to admit her, this same Gisilfrid gave him ten talents so that he might accept the woman with her field and permit the income from this same possession to serve for the cultivation of the aforementioned vineyard. All this was done with appropriate witnesses watching in the name of the Father and Son, and Holy Spirit, Philip, Gregory, and Gebhard.

4.39. After this, when quarrels broke out between the abbot and this Gisilfrid, he removed his son, who had already been made a monk, from the monastery and alienated the estates that he had given, that is, Teuringen and Jettenhausen. Nevertheless, he himself remained in the monastery in the habit of the bearded brothers, and died not long after this and was buried at the monastery. After his father's death, moreover, the son took up arms and claimed an unjust inheritance.

4.40. ABOUT ABBOT GEBINO. At the same time, since Abbot Uto of Wagenhausen[71] fell into disrepute, he was deposed, and Gebino was brought there from Petershausen by Bishop Ulrich II and ordained abbot of that place.[72] After he led that monastery capably for some years, the new monastery of Fischingen was entrusted to him, and he initiated the monastic life there.[73]

4.41. ABOUT ABBOT WALTRAM. After a short time, unable to endure the work, Gebino abandoned Fischingen. Abbot Conrad, called upon once again by Bishop Ulrich, made Waltram abbot of that place in Gebino's stead.[74] Waltram began to build a new church there from the ground up, and acquired many decorations and implements for it.

4.42. ABOUT THE ORGANS. After this, Abbot Conrad employed a certain monk called Aaron, a priest from Kamberg, most skilled in the arts of music. This monk built him an organ with a most elegant

---

70 Trutlind and her donation of land in Fischbach are commemorated in Petershausen's twelfth-century necrology on 21 September: MGH Nec. Germ. 1, 675.
71 Abbot Uto of Wagenhausen (r. 1119 – c.1127).
72 Abbot Gebino of Wagenhausen (r. c.1127–1156), uncle of the chronicler.
73 Around 1138, Gebino temporarily left Wagenhausen to get the new monastery of Fischingen up and running. This effort ended in failure, and Gebino returned to Wagenhausen and resumed his abbacy there until 1156. His successor Waltram, not Gebino, is generally considered to have been the monastery's first abbot.
74 Abbot Waltram of Fischingen (r. 1138–1146).

sound and installed it in the south side of the basilica. He had already built an instrument of this type for the church of Constance under the patronage of Herman, who was then interim bishop and *custos* of the church.[75]

HERE ENDS THE FOURTH BOOK

75 Bishop Herman I of Constance (r. 1138–1165).

TRANSLATION OF THE RELICS OF ST. GEBHARD (T)

Introduction

The translation in 1134 of the relics of Petershausen's episcopal founder Gebhard II is represented as a high point in the history of the monastery, the culmination of all of the history that has come before.[1] Through the ritual relocation of the holy body in the hands of the present bishop, Gebhard II was made a saint.[2] The event itself, as the Chronicle tells us, was preceded by extensive and vital repairs to the basilica that Gebhard himself had constructed over 150 years before. Employing the common rhetoric of monastic reform, the chronicler describes the just-in-time repair of faulty foundations and a cracking façade. Even the body of the soon-to-be saint needed to be rescued from the neglect of the monks and the dampness seeping into his crypt. This rescue is a part of a reform still-in-progress, with Abbot Conrad as its champion, fifty years after the arrival of the monks from Hirsau.

Both the structure of the manuscript and the shape of the text itself suggest that the chronicler initially intended this short book to close the work. The red initial at the opening of the Translation parallels those that open each of the previous books, and like these preceding books, it opens with a red *incipit* and ends with a red *explicit*. As will be noted in the three final sections of the manuscript, the Translation is that last portion of the CP that is primarily retrospective. The series of *ad hoc* additions (A), and Books Five and Six lack any discernable narrative arc. These final three sections following the Translation are structured more in the manner of annals than a chronicle, with sporadic entries made as events dictated.

---

1 On relic translations, see Bartlett, *Why Can the Dead Do Such Great Things?*, 282–295.
2 While Bishop Conrad of Constance's canonization was confirmed Pope Callixtus II in 1123, no such papal bull survives for Gebhard II. On the continued role of local bishops in awarding the title of saint in the early twelfth century through the translation of relics, see André Vauchez, *Sainthood in the Later Middle Ages* (Cambridge: Cambridge University Press, 1997), 22–27.

Translation

T.1 [5.1]. HERE BEGINS THE TRANSLATION OF THE BLESSED BISHOP GEBHARD. The following seems to distinguish between the death of the just and the death of sinners: the names of sinners are not remembered much among good men, while the just are remembered with praises and will be kept in eternal memory. Indeed, the death of sinners is most unfortunate, while the death of his saints is precious in the sight of the Lord. For God, who rewards the good ungrudgingly, not only ceaselessly rewards the merits of saints in heaven, but also on earth. When we see miracles occurring near the bones of the dead, the living entreating help from the dead, ornate churches built in their name, estates and gifts accumulated, the containers of their ashes splendidly decorated, and their memories celebrated with praises, what else but some great reward is being shown for human contemplation on earth? What, moreover, about the spirit of these men? As I will say briefly, *thou shalt hide them in the secret of thy face, from the disturbance of men* [Ps. 30:21]; truly they who enjoy glory and honor in the sight of God and the angels are hidden *from all disturbance of men*. But even though these rewards are already ineffable, for God they are not sufficient to reward his elect, so he adds yet more. He does not allow their bodies to be interred under the earth; he wishes them to be exalted above his altar. And if there were an even more honorable place, I believe God would place them there.

Hence while the body of the blessed Gebhard, confessor of Christ, former bishop of Constance, and founder of the monastery of Petershausen, was at rest beneath the earth in the manner of the dead for around 142 years, faithful God, who never forgets, frequently adorned the place of his tomb with miracles. When the basilica itself was on the verge of collapse from splitting cracks on all sides on account both of old age and the fragility of its foundation, at the urging of Hugo, a canon of the church of Constance, the venerable Abbot Conrad undertook to restore it. The force of storms had entirely eroded all of the mortar from the pediment that rises from the western side into the steeple, and the bared stones with their unseemly blackness made the whole building look hideous. He set out to restore this first, and he made a new and larger window, in which the glass-maker Werner, a servant of this same monastery, placed a glass window of his own making. Higher on this same wall he set two other windows on either side, where there had previously been two very small round windows. He sealed the cracks and holes with new mortar, and he removed and completely whitewashed over the paintings that had lost their beauty to old age. He demolished the old altar – which was very small and hollow, formed from only five square stones, and held no saints' relics, contrary to church custom – and built a new one that was larger and higher.

T.2 [5.2]. Abbot Conrad also built an exceedingly beautiful tomb from four stones, and above it a new altar, doorway, and stairway ascending to the altar and choir.

T.3 [5.3]. In the year of the Virgin Birth 1134, 152 years after the founding of the monastery, in the twelfth indiction, Abbot Conrad summoned the venerable Bishop Ulrich II of Constance, and he opened the tomb of the blessed Bishop Gebhard and found the precious treasure of his body, more prized than any pearl. Indeed, this tomb had been very carefully secured. It was in the southern side, next to the entrance of the crypt, and at its head was a plaster image of the Cross and an altar of St. Benedict. On the wall to its right was the image of the holy bishop himself, and on either side of him were the images of his attendants, as if assisting him at the altar, and columns, arches, vines, and the likenesses of birds and sheep were most charmingly formed out of plaster. To its left was a panel, which was positioned obliquely from the four stones and rose above the floor by two hand widths, and there was likewise another panel at his feet higher than the rest, and above this a wooden shelf holding seven candlesticks.[3] Above the tomb was a stone, which lay below the aforementioned items. After removing this stone, we found a slab of the hardest stone, to which two iron rings were secured with lead. Underneath was found the body of the saint, still wrapped in priestly vestments; most of these had rotted, but they clung to the bones because no hand had touched them. But when they began to be touched, they immediately fell apart, except for the stole and the upper part of the chasuble, which had been made from yellow fabric the color of a crocus. Of these, some part remained intact.[4]

T.4 [5.4]. One hundred and fifty-two years after the founding of the monastery,[5] Bishop Ulrich arrived, as well as abbots from seven other

---

3 cf. CP 1.52.

4 This account of a crumbling body wrapped in rotting liturgical vestments stands in strong contrast to the chronicler's description of Gebhard's body in the *Life of Gebhard* 1.23 – a more standard account that includes a heavenly scent (*fraglantia*) rising from the corpse. On the incorruptibility of the bodies of the saints in the Middle Ages, see Bartlett, *Why Can the Dead Do Such Great Things?*, 100–101.

5 i.e., in 1134.

monasteries, at the invitation of Abbot Conrad of the oft-mentioned monastery. A multitude of clerics, monks, and other faithful people gathered, and with tremendous joy and exultation, with hymns and praises, they honorably translated the bones and ashes of the blessed confessor of Christ, Bishop Gebhard, from their previous location at the tomb, and with the remains set in the sarcophagus, they processed around the perimeter of the monastery. They afterwards placed them in the new tomb with great honor.

T.5 [5.5]. ON THE DEDICATION OF THE ALTAR OF THE HOLY CROSS. On this same day, that is 27 August, which was his birthday, in the twelfth indiction, the altar over his tomb was dedicated in honor of our Lord Jesus Christ, the most Holy Cross, Mary the Mother of God, St. Gebhard, St. Benedict, and the other saints whose relics were kept there: relics of the holy apostles Peter, Paul, Andrew, Philip, Bartholomew, and the holy martyrs Fabian, Callixtus, Felix, Apollinaris, Blaise, Denis, Pelagius, Sebastian, Vitus, Cyricus, Agapitus, Protus and Hyacinth, Maurice, Candidus, Maximus, Fidelis, and the holy confessors Gregory, Nicholas, Gaugericus, Gall, Barbatian, and saints Mary Magdalene, Digna, Sophia, and Walburga.

T.6 [5.6]. ON THE DEDICATION OF THE BASILICA OF POPE SAINT GREGORY. On the following day, they dedicated the basilica itself in honor of the Holy Trinity, the most victorious Cross, and the saints Philip the Apostle, Pope Gregory, and Bishop Gebhard. These relics were kept in the altar itself: relics from the Cross of the Lord, from the vessel in which Longinus received the blood of the Lord, from the tree that the Lord planted, from the hair and veil of St. Mary, Mother of God, from the basilica of St. Michael the Archangel, which was itself dedicated on Mt. Gargunas, of John the Baptist, and the holy apostles Peter, Paul, Andrew, Jacob, Philip, Bartholomew, and the holy martyrs Pope Alexander, Pope Callixtus, Pope Fabian, Pope Marcellus, Pope Felix, and bishops Apollinaris, Denis, Blaise, Erasmus, Lambert, and the other martyrs Pelagius, Gregory, Maurice, Candidus, Sebastian, Cyricus, Vitus, Pancras, Christopher, Hermes, Cosmas and Damian, Agapitus, Crispin and Crispinian, Tiburtius, Protus and Hyacinth, Chrisantus, Fidelis, Castus and Desiderius, Carpophorus, Amand, Anianus, the priest Polycarp, Heraclius, Constantius, Julian, Nicander and Marcian, Maximus, Pergentinus and Laurentinus, and the holy saints Pope Leo, Pope Gregory, bishops Nicholas, Boethius, Maternus, Maximinus, Gaugericus, and Gebhard, likewise of Gall,

THE CHRONICLE OF PETERSHAUSEN: RELICS OF ST. GEBHARD

Barbatian, and the holy virgins Agatha, Lucia, Cecilia, Daria, Brigid, Walburga, and the other saints Mary Magdalene, Felicity, Digna, and Sophia. This was done joyfully and with glory during the time of Pope Innocent II[6] and august Emperor Lothar II,[7] in the tenth year of his reign, in the twelfth indiction, 28 August.

---

6 Pope Innocent II (r. 1130–1143).
7 Emperor Lothar II (r. 1125–1137; crowned emperor in 1133).

ADDITIONAL ENTRIES (A)

Introduction

Between 1136 and 1161, the chronicler added additional material *ad hoc* to the manuscript. The entries that follow the Translation are preceded neither by a new book number nor an incipit. It is almost as though, having completed the original work, he simply could not resist adding further material to the manuscript, including a seven-chapter *excursus* on the Life of Blessed Ratpero,[1] a saint whose oratory was located on land then owned by Petershausen. Some of this added material comes in the form of annals, in chronological order in 1139, 1142, 1143, 1146, and 1147, with each short entry beginning with a standard, "in the year of the Incarnation of the Lord..." This annual reporting was interrupted for comments on events of supra-regional importance; after the entry for 1147, for example, the chronicler added six chapters on the Second Crusade and Wendish Crusade,[2] including Bernard of Clairvaux's visit to Constance to preach it, and the involvement of some of Petershausen's own men who joined the crusade and had not yet returned.[3] Several chapters that describe the death of religious women and men and other later entries offer a rare acknowledgment in the CP of religious women and men of various sorts at Petershausen, including those the chronicler identifies as hermits and *inclusi*.[4] After a brief return to the annalistic format for 1156, the chronicler dwells at length on the events of 1159, notably giving a dramatic eyewitness account of the catastrophic fire that destroyed most of the monastery in June of that year.

The *ad hoc* nature of the expansion of the text is reflected in the underlying structure of the manuscript itself; whereas the Prologue through the Translation were copied as a finished work into uniform four-bifolium parchment gatherings, A is a composite of single parchment

---

1 d. c. 1034; CP A.5–A.11.
2 1147–1149.
3 CP A.21–A.26.
4 CP A.12–A.15, A.30–A.31, A.42.

leaves and two-bifolium extensions.[5] When more space was needed to finish an entry, the chronicler simply appended a sheet or two of parchment. Any remaining blank space seems to have invited further additions, and the manuscript expanded irregularly in this way over a period of twenty-five years. There are clearly changes in ink color and the cut of the pen during this time, as one would expect, but the gradually aging hand of the chronicler persists.

The addition of material without a new book number resulted in confusion with the numbering of the subsequent books. Although there was no *incipit* to signal the beginning of a new section of the manuscript, there is an *explicit*: "Here ends the Fifth Book." The confusion is immediately apparent when the following *incipit* – on that very same line – announces, "Here begins Book Five." The entries between the end of the Translation and the beginning of the next designated book comprise a *de facto* book. There are thus two Book Fives: a *de facto* Book Five, which we designate as A (83v–92r), and a designated Book Five (92r–94v). A very brief Book Six then follows from folio 94v to the last entries on folio 96v. None of the earlier published versions of the CP have taken this structure into account, but rather cite scribal error and renumber the books in sequence. To reflect the original intention of the chronicler and to make clear the process by which he created the CP, however, we have opted for a new system of book, section, and chapter numbers beginning with the translation (T). When our numbering differs from that of Abel and Weiland (1868) and Feger (1956), we give their designations in square brackets. We have also provided a concordance of chapters in Appendix 2.

A.1 [5.7]. In these days, a powerful infirmity raged within this same community, from which, I confess, I myself was miraculously freed by the merits of Blessed Gebhard. For I had given my spirit to mobility, but as often as I determined to leave the monastery, just as I used to, I was prevented from doing so by a terrible infirmity. When, despairing of strength, I would settle my soul, I would immediately grow a bit stronger. But whenever I stubbornly tried to engage in this former error, I fell to the ground, stricken with a severe punishment. As God is my witness, this often befell me in those days. But seeing that Gebhard's tomb, once it was opened, offered a clear view to all who

---

5 For a complete description of the quire structure of the manuscript and a discussion of that structure as a reflection of the changing nature of the text of the CP, see Beach, *Trauma of Monastic Reform*, 150–158.

approached, I too drew near, hoping that I might be strengthened a bit by the sight of the holy body. That night, I was exhausted by such a great infirmity that I was unable to attend Vigils and I lay nearly senseless during the solemnities that followed. Utterly terrified by this blow – for I knew what it portended, since I was not totally out of my senses – I dared not draw any closer, but I removed myself from anywhere the holy bones were taken (for they were later dried in the sun so that they might not be destroyed by rot), and I dared not touch nor even look at them. When no proffered medicines helped me, and time had passed, and no good fortune aided me in my difficulty, my spirit waned, my mind settled, and I renounced mobility. And thus, as though already reconciled to my Lord, I boldly asked Herbert, the *custos* of the church, to give me a tooth of St. Gebhard, and I placed it in a chalice and poured water over it, and I drank this and was immediately healed. From then on, down to the present day, countless men have been freed from fevers by such a drink.

A.2 [5.8]. ABOUT THE BELLS. After this, Abbot Conrad had a rather impressive bell made. Herbert, the *custos* of the church, had a second bell made, and I had a third small one made, dedicated to St. John. After they were sprinkled with holy water and anointed with holy oil, one was christened Hosanna, the other Alleluia, and the third Benedicta. He then built a bell tower over the church, since before this the bells had hung between four columns next to the church.

A.3 [5.9]. ON THE DEDICATION OF THE ALTAR OF ST. PETER. In the year of the Incarnation of the Lord 1136, in the fourteenth indiction, on 16 November, the altar of St. Peter the Apostle was dedicated by the venerable Bishop Conrad II of Chur.[6] The altar contained the relics of these saints: John the Baptist, Peter and Paul, John the Evangelist, Matthew, the Holy Innocents, Pope Clement, Pope Callixtus, Pelagius, Maurice, Vitus, Pancras, Hippolytus, Sebastian, Agapitus, Cosmas and Damian, Christopher, Genesius, and the confessors Martin, Nicholas, Gebhard, Benedict, Gall, and the virgins Agnes, Lucia, Eugenia, and Scholastica.

A.4 [5.10]. It came to pass that the priest Henry, who administered the oratory of St. Mary at Rötsee,[7] departed this world, and Abbot Conrad immediately sent the monk Albert there, a man quite suited to

---

6 Bishop Conrad II of Chur (r. 1142–1150).

7 Rötsee is a small lake in Allgäu, a region within the medieval Duchy of Swabia.

the task, so that the divine service in that place might possibly improve a little through him. When this man died after a few years, Conrad sent another Albert, who was younger, with this same hope. This is the place where the venerable Ratpero had first dwelled, as I said much earlier, and where he had built a church.[8] I will try to add something worthy about his deeds to this work, lest such a man's merits, already scarcely preserved in the memory of men, pass entirely into oblivion.

A.5 [5.11]. THE LIFE OF BLESSED RATPERO. It is said that the man of God Ratpero was born of noble and pious parents from Thuringia. His entire family line is thought to be ornamented and completed in him, as if by a golden clasp. He left his homeland and made his way to Alemannia and entered the circle of the most holy Bishop Ulrich of Augsburg,[9] and lived there for a long time under his direction in the regular life, since that same bishop at that time led the monastery of Kempten.[10] Since he was thus united in friendship with this holy bishop and was instructed by him in every good work, it happened that at a certain time they traveled together, and they reached an area bordering on Rötsee. When they were resting in a meadow after lunch, the bishop awoke after a short nap and, through the spirit, foretold to blessed Ratpero that there was a certain place nearby that would be improved by his labor, and where he would await the Day of Judgment. After the man of God Ratpero heard this prediction, he immediately turned his spirit resolutely to this business. Wisely, he began to go before the nobles of these same regions, since they might wish to grant him the place destined for this work. But when he was scorned by these men, he uttered curses against them, and it is thought that because of this their posterity was wiped out, just as it is written: *the seed of the wicked shall perish* [Ps. 36:28].

A.6 [5.12]. Therefore, so that the omnipotent God might fulfill the prophecy that he deemed worthy to tell to his servant Ratpero through the mouth of his servant Ulrich, he inspired a certain nobleman named Berengar to assent to Ratpero's plan and desire. Berengar thus gave him a place from his estates, now called Rötsee, which was then barren and deserted, but is now a fertile and lovely site. Long ago, as it is told, there lived in this place an exceedingly cruel thief who committed most

---

8 cf. CP 3.41.
9 On St. Ulrich I of Augsburg, cf. CP 1.28.
10 Ulrich was Abbot of Kempten in Allgäu (f. 752) from 941 to 962.

monstrous robberies all around. He had a kind-hearted wife, but she did very little good out of fear of her husband. One day, when her husband was away, a certain pilgrim came to their little dwelling, sought hospitality, and desired to stay the night there. The woman responded that she would gladly offer him hospitality, but that she feared her husband, because he was a tad belligerent. And although the pilgrim begged her insistently, she dared not offer him hospitality in her husband's absence. Finally overcome by his petitions, the woman received him. She dared not house him openly, however, but sent him up to the top of the house and hid him under the roof. When her husband came back in the night, he brought with him a lovely young virgin, modestly dressed, and he lit a large fire and hung a cauldron filled with water over it. When the water boiled, he undressed the girl and threw her into the boiling water. When she was thrown in, she is said to have cried out: "Woe! Have mercy on me because of my virginity!" When his wife saw this wicked crime, she exclaimed: "Woe, woe – there is a man hiding under the roof!" The pilgrim saw what they were doing, and he broke out through the roof and fled. And when the thief realized that he had been discovered, he fled the place immediately. The bones of the virgin are buried in this same place.[11]

A.7 [5.13]. Blessed Ratpero, having received this same place from Berengar of Arnach, began to build a church there, but with unending effort, because he had nothing other than his hands to carry out this enormous work. Nevertheless, with the help of God, who says *Trust in the Lord, and do good...* [and] *Delight in the Lord, and he will give thee the requests of thy heart* [Ps. 36:3–4], he laid the foundation for a church of magnificent workmanship, and saw it all the way to completion.

A.8 [5.14]. The man of God endured many persecutions and injuries from the clerics living nearby to such an extent that they even incited Bishop Warman of Constance[12] against him. After afflicting Ratpero with many injuries, the bishop finally expelled him from the place. But *the Lord is near to those who are of a contrite heart: and he will save the humble of spirit. Many are the afflictions of the just; but out of them all will the Lord deliver them* [Ps. 33:19–20]. For it happened that after he expelled the man of God, Bishop Warman proceeded to Rome and he

---

11 This story contains a number of folkloric elements, but the source of the tale is unknown.
12 Bishop Warman of Constance (r. 1026–1034).

died on this journey along with everyone accompanying him. He was succeeded as bishop by Brother Eberhard,[13] who was always most merciful and kind toward the blessed man Ratpero. For this same man of God, expelled from Rötsee, had moved to another place and built an oratory for himself there. But he was kindly called back to the original location by Bishop Eberhard, and thereafter he lived in that very place in the service of God. And this same bishop dedicated the church that the man of God had built in honor of holy Mary, Mother of God, and he helped Ratpero in any way he could. The man of God, however, gave this place to the church of Constance, because he hoped it would thus be better promoted in the service of God.

A.9 [5.15]. There was a very small forest near the oratory, from which a small amount of wood could be obtained for necessities. When certain bad men despoiled it against his will and obstinately refused to stop despite his frequent pleading, he prayed to the Lord that he might flood the place with water, lest the men further burden it with such thievery. Miraculously, water immediately began to rise up and cover the wood, and it made a beautiful pool that can be seen to this day, on account of which this place is called Rötsee.

A.10 [5.16]. He populated these same waters with little fish to support the inhabitants, but certain evildoers often caught them, and the man of God was moved to utter curses against them. While they were fishing again one day, one of them fell overboard and, overcome by the water, sank into the depths. The man's body was sought everywhere throughout the lake by his friends with the greatest diligence and through many delays – so that they might deliver him for burial – but it was not found anywhere. At last feeling remorseful, they began to entreat the man of God to consider granting pardon to the deceased man and to show them where they ought to search for his body. He immediately granted pardon, and through the Spirit, he pointed out the location. They hastened to the designated place and found the body there, standing upright under the water not far from land. After dragging him out by his hair, they gave him over to be buried.

A.11 [5.17]. After many struggles and labors, the blessed Ratpero, filled with the Holy Spirit, departed to the Lord on 26 July.[14] His body

---

13 Bishop Eberhard I of Constance (r. 1034–1046).
14 C. 1034; Ratperto is named in Petershausen's twelfth-century necrology on 26 July. See MGH Nec. Germ. 1, 673.

rests honorably buried in the church that he built, where to this day he does not cease to offer favors to many people.

A.12 [5.18]. ON THE PRECIOUS DEATH OF THE RIGHTEOUS.
There was a certain sister at Petershausen who was illustrious in serving God in pious widowhood for many years in all goodness, and at the end of her life she was consecrated with the holy veil. She was called Adalheid. When the end of her life drew near and she lay in bed seized with sickness, one day she looked up with raised eyes and said: "Oh what a great light I see shining up above!" The religious woman watching over her responded: "Do you see a light, dearest sister?" And she said: "I do indeed see a most splendid and elegant light." After saying this, she immediately closed her eyes and, for the few remaining days that she lived, she never again saw temporal light after having seen spiritual light, and thus she passed away.

A.13 [5.19]. There was in this same monastery another religious woman, a virgin named Meginrat, who had persevered in the greatest chastity and goodness until she was mature in years, and although neither nourishment nor clothing was given to her by the monastery, she nevertheless labored and served of her own free will in all things and generally led a blessed life in extreme poverty. When she approached the reward for her hardship, she lay burdened with sickness for several days with great patience, silence, and purity. As the hour of her departure approached, she lifted her eyes on high and said: "How wonderful, most holy Lady Mary, that you were willing to come here!" And after saying this, she lowered her eyes and reverently departed.

A.14 [5.20]. There was another woman by the name of Regilind who one day, even though she was sick, lay keeping vigil by herself late at night. She began to smell the pleasant scent of burning frankincense and she marveled silently at such a sweet fragrance. But she worried that she now had to depart this world, and she grieved exceedingly, as she herself often later reported, that she saw none of the sisters there with her at that time. And behold, a venerable old man with white hair appeared to her, took her by the hand and led her through a most lovely green land filled with brilliant light and every beautiful thing. There she saw countless people with the brightest appearance, clothed in gilded garments, who ascended ever higher to the heavens for a short while as if in chariots, and the higher she looked the brighter the light was. She also heard them asking who would be the person to cross over through them, and others answered that St. Martin would cross over,

THE CHRONICLE OF PETERSHAUSEN: ADDITIONAL ENTRIES

and again they said: "He is considered worthy of all honor and reverence."[15] The old man reported, moreover, that there were more splendid places ahead where she was not taken. The guide spoke nothing of this to her, but immediately after she saw this vision she was returned to the land of the living.

A.15 [5.21]. Earlier, during the time of Abbot Theodoric, there was a certain bearded brother named Lanzilin, indeed despised and small in stature, but with particular[16] simplicity. He often worked as the assistant to the gardener. When a fatal illness seized him, the priest fortified him with the body of the Lord and holy oil and stood there with others by his bed. Lanzilin then began to speak with a clear voice: "Where is the holy Apostle Peter, who was just standing here? Look! I saw him appear there just now!" And it happened that he happily departed this world shortly afterward.

A.16 [5.22]. In the year of the Incarnation of the Lord 1139, Pope Innocent [II] held a council of unprecedented size in Rome.[17] As it was reported, 800 bishops and 1,000 abbots with countless clerics and laymen were present at this council. Among the many useful decrees was one forbidding arson, which has been carefully observed for many years now.[18] Abbot Conrad was present at this synod, and when he returned he brought back two cloaks, from which he made two copes.[19]

---

15 Petershausen's religious women may have had a special interest in St. Martin, as they likely used a double chapel dedicated to St. Martin and St. Oswald (upper, consecrated in 1129) and St. Mary Magdalen and St. Fides (lower, consecrated in 1134), built during the extensive construction campaign undertaken under Abbot Conrad. See Beach, *Trauma of Monastic Reform*, 87.

16 Mone (1848), 165, reads praecipia for praecipua.

17 This was the Second Lateran Council (1139), the primary purpose of which was to resolve a papal schism that had arisen after the death of Pope Honorius II in 1130, although the rival Pope Anacletus II (r. 1130–1138) had died the previous year.

18 Canon 18 specifically prohibited arson and set excommunication as a penalty for this crime. See Norman P. Tanner, ed., *Decrees of the Ecumenical Councils*, 2 vols. (Washington, DC: Georgetown University Press, 1990), 1: 201. That this decree is the only one mentioned among many notable pronouncements is in keeping with the chronicler's repeated interest in monastic fires in his writings, even prior to the one that destroyed much of Petershausen in 1159 (cf. CP 4.14, 4.15, and 4.17).

19 A cope is a long liturgical vestment generally made of silk or other fine cloth. The semicircular garment is open at the front and fastened with a clasp at the breast. It is characteristic of the chronicler's interest in matters related to the performance of the liturgy that he mentions these cloaks and the creation of vestments from it rather than any other details of Conrad's experience at the council.

A.17 [5.23]. In the year of the Incarnation of the Lord 1142, Provost Hugo of Constance gave five talents and bought a small estate in Altheim, which Gisela of good memory had earlier given to the monastery. And once the aforementioned Hugo had purchased this estate from Abbot Conrad, he returned it again in the presence of the brothers and many others, and he bequeathed it to the monastery on the condition that every year on his death (that is, on 17 April) the whole community should be served from this estate as far as is possible.

A.18 [5.24]. In the year of the Incarnation of the Lord 1143, the priest Gering gave the monastery, with the hand of his advocate Henry into the hand of our advocate Conrad, two small estates – one in Schiggendorf and the other in Wangen in the *pagus* of Linzgau when Henry of Heiligenberg was count – without any contradiction and by legitimate transaction in the presence of many suitable witnesses. This same Gering, coming to the monastery, fell ill and was treated kindly until his death.[20] In this same year, Gundelo of Constance gave his estate in Gebhardsweiler and at the same time presented his daughter to the monastery.

A.19 [5.25]. In the year of the Incarnation of the Lord 1146, a great famine oppressed the people far and wide, and because of this certain people from Triboltingen and Tägerwilen, compelled by scarcity, handed themselves over to the monastery.[21] They gave themselves and their meager property to the monastery, but some of them could not complete this trade, since their holdings were tributary to Reichenau.[22]

A.20 [5.26]. In the year of the Incarnation of the Lord 1147, Abbot Conrad renovated the doors of the church. He also restored and

---

20 The priest Gering and his donations are commemorated in Petershausen's twelfth-century necrology on 4 January: MGH Nec. Germ. 1, 665.

21 This widespread famine extended from 1145 to 1147.

22 Self-donation (also called autodedition) was not uncommon in southern Germany during this period. Most commonly, self-donors would adopt a tributary status as *censuales*, typically paying a small fee of five *denarii* per year to retain a semi-free status, although self-donation into direct servitude was possible. When specified in monastic cartularies, the most common motives listed were piety and protection from the predations of others. This instance is significant as one of few specifying scarcity and poverty as the motive. Because *censuales* received no material benefit beyond legal protection, it can be inferred that these people gave themselves into direct servitude in order to receive rations from the monastery. For English-language works addressing the phenomenon of autodedition, see Sutherland, "Mancipia Dei," and Alice Rio, "Self-sale and Voluntary Entrance into Unfreedom."

THE CHRONICLE OF PETERSHAUSEN: ADDITIONAL ENTRIES

expanded the chapel of St. Ulrich and decorated it with most excellent paintings. Bishop Herman of Constance dedicated this chapel on 21 December in honor of Bishop St. Ulrich, the martyr St. Afra, the Holy Cross, and the holy Virgin Mary. Moreover, the altar contained the relics of St. John the Baptist, Peter and Paul, Bartholomew, the apostles Simon and Matthew; the martyr Stephen and the protomartyrs Blaise, Pelagius, John and Paul, Hippolytus, and Sebastian; the confessors Pope Gregory, Nicholas, Conrad, Gebhard, Gall and Magnus; the holy virgins Mary Magdalene, Agatha, the Eleven Thousand Virgins, Fortunata, and Eutropia.

A.21 [5.27]. THE EXPEDITION AGAINST THE HEATHENS.[23] And it came to pass in the time of King Conrad[24] that Pope Eugenius[25] sent letters to Louis,[26] king of the Franks. Abbot Bernard of the monastery that is called Clairvaux,[27] as well as other men, travelled through Gaul and preached that everyone, both old and young, who wished to obey the will of God should march under arms to bring battle to the heathens and especially against a certain bloodthirsty tyrant who had invaded the city of Edessa (which was once called Rages).[28] This tyrant either killed or captured all the Christians he found there, and he plundered, polluted, and ruined the sacred things of God. Therefore, when this news was made known, there was a great commotion in the region. Thus King Conrad[29] of the Romans and King Louis of the Franks, with their dukes, counts, and many other nobles, as well as an innumerable host of people from diverse regions, and also very many people from the monasteries, offered themselves to God and promptly joined this march with their men eagerly and with devout mind. An exceedingly large

---

23 That is, the ill-fated Second Crusade (1147–1149).
24 King Conrad III (r. 1138–1152).
25 Pope Eugenius III (r. 1145–1153).
26 King Louis VII of France (r. 1137–1180).
27 Bernard of Clairvaux (1090–1153). Bernard was already famous for his role in promoting the rising Cistercian movement and for his advocacy for the Knights Templar (founded 1119, gained papal recognition in 1139). Bernard travelled across France and Germany promoting the crusade, personally recruiting Louis VII and Eleanor of Aquitaine (1122–1204), as well as Conrad III. Bernard also advocated for the Wendish Crusade described in CP A.26.
28 Imad ad-Din Zengi, the Seljuk atabeg of Aleppo and Mosul (r. 1127–1146), conquered the Christian County of Edessa in 1144. This was the first of the Crusader States to fall. By the time of the Second Crusade, Zengi had been succeeded by his heir Nur ad-Din (r. 1146–1174).
29 King Conrad III of Germany.

army thus proceeded under arms through Pannonia and the forests of Bulgaria, with a great multitude of ships on the Danube transporting weapons and whatever else was necessary.[30] And when they arrived in Greece they were received with honor by the king of the Greeks,[31] and they were led by his duke into the vast desert so that they might arrive, as they planned, at the land of the gentiles. One day they set their camp in a certain place where they were divided by a valley and, exhausted after pitching their tents, they settled down to rest. Behold, a great flood suddenly came in the dead of night and, rushing violently, swept whatever it encountered in the valley into the sea.[32] This first misfortune was an omen of many later calamities. For when they first set out humbly and peacefully in fear of God, all good fortune came to them. But later, when they were carried away by arrogance and began to look to plunder, they were consumed by diverse calamities.[33] For when they advanced through the desert and did not find food, many perished from starvation, and others, laboring in hunger, were lost – either killed by the heathens or reduced into captivity. Some were also crowned with a glorious martyrdom. When King Conrad saw that he could in no way achieve his purpose, he returned to the king of the Greeks in Constantinople, who led him over the sea to Jerusalem in a ship.[34]

30 Although a sea route would have been faster and more economical, the crusade leaders were apparently eager to follow the same route taken in the First Crusade (1096–1099).

31 The Byzantine Emperor Manuel I Comnenus (r. 1143–1180).

32 This flash flood that struck the German encampment on the plains of Choirobacchoi, west of Constantinople, in the early morning of 8 September was widely reported in both Latin and Greek sources. See, for example, the eyewitness account of Bishop Otto I of Freising (r. 1137–1158) in his *Deeds of Frederick Barbarossa* 1.46 (trans. Charles Christopher Mierow, New York: Columbia University Press, 2004, 80–81) and the account of Byzantine historian John Kinnamos (d. post-1185) in his *Deeds of John and Manuel Comnenus* (trans. Charles M. Brand, New York: Columbia University Press, 1976, 63). Both Otto and John describe widespread destruction and attribute the disaster to divine judgment against the crusaders. See Jonathan Phillips, *The Second Crusade: Extending the Frontiers of Christendom* (New Haven: Yale University Press, 2007), 245–246.

33 Here the author echoes the common explanation championed by Bernard of Clairvaux, that the failure of the crusade was due to the unworthiness of the crusaders.

34 The forces led by Conrad were defeated in a series of skirmishes against the Turks culminating in the second battle of Dorylaeum on 25 October 1147, in which Conrad was himself wounded. After retreating to Constantinople, however, Conrad joined his remaining forces with the French crusaders and would ultimately continue on to Jerusalem. Phillips, *The Second Crusade*, 251–255.

THE CHRONICLE OF PETERSHAUSEN: ADDITIONAL ENTRIES

A.22 [5.28]. ON THE BROTHER OF THE KING. The brother of the king, Bishop Otto of Freising, had already departed from the army that was following the king some time before, and he wished to cross to Jerusalem by the King's Road. He had with him thirty thousand soldiers from the army. An army of heathens then encountered them and killed nearly everyone.[35]

A.23 [5.29]. ON THE KING OF THE GAULS. King Louis of the Franks also marched separately[36] with great ambition, with his wife[37] and his army, to the city of Antioch, and there he was honorably received by the prince of the city.[38] While he was resting there for a few days, as it is said, his wife was seduced by the prince of the city,[39] and the king barely managed to escape with a few men. He came to Accaron, where King Conrad graciously received him. He was later reconciled to his wife when she returned to him.

A.24 [5.30]. ON THE CAMPAIGN AGAINST DAMASCUS. After these things, King Conrad made for Jerusalem with a great army and was most dutifully received by the king and clergy of this city. The king immediately agreed on a campaign with the two kings and their armies against Damascus.[40] When they besieged Damascus and were about to storm the city, the soldiers of God were corrupted with bribes from those who were inside the city, and they led the army away and left without attaining their end.[41]

A.25 [5.31]. ON OUR MEN. Certain men set out from our monastery on this expedition and still have not returned. Many of the Christians

---

35 Otto and his forces were ambushed near Laodicea on 16 November 1147. Otto himself survived the battle.
36 *Sequestratim* – not *sequestratus* Feger (1956) or *sequestrati* (Abel and Weiland (1868)).
37 Eleanor of Aquitaine (1124–1204).
38 Raymond of Poitiers, Prince of Antioch (r. 1136–1149), who was also Eleanor's uncle.
39 Rumors of sexual relations between Eleanor and her uncle Raymond may have arisen from her threat to annul her marriage to Louis if he did not take Raymond's plan to attack Aleppo, prompting Louis to place Eleanor under house arrest and depart to rendezvous with Conrad.
40 Notably, Damascus was at this time allied with Jerusalem, but Nur ad-Din had recently married the daughter of the atabeg of Damascus, prompting fears of an impending betrayal.
41 The four-day siege of Damascus was in fact a tactical disaster, as the Christian army surrendered a defensible position to make a failed assault on a weak portion of the wall.

who were abducted as captives of the heathens, however, were ransomed by the Armenians and allowed to return to their homeland.

A.26 [5.32]. ON THE CAMPAIGN OVER THE ELBE. Duke Conrad of Zähringen[42] decided that he and innumerable others, for whom the aforementioned march to the Holy Land seemed too difficult, should march through Saxony against those pagans who dwelled across the river Elbe.[43] When they arrived there, they found the land impassable, very marshy, and full of swamps. Indeed, the inhabitants of this land did not dwell together, but were dispersed, such that they could not be found easily. Therefore, the army of Christians, exasperated by their ignorance of the area, returned without having had any effect.

A.27 [5.33]. In these times, pressed by poverty, our men removed the silver from the columns of the high altar and spent it.[44] They also built a very high and rather nice bell tower in these same times. They also renovated the portico in front of the church with new structures and paintings.

A.28 [5.34]. ON THE DEATH OF ABBOT WALTRAM. During this time, when Abbot Waltram of Fischingen was performing many good deeds, he lost his sight. Once he had returned to our monastery, his sight was restored with medicine. He then remained in the congregation in good monastic life and finally rested in a blessed end.

A.29 [5.35]. ON THE DEATH OF ABBOT GEBINO. In the year of the Incarnation of the Lord 1156, Abbot Gebino of Wagenhausen, gripped by a long sickness, saw in visions – I know not whether real or imagined – certain people as if they were standing before him. Sometimes he saw venerable men, and he would order those standing around him to make space for them. Sometimes he saw abominable grotesques,[45] which he ordered to leave in a clear voice, and he even drove them off with the staff that he held in his hand. When he was about to die, with the entire community gathered together, he prayed for pardon for them and asked that they might do the same for him.

---

42 Duke Conrad I of Zähringen (r. 1122–1152).

43 This was the Wendish Crusade (1147), a campaign against the Slavic Wends, authorized by Bernard of Clairvaux and Pope Eugenius III. Unlike the contemporary crusade to the Holy Land (and the First Crusade before it), the objective of the Wendish Crusade was the forced conversion of the native population.

44 Presumably this need originated from the continued famine (cf. CP A.19).

45 These terrible creatures (*tetras*) are grammatically feminine in the Latin.

Another man, called Folmar, also experienced many visions in his last hours.

A.30 [5.36]. ABOUT THE HERMITS. And now I return briefly to matters raised earlier. Certain of the brothers – namely Winhard and Marquard, who were both illiterate, and the priest Dietrich – zealous for the solitary life, retired into a hermitage and there led a strenuous life, but at different times and places. All of these men died in good monastic standing.

A.31 [5.37]. ABOUT THE ENCLOSED. Also the monk Walcher, and the bearded brothers Meribod and Hartman, the deeply religious woman Judinta, and Bertha from the sisters had themselves enclosed. Almost all of the men were of such uncivil temperament[46] that they had not been able to remain easily in community.[47]

A.32 [5.38]. In the year 1159, Burchard of Hausen died and left the estate that he possessed in Bichtlingen to the monastery.

A.33 [5.39]. At the same time, because a certain fuller in the monastery had long before lost most of his hearing, he came to the tomb of Blessed Bishop Gebhard on a certain day, and when he was able to hear neither the ringing of the bells nor the voices chanting the Psalms, he put his head down on the tomb and began to pray tearfully that St. Gebhard might deign to restore his hearing by interceding with God. Thus after a little while, before he left the tomb, he began to hear all things clearly and to recount the miracle in a clear voice to all who wanted to hear, and to glorify God and St. Gebhard. This gift remains to him to this day, and he tells the story happily to everyone around him.

A.34 [5.40]. ABOUT HAIDGAU. In the year 1159, an estate that the monastery possessed in the village of Haidgau was sold for sixty talents. With this money, a small part of the estate in Tägerwilen was redeemed, and a large debt that was owed to a certain noble woman in Constance was paid off.

A.35 [5.41]. ABOUT MIMMENHAUSEN AND AASEN, AND THE GOLD PANEL. In that same year, an estate that the monastery of St. George the Martyr in the Black Forest possessed in the village called Mimmenhausen was offered for sale. Since our monastery

---

46 The chronicler expressed a similarly negative view of contemporary *inclusi* in his review of various forms of religious life (CP P.21).

47 Feger (1956) (*contra* Beach) places the end of the work of the original chronicler here; Feger (1956), 230, n. 37a.

had an estate that Gerald of blessed memory had donated in that same village (in addition to himself and his other estates, namely Reute, Escherichsweiler, and Neufrach), we endeavored with great effort to acquire it.[48] To this end, the panel on the eastern side of the main altar of St. Gregory, facing the choir, covered most pleasingly with gold and gems, was stripped of gold. {In the middle of this panel was a circle very heavily decorated all around with precious gems, in the middle of which was a most beautifully rendered image of our Lord Jesus Christ seated in majesty. Around this were cherubim, each with four faces atop one neck and six wings, and there were also wheels with wings and eyes.[49] There were also nine rows of angels holding bowls in their hands, and the *four and twenty ancients casting their crowns before the throne of the lord* [Apoc. 4: 4, 10, somewhat freely]. There were also images of the four evangelists each rendered most beautifully in electrum[50] and encircled with many gems, and also many other images in electrum, and a boss with a grape-vine motif. The whole piece was made with the most beautiful workmanship and the best gold, such that it would have delighted you to see. This panel was stripped of its most precious covering in the year of the Incarnation of the Lord 1159, on 27 April, in the eighth indiction. Thus all of the gold and silver decoration in the church of St. Gregory was expended. For there were, as I myself have seen, two panels – one gold, the other silver and gold – four silver-covered columns of the ciborium,[51] a very precious silver censer, and more than nine chalices. All of these were expended in our days.[52]} Thus with the gold that was taken from the aforementioned panel, the estate that the monastery of St. George owned in Mimmenhausen, was purchased. The property that we owned in Aasen was also given for this estate, which Duke Berthold [II] of Zähringen, the brother of Bishop Gebhard III, had given to us at some point in return for the hospitality that he had violently demanded of us.[53]

48 cf. CP 2.25.
49 Ezek. 10:9–14.
50 Electrum is an alloy of gold and silver.
51 The ciborium and its columns are first described in CP 1.18 and 1.19.
52 There are numerous reports of the expending of treasure in the CP, which seems to have been of particular concern to the chronicler: CP 1.19, 1.20, 2.11, 4.13, 4.21, 4.34, A.27, A.35, 5.12, and 6.2.
53 Berthold II of Zähringen (c. 1050–1111, Duke of Swabia from 1092 to 1098). For further references to the House of Zähringen, see CP 2.31, 2.48, and A.26.

THE CHRONICLE OF PETERSHAUSEN: ADDITIONAL ENTRIES

A.36 [5.42]. ABOUT THE FIRE. Therefore when they had been freed from all debt in this unusual way, albeit with great loss, and both this place and the entire monastery had been greatly improved, it happened just as it is written: *the spirit is lifted up before a fall* [Prov. 16:18]. For there was a certain little room connected to the infirmary in which there was a furnace, and on both sides of it some straw {in which the brothers very often reclined and took their leisure with illicit food, drink, and chatter}. There the boys of the monastery carelessly lit a fire, which spread to the nearby straw, and it quickly spread through the entire monastery and also the church of St. Gregory, and the blaze likewise consumed all of the buildings of the monastery. The brothers, sitting down to dinner after Vespers, were thrown into uproar by this dangerous news. They forgot everything that they had in their hands, all of which was also consumed by the fire, ran about {and carried out whatever furnishings they were able to grab}.[54] But not believing that God would permit the church of St. Gregory to be consumed by the fire, they carried things out without much concern, until many of the things that they could have carried out were consumed by the fire, both manuscripts and furnishings. Thus, the main altar and all of its ornaments were consumed, and in the altar a reliquary covered with silver that once held the arm of St. Philip the Apostle, the top of which was a very beautiful piece of red marble, and also the many other relics contained in the altar, particularly those of St. Apollinaris and Aubertus and many other saints, which were all destroyed together. The blaze destroyed the ciborium with all of its ornaments, from which hung a pyx covered with gold and silver containing the body of the Lord, many other very beautiful reliquaries, a most beautiful crucifix in which there were many relics, the chancel railings, which were decorated all over with the most beautiful images of wonderful workmanship, the altar before the cross, the choir, which had been built with splendid workmanship, many rather beautiful lecterns, many rather good manuscripts, many precious dorsals and altar cloths, seven chapels, the chapterhouse, whose benches were all decorated with various coverings for the solemnities of Pentecost, a rather nice Rule

---

54 This text was struck out by a later reader, perhaps noting the contradiction between the account of the panicked monks running about grabbing things and the assertion that the monks were slow to remove property that could have been saved from the flames because of their belief in the power of Gebhard II to protect the monastery from fire.

containing two martyrologies – one of the saints and the other of the dead[55] – a Gospel book, Isidore's Sentences, the refectory with all of its utensils, the kitchen and cellar with all that was in it, a rather nice *armarium* and the many things that were stored in it, the dwelling of the lord abbot with many rather nice pieces of furniture, and the best manuscripts both for the altar and for the Divine Office, which were beautifully decorated. Many incomparable bells, cymbals, and organs perished. But the sacristy and the repository of books were just barely saved with the things that were in them. It was, indeed, a miserable thing to see. The dormitory of both the monks and the exterior brothers was destroyed, and many were miserably left without clothing. The sisters' dwelling, which the blaze did not touch, was nevertheless immediately evacuated and the women entirely dispersed.[56] Even some of the monks were sent to whichever other monasteries could receive them.

A.37 [5.43]. In the year of the Incarnation of the Lord 1159, 177 years after the monastery was founded, in the seventh indiction, on the second day of the month of June, on Tuesday of the holy week of Pentecost – when the Holy Spirit came down upon the apostles of Christ in fire, not consuming, but illuminating – fire came down upon us, but just as we deserved, consuming and devouring, casting down walls and shattering unyielding stones.

After the fire was put out, both men and women, great and small {and indeed even some of the monks} rushed in and carried off, like grave plunder, everything that they could grab in gold, silver, and other metals that had survived the flames. But the *custos* and the other brothers were so stricken with immense grief that they were not attentive and did not take notice until almost everything of value had been carried off, and the great loss went on for many days.

A.38 [5.44]. Along with the rest came a certain woman from Constance, and she went up to the altar of St. Gregory, which was

---

55 This was Petershausen's chapter book, a manuscript used for the liturgy of the naming of the names of the dead in many Hirsau-influenced communities. Twelfth-century chapter books still survive from Wagenhausen, including one that contains entries made by the chronicler himself (Budapest Széchényi-Nationalbibliothek, Codex Latinus 514).

56 That the women's community did not burn, despite the intensity of the fire, suggests that it was set at some distance from the men's precinct – one of the few hints as to the physical location of the female side of the monastery.

THE CHRONICLE OF PETERSHAUSEN: ADDITIONAL ENTRIES

entirely burned and destroyed, and collected some of the ashes of the saints that had burned in the altar and brought them home. She had a small son, crippled by weakness in all of his limbs. She prepared a bath for him and threw in some of the saints' ashes that she had carried, and she put the boy in and bathed him. Because of this, he immediately began to improve, and in a short time he attained full health.

A.39 [5.45]. The Divine Office was held at that time in the chapel of St. Fides, since only this altar and the altar of St. John the Baptist were found to be undamaged, and all the reliquaries of the saints and the sarcophagus of St. Gebhard were carried there. A woman from another village came there, carrying her small son in her arms. One of the boy's arms was hanging in such a way that he had not been able to lift it for many days. She placed him on the sarcophagus, and, to her great joy, he was healed not long after.

A.40 [5.46]. Our predecessors some time ago prophesied that this place would never be burned by a fire, but as the Lord threatens through Jeremiah: *And I will suddenly speak of a nation and of a kingdom, to build up and plant it, if it shall do evil in my sight, that it obey not my voice: I will repent of the good that I have spoken to do unto it* [Jer. 18: 9–10].

A.41 [5.47]. In those days, the rigor of discipline and of the work of God was lacking among us, as it is written: *they were separated, and repented not* [Ps. 34:16].

A.42 [5.48]. There was a certain venerable priest, an *inclusus*, in the area. During his prayers, he lamented the demise of this place and said: "Lord, why did you permit such a bad thing to happen to such a place?" He immediately heard a voice saying to him: "Because they themselves took away the beauty of my house."[57]

A.43 [5.49]. ON THE RESTORATION OF THE BUILDINGS.
Therefore, after nearly everything that was old or newly constructed or gathered had been consumed, Abbot Conrad and Prior Herman rose up and manfully prepared themselves for the restoration of the aforementioned things. And the remaining brothers assisted them, some by joyfully carrying burdens, others by going around the regions with saints' relics and entreating both rich and poor for aid in the reconstruction

---

57 Feger (1956) argues (*contra* Beach) that this is the end of the work of the first continuator; Feger (1956) 238, n. 48a.

of the monastery that was consumed by fire.[58] Therefore, from such contributions they first began to build a dwelling for the abbot and two chapels, one atop the other – the upper chapel in honor of St. Martin and St. Oswald, and the lower in honor of St. Mary Magdalene and St. Fides the virgin and martyr.

A.44 [5.50]. The commemoration of the dedication of St. Fides continued just as before on 22 November,[59] since that altar was found intact, and there they held the Divine Office.

They also built two refectories, one above the other, as well as a kitchen, cellar, winepress, calefactory, infirmary, chapel of St. Mary, chapterhouse, and dormitory. For this they burned limestone[60] at great cost in the woods near Dettingen, and they felled a great flow of large logs and other timbers in the forest near Bregenz, which more than fifty oarsmen brought to us over the wide river. Other monasteries also sent gifts with good will: a good altar cloth and a wagonload of wine from the monks of Hirsau; a chalice from the monks of the Abbey of St. Peter; a chasuble, an alb, and a stole from Zwiefalten; and other small gifts from other monasteries, which were all accepted in the name of God.

A.45 [5.51]. In the year of the Incarnation of the Lord 1161, in the ninth indiction, on 8 December, a chapel was dedicated to St. Mary next to the infirmary by the venerable Bishop Herman of Constance, with Abbot Conrad assisting, in the name of the Holy Trinity – that is, the Father, the Son, and the Holy Spirit – and in honor of the most Holy and Victorious Cross. And because an earlier chapel had been dedicated in honor of St. Michael, and another chapel above the first had been built in honor of St. Andrew the Apostle, where the exterior brothers sang,

---

58 While such relic-based fundraising journeys, or relic quests, were a common occurrence in France, this is a rare reference for Germany. For the phenomenon in France, see Pierre Héliot and Marie-Laure Chastang, "Quêtes et voyages de reliques au profit des églises françaises du Moyen-Âge," *Revue d'histoire ecclésiastique* 59 (1964): 789–822; Pierre Héliot and Marie-Laure Chastang, "Quêtes et voyages de reliques au profit des églises françaises du Moyen-Âge," *Revue d'histoire ecclésiastique* 60 (1965): 5–32; Reinhold Kaiser, "Quêtes itinérantes avec des reliques pour financer la construction des églises (XIe–XIIe siècles)," *Le Moyen Age: Revue d'histoire et de philologie* 101 (1995): 205–225.

59 Originally dedicated 22 November 1134; cf. CP 4.31.

60 Limestone was burned in kilns to produce a substance known as quicklime (calcium oxide), which may have been used to make the cement and plaster needed for the construction.

and these had already been destroyed in the fire, these three celebrations now had to be held in this one chapel. And they dedicated it in honor of Mary the holy Mother of God, and St. Michael the Archangel, and also St. Andrew the Apostle and these other saints whose names are listed below: John the Baptist, the Holy Cross, the Apostles Peter and Paul, Jacob, Philip, Bartholomew, John the Evangelist, Jacob, Thomas, Simon and Jude, and Matthew; Stephen the Protomartyr, the Holy Innocents, the martyrs Fabian and Sebastian, Clement, Blaise, Apollinaris, Gregory, Maurice, Boniface, Vitus, Hippolytus, Eutyches, Pope Felix, Pelagius, John and Paul, Cyriacus, Pope Callixtus, Cosmas and Damian, Protus and Hyacinth, Bishop Dionysius; and of the martyrs Pancratius, Eugenius, Genesius, and Agapitus; Pope Gregory, Pope Sylvester, Bishop Martin, Bishop Nicholas, Bishop Augustine, Bishop Lull, Bishop Ulrich, and Bishops Conrad and Gebhard; the confessors Benedict, Gall, Magnus, Othmar, Wicpert, Maximus, Leonard, and Aegidius; the virgins Mary Magdalene, Agatha, Agnes, Caecilia, Lucia, Margaret, Barbara, Scholastica, the Eleven Thousand Virgins, and part of the head of St. Walburga.

A.46 [5.52]. A certain knight by the name of Helias who was passing through came to Wollmatingen and was there mortally wounded by his enemies. He immediately sent word to the monastery and called upon the brothers and commended himself to them resolutely. He gave his horse and the small estate that he had in the *pagus* of Hegau, in the village of Lohn, and asked that he be buried in the monastery, and this was done accordingly.[61] For when he died, he was carried to the monastery, and the bishop buried him honorably and established that every year thereafter on the same day as the dedication of this chapel, as far as possible, the brothers should be served communally from the little estate that had been given by the aforementioned knight Helias, who was a ministerial of St. Mary the Mother of God and of the holy church of Constance. He also gave this property as an endowment for this same oratory.

A.47 [5.53]. On that same day Bishop Herman also dedicated the chapel of St. Martin and restored the relics that had been there before, which were listed above.[62] From that day forward, they conducted the

---

61 Helias is commemorated on 8 December in Petershausen's twelfth-century necrology. MGH Nec. Germ. 1, 677.
62 cf. CP 4.30.

Divine Office in the aforementioned chapel of St. Mary. The expense for these buildings came entirely from the gold that was left over after the purchase of the estate in Mimmenhausen.[63]

HERE ENDS THE FIFTH BOOK [sic]

---

63 cf. CP A.35 for initial purchase of Mimmenhausen. This gold would have been surplus from the sale of many of the monastery's treasures.

BOOK FIVE

Introduction

Book Five, which covers the years from 1160 to the death of Abbot Conrad in 1164, opens with a return to the destruction of the fire of 1159 and its aftermath, and then moves on, as in A, to recount a variety of events of local and regional importance. In the course of Book Five, however, a new narrative voice emerges. Whereas the assessment of Conrad and his work on behalf of the monastery evinced in previous books was uniformly positive, this new voice is suddenly and surprisingly critical, particularly from CP 5.8 on. In CP 4.29, for example, the chronicler notes the beauty of the new abbatial residence that Conrad built. In CP 5.11, however, we hear that these expensive new buildings were undertaken "against the will of all," and that in the course of the building, the new abbot darkened the refectory by blocking two of its windows to build himself a privy, and cut down the old fruit trees in the atrium.[1] And the criticisms do not stop with Conrad's building projects. Before he even became abbot, we now read, Conrad had betrayed the trust of a friend who had entrusted him with the care of a large sum of money by spending it,[2] and other accusations of the misuse of funds follow. Money loaned to the community is stolen and cannot be repaid on two separate occasions, and a farce of justice culminates in a riot that forces Conrad to quit the monastery for days.[3] This shift in tone suggests that, by CP 5.8, a new author has taken charge of the text, a continuator who makes it his business to return to events well over thirty years in the past. As noted above, the chronicler may have set the work aside in 1164 to succeed Conrad, taking up the office of abbot as Gebhard I, leaving the text in the hands of another monk of the community.[4] Or with Abbot Conrad dead, was the original chronicler now

---

1 CP 5.11.
2 CP 5.8 and 5.10.
3 CP 5.9.
4 The writer of CP 5.12 assumes the same authorial persona as the author of the previous books while acknowledging his repetition of an account originally recorded in A.36.

free to speak his mind even more freely, particularly with regard to the late abbot?

Book Five [sic]

5.1 [6.1]. When the fire raged in the church of St. Gregory, the blaze had such force that the liquefied bronze of the large bells melted away like water and, falling from on high down to the ground, scattered into such small bits that only a portion of these was later recovered.[5] From these, new bells were later recast. Some of these immediately shattered, but others still remain. They prepared many wooden and iron tools for clearing away the great piles of stone and wood. The columns and squared stones were fractured from the heat and were rendered almost useless, and none of these could remain in place. A certain lady named Matilda purchased some of these columns with their capitals and bases.

5.2 [6.2]. THE REDEDICATION OF THE CHAPEL OF ST. JOHN THE BAPTIST. Earlier, that is in the year of the Incarnation of the Lord 1160, Bishop Herman of Constance dedicated the cemetery chapel of St. John the Baptist on 26 December and restored the relics that had been there before, as noted above.[6]

5.3 [6.3]. THE RESTORATION OF THE CHURCH. In the year of the Incarnation of the Lord 1162, in the tenth indiction, on 16 May, while Emperor Frederick [I] reigned and Bishop Herman presided over the church of Constance, under Abbot Conrad, on the eve of the Ascension of the Lord in the third year after the monastery burned down, the first foundation was laid for a new structure for the church of Pope Gregory in the same place where Bishop St. Gebhard the founder had originally built it, and the lintel of its entrance was positioned to face the cloister on the western side. At that time the Roman church was without a clear leader, since two had usurped it for themselves, that is, Alexander and Victor. The emperor favored Victor, while the Eastern Church favored Alexander.[7]

---

5 Among these bells were likely those commissioned by the chronicler and Abbot Conrad (cf. CP A.2).

6 cf. CP 4.32.

7 This describes the Alexandrian Schism, which arose after the death of Pope Adrian IV in 1159 and would last until 1178, well after the end of the original chronicler's contributions to the Chronicle. The schism began when two rival popes were elected: Alexander III (r. 1159–1181) and Victor IV (r. 1159–1164). Barbarossa declared his support for Victor the following year at the Council of Pavia, with the

THE CHRONICLE OF PETERSHAUSEN: BOOK FIVE

5.4 [6.4]. During this time, Emperor Frederick besieged the city of Milan, and great hunger soon compelled its citizens to surrender.[8] Thus gripped by fear on account of the fall of Milan, since it was the strongest of all the cities of Italy, every city that had rebelled offered inestimable sums to the emperor for his favor. From these and other funds that he had acquired by any means during the campaign, Frederick determined that a tenth should be donated in alms to monasteries throughout Italy and Germany. He thus sent us five marks. Thereafter gradually raised up day-by-day, the basilica of St. Gregory was rebuilt under the direction of a certain Wezil, a former cleric from Constance.[9]

5.5 [6.5]. At this time the small estate in Lippertsreute, which Rudiger had given with the hand of his son Eigilward and the hand of his lord Conrad, the advocate of Heiligenberg, was sold for six talents.

5.6 [6.6]. In that same year, that is 1162, on his return from the revolt of the city of Milan, Emperor Frederick held a conference in a city called Toul, and then again in Ulm, and a third in Constance.[10] He then gave us five more *libras* of silver.[11] Duke Henry of Saxony,[12] who at this

---

    support of most imperial bishops. His support for Victor was politically motivated, as the anti-pope had been elected by cardinals favoring a renewal of the papal alliance with the emperor (which had broken down in 1156, when Adrian IV allied with the Norman King William I of Sicily (r. 1154–1166) against the emperor in the Treaty of Benevento after Barbarossa failed to assist Alexander in reclaiming Rome from control by a local commune as he had agreed to do in the 1153 Treaty of Constance). Despite Victor's death in 1164, the schism would end only in 1178, when Victor's successor Callixtus III (r. 1164–1178) submitted to Alexander III following the Treaty of Venice (1177) contracted between Alexander and Barbarossa. For more on the Alexandrian Schism, see I. S. Robinson, *The Papacy, 1073–1198: Continuity and Innovation* (Cambridge: Cambridge University Press, 1990), esp. 79–84, 464–484.

8 Frederick suppressed the revolt of Milan on 6 March 1162. The city had been in open revolt against Frederick since 1159, when he attempted via his legates to infringe upon the right of the Milanese to appoint their own consuls. See Freed, *Frederick Barbarossa*, 237.

9 This may refer to Wetzel, a supporter of Arnold of Brescia. See Karl Schmid, *Graf Rudolf von Pfullendorf und Kaiser Friedrich I* (Freiburg im Breisgau: E. Albert, 1954), 57, n. 44.

10 Frederick was in Constance from 24 to 27 November 1162.

11 We have here elected to leave *libras* untranslated to avoid potential anachronism regarding the economic value of a "pound."

12 Duke Henry III of Saxony (r. 1145–1180), aka Henry the Lion, the Welf cousin to Frederick Barbarossa. Also Duke of Bavaria (as Henry XII) from 1156. Henry, who died in 1195, lost both duchies in 1180 at the hands of Barbarossa, but the two were close allies until 1174.

time separated from his wife,[13] also gave us five more *libras* of silver. In the same year, Henry of Neufrach gave us the small estate that he had in Moos.

5.7 [6.7]. In the time of Abbot Berthold, there was a certain vesterer among us, who on account of his insolence was accustomed to give insulting replies to the brothers when they sought something from him, and he did this frequently. It happened on a certain day that some of the exterior brothers demanded something troublesome from him, and he replied harshly. Swept into a frenzy, they rushed him and struck him to the ground and began to beat him with both fists and clubs until everyone had had enough. On account of this, they were expelled, excommunicated, and detested by all, since this great scandal then spread far and wide. At long last, at the petition of the bishop and of many others, they were allowed to do penance and were readmitted. They were shorn and beaten publicly in Constance, with the clergy and people observing, and they were ordered to go around to every monastery in the diocese to confess their guilt and shame openly before all.[14]

A similar thing befell two exterior brothers who treated two interior brothers poorly not long ago; they were compelled to do public penance, and the bishop, clergy, and people with many petitions were scarcely able to request that they be readmitted. I mention these things as a cautionary tale.

5.8 [6.8]. Before Conrad was made abbot (when he was still chaplain under Abbot Berthold), a certain layman entering the religious life conferred a portion of his wealth to the monastery, but he wished to hold on to a certain part for himself and his posterity – in the manner

---

13 Clementia of Zähringen (d. 1175), whom Henry had married in 1147. Clementia was the daughter of Duke Conrad I of Zähringen, mentioned by the chronicler in CP A.26 in the context of the Wendish Crusades. Henry divorced Clementia because her brother Duke Berthold IV was at that time in conflict with Barbarossa, then Henry's ally.

14 This chapter repeats the same story that had been erased in CP 4.11. In this retelling, the cellarer (*cellerarius*) has become a keeper of the wardrobe (*vestiarius*), and Bertha of Bregenz and her intervention in the conflict are omitted. This may be a function of the fact that this comital family had died out with the death her son, Rudolf, around 1160. Alternatively, if the newly critical authorial voice reflects a change in author (a possibility discussed on pp. 177–178 above), this may also account for the discrepancies between the two accounts.

of Ananias and Sapphira.[15] He entrusted guardianship of it to Conrad as his friend. A few days later, Conrad was made abbot and spent all of this money to build his residences.[16] When the layman demanded his money back, Abbot Conrad terrified him with great indignation and afflicted him with many insults, returning to him nothing at all except many evils.

5.9 [6.9]. Similarly, when Bishop Conrad of Chur[17] remained here for a period and charitably loaned us his money, the doors to the place where the money was stored were broken into at some point and the money was stolen. We were all afflicted with anguish because of this, and there was a great investigation among us. It was decided that a verdict should be sought as to who among us had committed this crime. Therefore, when this tribulation weighed heavily on everyone, both young and old, a certain young blacksmith was immediately found, who had never even been near the place where the money had been, nor did he know or had he heard that it was kept there or had ever been there at all. Therefore, as it was said, this was done so that he might secretly take the money from the thief and return it, saying that he had stolen it. When he openly confessed to this before all the brothers, almost everyone rushed at him, even though the abbot was present, and grabbed him, punching him and pulling his hair, until they had enough, and then they expelled him. They made a great uproar with various complaints, and both the bishop and the abbot departed the monastery with great indignation. After many days, once the furor had died down, they returned.

A priest of Constance likewise loaned us his money. When he demanded it back, he realized that a certain part had been stolen. Thus roused to indignant fury, he inveighed against us all with many abuses and insults.

5.10 [6.10]. Another man also entrusted money to us, as we related much earlier.[18] Because we had unknowingly spent this money, when he

---

15 Acts 5:1–11; this married couple kept for themselves part of the proceeds from selling a piece of their property, rather than donating all the money to the common fund for the followers of Christ. Once again, the chronicler is comparing the common monastic life with the common life observed by the primitive church [Acts 4:32–37].

16 cf. CP 4.29.

17 Bishop Conrad I of Chur.

18 cf. CP 4.36. Notably, none of the negative aftermath of this deception was recorded in this earlier account. If this is indeed a new author, he must here be assuming a corporate "we" in referring back to CP 4.36.

returned and asked for it back, we skillfully managed to divert him with the monastery's possessions. Both Conrad and his brother,[19] whom he had brought away from Ursberg where he first took the habit, were nevertheless accused of all of these crimes. For this reason, and for other crimes, his brother was expelled from the office of prior. Later when he was made abbot of Fischingen, after a short time he also left from there and wandered through many monasteries in Bavaria. In the end, he was appointed abbot of Mehrerau in Bregenz.

5.11 [6.11]. When Conrad was first ordained abbot, against the will of all he built expensive dwellings for himself while we, as usual, were in dire need.[20] He darkened our refectory by building his privy next to it and obstructing the two windows above the main table. He also destroyed an atrium with many large fruit-bearing trees.

5.12 [6.12]. In addition to a good farmstead in Ailingen and many excellent vineyards in Allensbach, he also purchased estates in Heiggau, Schnetzenhausen, Dotternhausen, Triboltingen, and Aasen. He despoiled the golden panel of the altar and stripped the ciborium of its silver. He broke apart many manuscripts and chalices, and he spent the silver of the censer. Nevertheless, he did all these things out of common necessity; but regarding these things I have previously turned my pen.[21]

5.13 [6.13]. Before Conrad was made abbot, he transcribed the *Hexameron* of Ambrose with his own hand, and he had the arm of St. Philip the Apostle covered in gold and silver. After he was made abbot, moreover, he had many other beautiful works made, which were all destroyed in the fire. Nevertheless, he then labored as much as he could for the restoration of the buildings and other useful things. He also purchased some small estates in Neuheim from tributary freedmen, and he established that both his anniversary and the anniversary of his predecessor and *nepos*, Abbot Theodorich, should be celebrated.[22] The

---

19 Conrad's brother Ulrich had served as prior of the newly founded Premonstratensian community of Ursberg from 1125 to 1136, and would serve briefly (1146) as abbot of Fischingen and later (dates unknown) as abbot of Mehrerau, despite his alleged crimes. On Ulrich's brief tenure at Fischingen, see Bruno Meyer, "Die Äbte des Klosters Fischingen," *Thurgauische Beiträge zur vaterländische Geschichte* 113 (1977): 103.

20 cf. CP 4.29–4.30 (where these construction projects are regarded favorably).

21 cf. CP A.35.

22 The meaning of *nepos* as it is used here is unclear. The term traditionally signifies a younger relative – most often grandson, nephew, or descendent, and sometimes

anniversary of Abbot Theodoric should be celebrated from these estates. And he decreed that on his own anniversary, which is [...],[23] ten *solidi* should be spent, and three *solidi* for his *nepos*. During his time as abbot and with his help, churches were renovated and dedicated, and oratories built in Aichstetten, Epfendorf, Oberwangen, Mimmenhausen, Neuheim, and Rheinhart. He also made two brass censers and some books, and finally a small room for storing books.[24]

5.14 [6.14]. In the year of the Incarnation of the Lord 1164 in the month of June, Abbot Conrad fell ill, and when neither medicine nor anything else that could be proffered to him helped, he reluctantly began to despair and gave us one rather good stole and bought back a jeweled and gilded chalice that he had earlier sold.[25] He also called for the bishop,[26] who was his friend, and some other great men. He discussed his affairs with them meticulously, as I believe, and he departed this world in the thirty-seventh year of his ordination, on 28 June, and on this same day he was honorably buried in the basilica near the entrance from the cloister.[27]

5.15 [6.15]. On this same day something remarkable happened. A certain bearded brother was healthy and spirited in all respects, except that he had a boil on his leg, from which much blood suddenly burst forth. The bleeding could not be stopped by any means, and he immediately collapsed and was barely able to receive the body of the Lord before he suddenly passed away.

---

cousin in medieval usage – but Theodoric (abbot from 1086 to 1116) was clearly not younger than nor even a close contemporary of Conrad (abbot from 1127 to 1164), and there is no other reference to any relation between the two.

23 Space was left open here in the manuscript for the insertion of the day of Conrad's anniversary. It may be that this section of the text was written just before his death, and the following text (which includes the anniversary date of 28 June 1164) just after.

24 This chapter evinces a distinct ambivalence about Conrad and his legacy, in contrast with the starkly critical view expressed elsewhere in Book Five. CP 6.3 is more favorable yet. It is possible, but purely speculative, that this abruptly more positive tone was penned in response to feedback from the original chronicler, if he indeed had handed the work over to a continuator when and if he became abbot.

25 cf. CP A.35.

26 i.e., Bishop Herman I of Constance.

27 Abbot Conrad is commemorated in Petershausen's twelfth-century necrology on 28 June. MGH Nec. Germ. 1, 672.

BOOK SIX

Introduction

With this short final book, the CP fades out rather than concludes. After opening with the election of Gebhard I to the abbacy in 1164, a continuator presses on briefly in the vein of the previous books, offering an account of the embellishment of various reliquaries,[1] a conflict with a local nobleman over land,[2] and a donation made by a noblewoman on behalf of her son.[3] After this final donation was recorded in 1164, no further entries were made until a new hand laments that a series of calamities befell the monastery in 1170. Three years later, another entry records the deposition of Abbot Gebhard and the laying of the cornerstone for the eastern part of church.[4] After this entry for 1173, a single scribe prepared two dated lines for each of the years from 1174 to 1211. Except for brief notices for 1202 and 1203, all of these lines were left empty. The will to continue the CP seems simply to have run out. On the *verso* of the last of these three blank pre-dated leaves, a fourteenth-century hand has added the names of Petershausen's abbots, a list that was updated into the sixteenth century.

6.1 [6.16]. In the year of the Incarnation of the Lord 1164, on a Sunday, 28 June, the brothers gathered together, and in a free election with no outsider interceding, they elected Gebhard – a worthy and unimpeachable man – and they made him their abbot canonically and regularly with great liberty. Bishop Herman also ordained him with the greatest honor during the feast of the Translation of St. Benedict, with all of the canons of the church of Constance and a multitude of people attending and supporting him with great enthusiasm. There was great joy, praise, and exaltation on account of such clear consensus among the brothers, because at that time there was great division among many in other

---

1 CP 6.2 and 6.3.
2 CP 6.4 and 6.5.
3 CP 6.6.
4 CP 6.7.

monasteries; they thus congratulated us exceedingly, because not one of us – neither old nor young – dissented from the others.

6.2 [6.17]. In the year of the Incarnation of the Lord 1163, our monk and priest Rudolf gathered a small amount of money from a collection from the faithful that had been made at his request for the use of the monastery, and he also adorned the arm of a soldier from the legion of Theban martyrs, the companions of St. Maurice, with gold, silver, and jewels.[5] Herman the Elder of Hirschegg brought this arm to our monastery, which he had acquired from a certain prior known to him from the monastery of Agaunum, when he visited this same monastery while proceeding from Italy.[6] This same Rudolf then bought back a good chalice, which Abbot Conrad had recently sold.[7]

6.3 [6.18]. In the year 1164, Abbot Conrad embellished the round reliquary of St. Gregory and the priest Otto restored the arm of St. Philip the Apostle where it had broken.[8] I will not cease to speak about Abbot Conrad of blessed memory, but will in fact relate certain examples of his diligence for posterity's sake. He was skilled in the art of poetry and music, and was of the best character. He had a clear voice, was friendly in conversation, had venerable gray hair, and was restrained in manner and word. He built many splendid things that were destroyed in the fire.[9]

6.4 [6.19]. At this time Count Rudolf of Ramsberg bought a fortress called Rheineck from Conrad of Heiligenberg, who had held it in benefice from the church of Constance.[10] And when he lived in this same fortress and remained there, he learned that the monastery of St. Gregory, called Petershausen, held property nearby that would be greatly advantageous for him. He began to discuss with Abbot Conrad how this property, which was called Rheingemünd, might be granted to him for a price until the end of his life, so that he might cultivate

---

5 On this relic, see CP 2.18.

6 cf. CP 2.18, where the story first appears; Herman's burial epitaph is recorded in CP 2.24.

7 That is, in 1159; cf. CP A.35.

8 This important relic of St. Philip is mentioned repeatedly in the CP: 1.13, 1.29, 4.10, and A.36.

9 Note that this continuator has returned to a positive assessment of Abbot Conrad, in contrast with the complaints about him voiced in CP 5.8, 5.10, and 5.11.

10 According to Karl Schmid, the counts of Ramsberg were identical with the counts of Pfullendorf. See Feger (1956), 254, n. 19.

the property and be able to have fodder and pastures from it. After his death, the monastery was to recover both this property in its entirety and everything that is found there at that point without any contradiction. He pressed them for all of this for a long time with rude demands and various promises until he persuaded the aforementioned abbot and the brothers to consent. He pledged to give ten talents – and he gave some of this, but in truth he still kept the rest – and he brought this property in Rheingemünd, neighboring his own, into his power. Over all of this the following privilege was written, and it was secured with his seal.

6.5 [6.20]. PRIVILEGE OVER RHEINGEMÜND.[11] "In the name of the holy Trinity, namely the Father, the Son, and the Holy Spirit. I Rudolf, Count of Ramsberg, make known to all persons who want to know, present and future, how I, favored by Divine Providence, began to negotiate with Abbot Conrad and his brothers at the monastery of Pope St. Gregory, which is called Petershausen, for them to concede to me the estate that the monastery is known to have in the place called Rheingemünd, because that same property is near to me and ideal for tending sheep, and my men are not able to avoid it without doing harm to the brothers. It seems better to me that I, Rudolf, give Abbot Conrad of Petershausen and the brothers of this same monastery ten talents, and that they grant to me the aforementioned estate in Rheingemünd with the condition that, in memory and confirmation of this agreement, they should mark and celebrate the anniversaries of my mother Adalheid and her brothers, and that I shall provide the monks with wine on that same day every year as long as I live, as a tribute and as a reminder of the present agreement. After my death, however, none of my descendants shall have any power at all over this same property, or anything then found there – neither herds, nor other goods, nor resources of any kind. But the abbot then presiding over the monastery of Petershausen and the brothers of this place shall have the property in its entirety, free of all contradiction, for the remedy of my soul, and the soul of my mother, and those of all of my progenitors. And I, Rudolf, had this document drawn up so that none of my heirs dare diminish my act or disturb the aforementioned brothers in this estate after my death. Carried out in the year of the Incarnation of the Lord 1163, with Emperor Frederick reigning, Herman as Bishop of Constance, and

---

11 The original charter survives in the Generallandesarchiv in Karlsruhe (#C 46). For a reproduction, see Schmid, *Graf Rudolf von Pfullendorf*, 48.

THE CHRONICLE OF PETERSHAUSEN: BOOK SIX

under Abbot Conrad (and I, Gebhard the priest, wrote this privilege in the first year of the abbacy of Gebhard[12]). The witnesses of this act are my wife Elisabeth, my brother Arnold, Rudolf of Güttingen, Count Albert, Rupert of Teuringen,[13] priest Albert of Tal, Diemo of Bregenz, Arnold of Kriessern, Berthold of Lustenau, and many others."

6.6 [6.21]. CONCERNING MATILDA. There was a certain lady named Matilda in Constance, who had a son named Henry with us, a well-educated priest who, alas, lay ill for a long time. This woman, out of love for her son Henry, paid us forty talents in an unusual way, with the condition that her son Henry should have usufruct over the farmstead called Owingen so that he could get from there what he needed but could not obtain from the common allotment, and that he should undoubtedly have this for aid in his illness until he recovers, as long as he should live. All of these things were confirmed by a most firm contract in the presence of Abbot Gebhard and the brothers of this monastery, with the following conclusion and confirmation, that after they die, the anniversary of each should be celebrated in its time with an office for the dead celebrated as a memorial, and that on that day, the brothers or the entire congregation should be charitably and abundantly served from that same estate. This same Matilda departed this life a few days later, on 11 April in that same year, and she had given us five more *libras* of silver and asked that she be buried among us, which was done with great honor. This took place happily in the year of the Incarnation of the Lord 1164,[14] with Emperor Frederick reigning, Herman as Bishop of Constance, and under Abbot Conrad.[15]

6.7 [6.22]. In the year of the Incarnation of the Lord 1170,[16] many calamities afflicted the monastery of St. Gregory, about which it wearies me greatly to say anything further.

---

12 i.e., in 1164.

13 Probably identical with the Rupert of Teuringen who left Petershausen after making his profession there as a monk and claimed land back from the monastery. Cf. CP 4.38 and 4.39.

14 The correct date must be 11 April 1165, since Abbot Gebhard was not consecrated until 11 July of 1164. See Feger (1956), 21.2.

15 Matilda and her donation are commemorated in Petershausen's twelfth-century necrology on 11 April. MGH Nec. Germ. 1, 669.

16 On the year of Abbot Gebhard's deposition, which took place between 1170 and 1173, see Krebs, "Quellenstudien," 528.

Abbot Gebhard was deposed, and this place was violently attacked and despoiled.

In the year of the Incarnation of the Lord 1173, the foundation stone for the eastern part of the church of St. Gregory was laid.

6.8 [6.23]. In the year 1202, the bishop of Würzburg[17] was murdered. In the year 1203, Philip moved against the landgraves with an army.

6.9 [6.24]. In the year of the Incarnation of the Lord 1249, the altar in the choir near the entrance to the monastery was consecrated on 14 February by the venerable lord Bishop Henry of Semgallen,[18] of the Order of the Friars Minor, in honor of the Virgin Mary and of all the saints. The relics enclosed there are as follows: the Cross of the Lord, the column on which the Lord was flagellated, the Sepulcher of the Lord, the linen in which the body of the Lord was wrapped, the garments of St. Mary, the garments of St. John the Evangelist, the relics of the holy apostles Peter and Paul, and of the apostles Andrew, Thomas, Bartholomew, and Jacob, Maurice and his companions, Gereon and his companions, Pelagius, Fidelis, Pope Callixtus, the martyrs Stephan, Lawrence, Sebastian, Pancras, Vincent, the confessors and bishops Gregory, Gebhard, Nicholas, Magnus, Benedict, and Leonard, of King St. Henry,[19] of St. Mary Magdalene, Margaret, the Eleven Thousand Virgins, the virgins Balbina, Torpeiadech, Patrialia and many other saints. At the request of the monastic community, the venerable Bishop Henry also established that this same dedication should forever be celebrated during the Octave of Easter, and to all those assembled with devotion for the aforementioned solemnities he granted an indulgence of a year and forty days for all of their sins, and to those who sought it worthily, he granted this indulgence for eight continuous days following the anniversary of the dedication in perpetuity. These things took place in the time of Pope Innocent IV,[20] of Bishop-Elect Eberhard of Constance,[21] with the assent and favor of Abbot Ulrich,[22] with the encouragement of Henry, monk and priest and guest-master

17 Bishop Conrad I of Würzburg (r. 1198–1202).
18 Henry of Lützelburg, Bishop of Semgallen 1247–1251; also Bishop of Kurland 1251–1263 and of Chiemsee 1263–1274.
19 Henry II.
20 Pope Innocent IV (r. 1243–1254).
21 Bishop Eberhard II of Constance (r. 1248–1274).
22 Abbot Ulrich I (r. 1248–1258).

THE CHRONICLE OF PETERSHAUSEN: BOOK SIX

of this church, and of other wise and honest persons, to the praise and glory and honor of our Lord Jesus Christ, who lives and reigns with the Father and the Holy Spirit as God, forever and ever. Amen.

The names of the abbots of Petershausen[23]
Pezilin[24]
Perriger [993–?]
Ellimbold [?–1003]
Walter [1003–1004]
Sigfrid
Erchimbold
Folmar [1043]
Albert [c. 1044, 1058–1060]
Siggo [1061–1062]
Arnold [1064]
Meinrad [1079, 1080–1081]
Liutold [1085]
Theodoric [1086–1116]
Berthold [1116–1127]
Conrad [1127–1164]
Gebhard [1164–1170/3]
Henry [1171–1182]
Eberhard [c. 1195, 1200–1218, c. 1222]
Conrad II [1225–1248]
Ulrich [1248–1258]
Henry II [1259]
Henry III [1289]
Diethelm [1292–1321]
Ulrich II [1321–1329]
Conrad III [1329–1339?]
Burkhard [1339–1342]
Johann I [1340–?]
Johann II [?–1352/1353]
Henry IV [1354–1360]
Burkhard Lüczler [1360–1386]
Henry Semly [1386–1391]

---

23 Dates given in square brackets supplied by the editors of this volume.
24 The name of Petershausen's first abbot is variously given as Pezilin and Perriger, a confusion reflected here in the listing of both names as individual abbots.

Johann Fryg [1392–1427], who ruled the monastery at the time of the great Council of Constance,[25] the first abbot of the monastery vested with a miter, who ruled the monastery of Petershausen laudably for many years and built great and splendid buildings and left copious worldly treasure for his monks.

Johann Amfeld [1426–1427], the second to be mitered, renewed the house of the *custos*; he lived six months in office.

Diethelm Wissz [1427, 1443], the third mitered abbot, bought for the knight Henrich Rogwiler and his brother Manzo a tenth with a winepress on the Egerd for 1800 Rheinish florins.

Johann Hir [1443–1451], the fourth mitered abbot, ruled competently, but did not live long after he was afflicted with leprosy.

Nicholaus Roschach [1451–1473], the fifth mitered abbot.

Martin Brülin [1489/1490, 1495], the sixth.

Johann Merk [1495–1524], the seventh mitered abbot, restorer of this monastery.

Andreas Berlin, elected 1524 [–1525].

Gebhard Dornsperger, elected 1526 [–1556], born in Stockach.

Christophorus Funk was elected in 1556 [–1580] on 8 July.

---

25 The Council of Constance, 1414–1418. In 1417, in the midst of the council, Petershausen hosted delegates from 133 German Benedictine abbeys for a meeting of the German provincial chapter of the Benedictine Order. See Philip H. Stump, *The Reforms of the Council of Constance: 1414–1418* (Leiden: Brill Publishers, 1994), 155–157.

Appendix 1

THE LIFE OF ST. GEBHARD

Translated and annotated by Samuel S. Sutherland, with Alison I. Beach and Shannon M. T. Li

Introduction: *The Life of St. Gebhard*

In CP 1.6, the Petershausen chronicler notes that he had previously written about Gebhard II's efforts to reclaim his portion of his paternal inheritance from his brothers in another work. Comparing the writing styles of the CP and the *Life of Gebhard*, there can be little doubt that this is the work to which he referred, which recounts this conflict in the *Life of Gebhard* 1.9. The chronicler's autograph of the *Life* has not survived. The only surviving copies date to the late Middle Ages, one copied by an anonymous scribe in the fifteenth century, and the second by one Felix Manilius in 1511. This sixteenth-century copy is now bound within University of Heidelberg, *Codex Salemitani* IX 42a, just after the autograph of the Chronicle.[1] While the two works are clearly the work of a single author and evince many of the same stylistic quirks, the Latin of the CP seems noticeably more polished. This may reflect the author's growth as a stylist between the two texts, or perhaps in writing the *Life*, the author simply had more frequent occasion to wax florid – which was never his strong suit – in keeping with demands of the genre of hagiography.

There are, however, some significant differences in content that cannot be reconciled by the order of writing alone. Perhaps much of this stemmed from a simple desire to avoid excessive repetition between the two texts, but it is nevertheless interesting to observe that, while many key details

---

1 See Wilhelm Wattenbach's introduction to the *Vita Gebhardi Episcopi Constantiensis*: MGH SS 10: 582–583. Digital access to the two surviving copies of the Latin text is available through the University of Heidelberg. *Codex Salemitani* IX 9 (fifteenth century): https://doi.org/10.11588/diglit.7328#0003 *Codex Salemitani* IX 42a, beginning at 98v. (1511): https://doi.org/10.11588/diglit.605#0212. (Date of last access: 22 December 2019).

appear in both, a number of items more appropriate to the CP appear only in the *Life* and vice versa. Only the *Life*, for example, reports that Gebhard reassigned his servants as specialists of various kinds with a special provision for inheritance.[2] On the other hand, there is no discussion of Gebhard's illustrious ancestry or of his miracle-working father in the *Life*, although these are elements central to the CP.[3] In some cases, rhetorical considerations may have dictated the logic of inclusion; both Gebhard's brother Liutfrid's deception in the division of their paternal inheritance and his hostile encounter with the relics of St. Ulrich of Augsburg feature in a broader narrative of family conflict in the CP, but would fit awkwardly at best in the *Life*.[4] For other discrepancies, there seems to be no plausible explanation beyond purely stylistic choice.[5]

Unsurprisingly, much of the *Life of Gebhard* recycles common hagiographic tropes and generally follows the conventions of the genre.[6] Among the more noteworthy hagiographical elements that feature in the *Life* is Gebhard's *furta sacra* of the head of St. Gregory, Petershausen's most prized relic.[7] Both the *Life* and the CP recount how Gebhard was given the head by Pope John XV when he traveled to Rome seeking a papal privilege for Petershausen (a story that is included in its entirety with identical text in both), but only the *Life* reports his dramatic escape from a crowd of Roman pursuers who were evidently unaware that this donation had been voluntary.[8] The conflict between the church of Constance and Petershausen over Gebhard's body appears only in the *Life*, although it could well have fit in the theme of such conflicts in the Chronicle.[9]

The second book of the *Life* catalogs Gebhard's many post-mortem miracles, with no overlap with those that feature in the CP.[10] Running

2 *Life of Gebhard* 1.19.
3 CP 1.1–1.3.
4 CP 1.5, 1.28.
5 *Life of Gebhard* 1.24; CP 1.53–1.54.
6 On the saint's Life as a medieval genre, see Bartlett, *Why Can the Dead Do Such Great Things?*, 518–546.
7 On religious meaning of holy relic theft, see Patrick J. Geary, *Furta Sacra: Thefts of Relics in the Central Middle Ages* (Princeton: Princeton University Press, 1991).
8 *Life of Gebhard* 1.16–1.17; CP 1.26.
9 *Life of Gebhard* 1.22–1.23.
10 CP 3.15, 3.2, and A.1. CP A.33, A.38, and A.39 also record miracles performed by the deceased saint, but these occurred after the *Life of Gebhard* was written.

APPENDIX 1: *THE LIFE OF ST. GEBHARD*

through these is an interesting undercurrent of skepticism about Gebhard's good character. As the author reports when recounting the first of these miracles, "even in those days some ignorant brothers disregarded his merit and disparaged his sanctity," prompting Gebhard to appear to one such brother and confirm that he is "not so contemptible" as his reputation would suggest.[11] Similarly, in the longest and most colorful of the miracles, a demon possessing a woman disparages Gebhard as "a pretender and seducer," in whom "there is said to be no sanctity," asserting that Gebhard will therefore be powerless against it.[12] While all of this could fit comfortably within the hagiographical *topos* of the deceased saint proving his or her merit, it may also reflect the author's attempt to rehabilitate the image of the founder of his monastery in the face of real doubt. After all, the phrase "even in those days" hints at the possibility that similar doubts lingered in the author's own day.

Here begins the preface to the life of blessed Gebhard the Second, Bishop of Constance, confessor of Christ, and founder of the monastery of Petershausen

1.0. When the Creator formed the first man in paradise, he gave him authority over that place with the salvific commandment that he beget spiritual offspring up to the full number of predestined souls, so that these – without any intervention of death – might ascend in body and soul to that place from which the wicked one fell with his followers. But the devil, riled up in jealous spite because the flesh would possess the glory that he had lost, seduced the man with deceitful persuasion. By promising divinity that he did not have, the devil stripped man of his immortality and the glory he already possessed. God detested the malice of the enemy more than the fall of man, however, and so recalled man to repentance but sentenced the deceiver to eternal punishment. He gave men leaders and masters whom he inspired through his Spirit to know what should be done and what should be avoided, so that these might guide the rest and teach them to proceed on the *paths of justice* [Ps. 22:3] and avoid the crooked roads. To this end, he promised them his arrival in the world, so that his flesh might free our flesh, and his

11 *Life of Gebhard* 2.1.
12 *Life of Gebhard* 2.5.

light might illuminate our blindness, we who were *dwelling* in *darkness* and *in the region of the shadow of death* [Isa. 9:2]. Moreover, he spoke prophecies first through the patriarchs, then through the Law, and finally through the various prophets, for these all were sent to foretell the arrival of the Savior in the flesh and to prepare the people to be perfected in the Lord.

But when the fullness of the time was come, God sent his Son, made of a woman, made under the law: That he might redeem them who were under the law: that we might receive the adoption of sons [Gal. 4:4–5]. But he did not come to call only those who were under the yoke of the Law, but also those who were without the yoke, saying to them, *"Take up my yoke upon you, and learn of me, because I am meek, and humble of heart: and you shall find rest to your souls"* [Matt. 11:29]. When he had fulfilled this dispensation for which he had taken on the flesh, he returned to the Father, from whom he had never truly departed through the unity of divine majesty. He did not leave his servants as orphans, but rather confirmed and fortified them with the consolation of his Spirit, and ordered them to preach and testify among all the nations so that they might accept repentance, remission of sins through the bath of regeneration, faith in Jesus Christ, entrance into the celestial kingdom, and everlasting glory. The first sowers of these words were the apostles, and next their successors, the priests of the Lord. Many of them fought for these words even to the point of blood, willingly enduring death for the Lord in order that they might deserve to partake of eternal life. They returned their entrusted talent with profit [c.f. Matt. 25:14–30] – some by offering themselves to the Lord as a living sacrifice upon the altar of the heart with fasts, vigils, and prayers, and others by spreading the word of life.

Among these was the most holy Gebhard, who, ornamented with the radiance of all virtues, glowed red over the German lands like a most brilliant star. He was so firm in probity of habits and chastity of life that the omnipotent God frequently brought about extraordinary things through his merit. I have not learned of all his deeds, but some few have reached my ears by the report of my elders which I desire to pass on to posterity as well as I can. Therefore, let no one criticize the superficiality of the words, let the unrefined language of what follows instill no contempt, and let the hearer not focus on who speaks or how he speaks, but rather on that about which he speaks. And let it not disturb anyone that I presume to write about that which I have heard but not seen, since even Luke and Mark composed their Gospels, and many of the

APPENDIX 1: *THE LIFE OF ST. GEBHARD*

holy fathers their writings, from what they had learned not by sight, but truly only by report. Indeed, the men by whose report I learned these things were of such character and so numerous that I could believe their words better than my own eyes. But in this my predecessors who saw and were present for these deeds that God worked through that man are to be faulted not a little, since they did not care enough to record these things in writing for the praise of Christ. But setting that aside, with God's help, let us come to the order of the narrative.[13]

HERE ENDS THE PREFACE

Here begins the life of holy Gebhard the Bishop of Constance

1.1. CONCERNING HIM WHO WAS CUT OUT FROM HIS MOTHER'S WOMB.[14]

Blessed Gebhard was born of a most noble lineage of the Alemanni, and indeed his father Otzo[15] was count of the Rhaetians. While his mother still carried him in her womb, she was seized by weakness, with death demanding its due. As she neared the end, she revealed to her servants the life she carried in her womb and asked that they cut into her belly after her spirit was carried off, remove the little infant, wrap him in a mass of warm fat, and carefully watch over him for the providence of God. Everything was done as she had requested. When the hour approached that the babe would have been born if he had been allowed to stay warm in his mother's womb, he cried out and thus they knew he should be unwrapped and rendered into the light. O miraculous works of the omnipotent God, who, as blessed John the precursor of the Lord said, *is able of these stones to raise up children to Abraham* [Matt. 3:9], for he nearly begat this pillar of his Church without the warmth of a woman's womb. Concerning this, that which the Lord said to the prophet Jeremiah can certainly apply: *Before I formed thee in the bowels of thy mother, I knew thee: and before thou camest forth out of the womb, I sanctified thee* [Jer. 1:5].

---

13 In both of the surviving late medieval manuscripts, the preface is followed by a table of contents that we have here distributed as headings for each chapter, although it is unclear whether the author originally included these as chapter headings or whether they were created by a later scribe. That the later CP (for which the original manuscript is preserved) does include rubric chapter headings of a similar style, however, suggests the former interpretation.
14 cf. CP 1.6. Gebhard was born in 949.
15 cf. CP 1.3–1.4.

1.2. ON HIS BOYHOOD. Therefore, they removed the babe and entrusted him to a nurse, and later handed the youth over to be educated.[16] Then the boy began to show his innately good character, and just as a very skillful bee collects honey from among many kinds of flower, so did he collect sweet teachings from the diverse pages of holy scripture in the beehive of his heart, from which he would later sweeten the throats of many people.

1.3. THAT HE CONVERSED WITH BLESSED CONRAD WHILE STILL A YOUTH. Moreover, when he grew out of boyhood and arrived at the cusp of youth, he began to seek the company of the servants of God, especially that of Bishop Conrad of Constance,[17] a blessed priest worthy in the eyes of God. He served Conrad as a very close attendant so that, from this man's probity, he might discover what still needed to be improved in his own habits. For he knew that it is written: *with the holy, thou shall be holy, and with the innocent man shall thou be innocent, and with the perverse thou shall be perverted* [Ps. 17:26–27]. He therefore also fled the company of depraved men, saying with the prophet: *my eyes were upon the faithful of the earth, to sit with me: the man that walked in the perfect way, he served me* [Ps. 100:6].

1.4. HOW IT WAS PREDICTED BY CONRAD THAT HE WOULD BE BISHOP. Moreover, the Holy Spirit deigned to foretell to the faithful that this man would bear the yoke of the Lord and become a father in his house. For on a certain day while the above-mentioned Conrad of blessed memory was sitting with his men, he had to depart for some purpose. As a joke, the man of the Lord Gebhard (who was always wont to jest) came and sat in the bishop's chair. Returning unexpectedly and seeing Gebhard occupying his place, the bishop grinned and, as it is told, said to him, "See, Gebhard, how quickly you wish to take my place? But it shall not be so, for the episcopacy is not destined for you after me, but for another. But after that man is taken up into heaven, the Lord has predestined you to be a leader and shepherd of his sheep." Indeed, the way things turned out proved this prophecy to be true.

1.5. ON HIS ELECTION. For after the most blessed Conrad was taken to the Lord, Gaminolf[18] succeeded him as bishop and ruled

---

16 Presumably as a student in the cathedral school in Constance; cf. CP 1.6.
17 Bishop Conrad I of Constance (r. 934–975).
18 Bishop Gaminolf of Constance (r. 975–979).

APPENDIX 1: *THE LIFE OF ST. GEBHARD*

for about four years. After he died, the clergy, senate, and people of Constance[19] unanimously chose Gebhard to be their shepherd.[20] Truly, a clear sign was given to show that this election was acceptable to the highest Shepherd and that this man was predestined by the Lord to be a shepherd for his sheep.

1.6. HOW THE IMAGE OF THE HOLY MOTHER OF GOD APPEARED TO HIM IN HIS DREAMS. For there was in that same church an image of Holy Mary the Mother of God carved in wooden panels, which seemed in a dream to offer the blessed man the pastoral staff and instruct him to feed the Lord's flock, and showed him the pasture of eternal life.

1.7. ON EMPEROR OTTO [II]. Emperor Otto, the second of this name, hearing of the death of the bishop of Constance and of the consensus of the people in the election of the venerable man Gebhard, congratulated him and sent him the pontifical staff and ring. And he enjoined the people of Constance to obey Gebhard with all submission and to rejoice that the Lord had given them this man as bishop. For this same man of the Lord was very close with the emperor, since he was Otto's close friend,[21] and for this reason the emperor was overjoyed to find an occasion to promote him to this office, since he had long desired to do so and deemed him most worthy in every virtue of life.

1.8. ON HIS UNCTION AND THE SANCTITY OF HIS LIFE. After this canonical election was completed and Gebhard was anointed with the oil of sanctification, which *ran down* from the head *upon the beard of Aaron* [Ps. 132:2], the man of the Lord began to imitate the example of the Good Shepherd – to avoid the perfidy of the merchant's servant and return his entrusted talent with profit [cf. Matt. 25:14–30], to busy himself in the complete exertion of his mind and to attend to every virtue, just as was proper for the Lord's steward: good, pious, modest, sober, chaste, and, to put it briefly, conspicuous in every virtue

---

19 The anachronistic term *senatus* may be used here in conjunction with *populusque Constantiensis* to invoke the ancient Roman formulation *senatus populusque Romanus*, in keeping with the mirroring of sacral spaces in Rome and Constance and perhaps other classical allusions made by the author – for example, the invocation of Caesar's famous divisions of Gaul in CP 1.1.

20 In 979. Gebhard II would serve as bishop until 995.

21 *Compater* could also mean godfather, but this relationship is not attested elsewhere and Gebhard was only six years older than Otto, who was born in 955.

and adorned with the universal dignity of manners. For he went from *virtue to virtue* that he might see the *God of gods in Sion* [cf. Ps. 83:8]. *With all watchfulness* he *kept* his *heart* [Prov. 4:23], heeding what the Lord said in the Gospel: *Blessed are the clean of heart: they shall see God* [Matt. 5:8]. He *became all things to all men, that* he *might save all men*; *and* he *did all things for* God's *sake, that* he *might be made* an heir *thereof* [cf. 1 Cor. 9:22–23], indeed the co-heir of Christ.

1.9. HOW HE COMPELLED HIS BROTHERS TO DIVIDE HIS PATERNAL INHERITANCE WITH HIM.[22] He was of most noble and wealthy parents who left his brothers and him a great multitude of estates, but because human avarice is not satisfied with riches, his brothers claimed all of it for themselves and gave Gebhard nothing from his inheritance. The man of God, however, not out of greed for the estates but burning with love for God, to whom he desired to donate these estates, demanded that his brothers give him his share of the properties. When they refused, he wrenched from them by force that they should divide everything equally, and he did not allow them to have anything that bordered his allotment. He carried these things out not with malice, but with divine zeal burning in his soul, lest perhaps his brothers hasten into spiritual danger by seizing for themselves something which had been unjustly usurped.

1.10. THAT HE BUILT A MONASTERY FROM HIS PORTION OF THE ESTATES.[23] Once this division of the inheritance was completed, the man of the Lord Gebhard, contemplating in his soul that which the Savior said in the Gospel: *go sell what thou hast, and give to the poor, and thou shalt have treasure in heaven* [Matt. 19:21], and unless he *renounce all that he possesseth*, he *cannot be my disciple* [cf. Luke 14:33], built from his estates the monastery of Pope St. Gregory on the banks of the Rhine River by the city of Constance. He assigned twelve brothers[24] to that place, where they persevered in the divine office day and night, and he arranged sufficient food and clothing for these men to be furnished from his resources. Therefore, he reserved nothing for himself from his earthly wealth, but faithfully expended all of it on Christ's poor, just as it is written: *he hath distributed, he hath given to*

---

22 cf. CP 1.6.
23 cf. CP 1.9.
24 CP 1.15 specifies that the first monk came from Einsiedeln Abbey, which likely also provided the other eleven mentioned here.

APPENDIX 1: *THE LIFE OF ST. GEBHARD*

the poor, his justice remaineth for ever and ever [Ps. 111:9]. He did *not lay up to* himself *treasures on earth,* where *he knoweth not for whom he shall gather these things,* [Ps. 38:7] *but* he *laid up to* himself *treasures in heaven, where neither the rust nor moth doth consume, and where thieves do not break through, nor steal* [Matt. 6:19–20].

1.11. WHEN THIS BEGAN. In the year of the incarnation of the Lord 983, in the fourth year of his episcopacy and in the eleventh year of the reign of Emperor Otto II, he began to construct this earthly house for the Lord from stone – this living man laying stone for an eternal, heavenly house, saying with the apostle: *"For, we have not here a lasting city: but we seek one that is to come"* [Hebr. 13:14]. He laid for himself a good foundation for the future, that he might embrace true life, which is in Jesus Christ.

1.12. ON THE REVIVAL OF THE MAN WHO FELL WITH THE SCAFFOLDING.[25] Once the man prospering in God had laid the foundation of the church and the whole work was started, he began to persevere with it every day. With God providing, the walls grew high enough that it was necessary for scaffolding to be erected, along which those carrying the loads would ascend and descend, and on which they could stand while doing their work. And behold, on a certain day a disaster suddenly struck out of nowhere, which greatly afflicted all the workers. For while they all were standing on the scaffolding, it happened that the supports on which they stood snapped and all the workers fell to the ground. The foreman who oversaw the construction was completely mangled and found as though dead. Although everyone was greatly afflicted with sadness on account of what had transpired, the man of the Lord Gebhard, confident in him who said *"Whatsoever you shall ask of the Father in my name, he may give it to you"* [John 15:16], ordered him to be lifted and carried into the oratory of St. Michael, which was nearby, and once everything had been cleared out of the way, he shut the door and gave himself to prayer. While he was praying, the broken man arose healthy, and Gebhard ordered him to get back to work, saying to him: "Truly, no one shall hereafter suffer spiritual

---

[25] cf. CP 1.12. The meaning of *vestibulum,* which is used once more in the body of the chapter, is not entirely clear in this usage. The term can have a number of possible architectural meanings that do not seem to apply in this case. From the context of the chapter itself, it seems likely the term is intended to describe the same structure as the *lignorum instrumenta,* which we have here rendered as scaffolding. In this we agree with the conjecture of Wilhelm Wattenbach, editor of the MGH edition.

danger on account of this collapse." And he ordered all the walls to be built high and straight without scaffolding, as is still seen today, such that the ceiling panels of this church seem to be suspended in the shape of a cross.[26] He decorated these ceiling panels with gilded bosses in the manner of the starry heavens, and he adorned the walls all around with various paintings. He depicted not only that which the prophet Ezekiel saw through the hole in the wall,[27] but also the works of the Savior done in either the Old or the New Testament for the edification of the viewers.

1.13. ON THE LOCATION OF HIS CHURCH, ITS DEDICATION, AND ITS SAINTS' RELICS. The site of this church was oriented toward the west and it was modeled after the design of the basilica of the prince of the apostles in Rome, on account of which this place is also called the House of Peter [Petershausen]. All around, he built truly suitable dwellings for the monks. Once everything was completed in the tenth year,[28] he dedicated the church in honor of Pope St. Gregory and gathered many magnificent saints' relics. Among these was the arm of the St. Philip the Apostle, which had been given to him by Emperor Otto III[29] along with many other relics which he assembled there with the utmost zeal.

1.14. THAT HE ACQUIRED A PRIVILEGE FROM ROME.[30] While he was gathering saints' relics and everything else pertaining to the divine cult from various locations all over with the utmost zeal, he also hastened to Rome for this purpose, that he might procure from the thresholds of the apostles both saints' relics and a privilege of liberty, which he also sought and obtained splendidly. For because he had already delivered the oft-mentioned monastery into the ownership of the prince of the apostles, he was worthy to receive such a privilege from his vicar John:[31]

1.15. THE PRIVILEGE OVER HIS MONASTERY.[32] "John, Bishop, Servant of the Servants of God, in the name of the holy and indivisible

26 cf. CP 1.48.
27 cf. Ezek. 8:7.
28 i.e., 992; cf. CP 1.24.
29 cf. CP 1.29.
30 cf. CP 1.25.
31 Pope John XV (r. 985–996).
32 cf. CP 1.27. The wording of the privilege is identical in both sources.

APPENDIX 1: *THE LIFE OF ST. GEBHARD*

Trinity, the Father, the Son, and the Holy Spirit: we wish it to be known to all believers in Christ how Gebhard II, worthy of love, bishop of the holy church of Constance and our most beloved brother, came to Rome to pray at the house of Peter, the Prince of the Apostles, and of Paul, and before our presence, and reported to us how he, moved by the prompting of God, has constructed a church of cenobites in honor of blessed Gregory, confessor of Christ, on the bank of the river that is called the Rhine. In this place he most illustriously established the rule of Abbot St. Benedict and his monastic brethren. There he most generously bestowed lands from his own estates, which came to him from his parents, as well as a portion from the estates of his sacred church, for the sustenance and income of those monks who cease neither day nor night to render praise to Christ assiduously in that same holy monastery. For these things he has begged this indulgence of our humility, that this aforementioned place remain forever under the protection and defense of St. Peter, and of us and our pontifical successors, such that no one, neither king nor duke nor margrave, nor even the bishop who holds that episcopate at the time, nor any other person may dare to alienate or in any way remove from that holy monastery all those things that were granted by the aforementioned Gebhard; but we grant that they are to remain secure, stable, and fixed forever. And also by this apostolic precept, at the request of our aforementioned brother, we prohibit in the name of our Lord Jesus Christ anyone to be placed over this monastery other than he whom the brothers assiduously serving God there elect by common consent; the bishop should take care to confirm the elected man with the sign of blessing. The same procedure should also be observed for the election of an advocate. If, God forbid, it should ever happen that the bishop of this sacred church proves to be a heretic or schismatic, the brothers of the aforementioned monastery may by the authority of the Apostolic See have the power to seek ecclesiastical rites wherever they recognize a catholic bishop, and that the unjust bishop may not presume to inflict some injury on them concerning this. For if, although we do not expect it, anyone, of whatever order or power, is tempted to disrupt in some way those things that were bestowed upon the aforementioned monastery by our aforementioned brother, or if he wishes to take away from the right or domain of this monastery, unless he come to his senses, he shall stand excommunicated from the body and blood of our Lord Jesus Christ and anathematized by all the sacred fathers and by us, and he shall not receive the viaticum at the end of his life, and even in death his name shall not by any means be recited during the solemnities of the Masses. Whoever through pious intention will stand as guard and keeper of this our precept shall forever deserve to attain the grace of benediction and eternal life from the Lord God and our Savior Jesus Christ. Amen. Written by the hand of John, the notary, regional, and official of the holy Lateran Palace. Given on 25 April by the hand of Bishop Gregory of the sacred church of Portus and librarian of the sacred Apostolic See, in the fourth year[33] of the pontificate of our most sacred Pope John XV."

1.16. THAT HE THEN ACQUIRED THE HEAD OF ST. GREGORY.[34] Among the other saints' relics that the pope gave the blessed man, he presented him with the head of the most holy Pope Gregory, but only a few of his closest associates were aware of this. Overjoyed at having received such a gift, the man of God quickly left the city, fearing what would have come to pass had he not been protected by divine mercy. For the Romans, realizing that they had been deprived of such a treasure and lamenting as though in mourning, all pursued the man of God as he left the city.

1.17. HOW HE CROSSED THE RIVER PO WITH DRY FEET. Sensing this, Gebhard began his escape. In his flight from Piacenza,[35] he arrived at the River Po, which he found had risen to an immense height, and he grieved that the ferry was on the other side of the river. Because he saw no one nearby who could bring the ferry back and he feared that his pursuers were about to catch up to him, he recognized then the only thing that could help, so he took refuge in the protection of prayers and cried out to God on the banks of the same river. Christ soon enlarged him who was invoking him in his tribulation, since *the eyes of the Lord are upon the just and his ears are open to their prayers* [Ps. 33:16, freely]. He said to the still-pleading man: "Behold, I am here." Gebhard therefore prayed to the mercy of omnipotent God and implored that, if it should be his will that these saints' relics reach their destination, he come to his aid in this moment of need. Amazing to say, he lowered himself into the Po, and a perfect ford appeared to the most holy man right through the middle of the river. Just as the Psalmist sang to the people of Israel: *the sea saw and fled: Jordan was*

---

33 i.e., 989.
34 cf. CP 1.26.
35 The narrative implies that Gebhard had made it as far as Piacenza (which sits on the southern bank of the River Po) before he learned of his pursuers from Rome.

turned back [Ps. 113:3] and: *thou hast conducted thy people like sheep, by the hand of Moses and Aaron* [Ps. 76:21], so also can I proclaim of this man that the Po *saw* him and *fled*, and *was turned back* from its course, and the Lord led his faithful through the many waters *by the hand* of his servant Gebhard. As soon as the man of God saw that the way had been made clear by the Lord, he proceeded with all his men and crossed with all alacrity. But one man, who was by no means a member of the saint's retinue, was made to cross after them, and once all the others crossed he found himself alone on the riverbed and was caught and drowned by the rushing waters, according to that which is written: *woe to him that is alone, for when he falleth, he hath none to lift him up* [Eccl. 4:10]. When this was told to the man of God, he said: "Don't let yourselves be grieved by this, dear ones, for we had to pay this fare here, on account of which we believe he was raised to the Lord. Let us complete our journey with joy, giving thanks to Christ." Truly, those who had been pursuing the man of God, seeing what had occurred, returned to their own homes. Who upon hearing these things is not astounded? Or who, being astounded, can believe that such a man sprang from the barren lands of the Alemanni, a man through whom God deigned to recreate ancient miracles in these times? For just as Moses crossed through the Red Sea with the Israelites, and Joshua, Elijah, and Elisha crossed through the Jordan River with dry clothes, so too did this beloved man of the Lord block the swift currents of the Po with the barrier of faith and cross with sure steps by a path that was previously inaccessible to human feet.

1.18. THAT HE ASSIGNED TWELVE BROTHERS TO THAT PLACE.
When he returned home, he diligently gathered the remaining twelve brothers appointed to that place, as I said above, and established Perriger as the thirteenth to lead them in place of Christ.[36]

1.19. THAT HE SELECTED ARTISANS FROM AMONG HIS SERVANTS, AND WHAT RIGHT HE CONSTITUTED FOR THEM.[37]
After these things he called together his servants and chose the best among them and made them cooks, millers, petty tradesmen, fullers, cobblers, gardeners, carpenters, and masters of every art. And he ordained for them that, on the days they served the brothers, they should be refreshed with bread from the brothers' provisions, *for the*

---

36 cf. CP 1.13, 1.15, 1.50.
37 cf. CP 1.11.

workman is worthy of his meat [Matt. 10:10]. Moreover, in order that they serve their masters with good spirit, he enhanced these men with the provision that when they or their successors die, their goods should not be taken from them, but their heirs should possess their inheritance undivided. But if someone from a different progeny should be added to their number, he shall not enjoy this benefit.

1.20. ON THE KNIGHTS HE ASSIGNED TO THE MONASTERY.[38] He also established other dependents[39] to serve on horseback, in order that these always be ready to ride whenever need arise and lend their horses to the brothers whenever a matter calls for it. The man of the Lord accomplished all of these things as if he were a winged creature full of eyes on the front and back,[40] with the result that the brothers serving Christ in that place, quite sufficiently furnished with all spiritual and physical necessities and freed for the contemplative life, left behind worldly life for the feet of God with Mary [cf. Luke 10:38].[41] Nor did he often disturb them in the active solicitude of Martha, just as it is written: *there is no want to them that fear him* [Ps. 33:10; cf. Rule of St. Benedict 2.36]. For he knew the scripture: *through poverty many have sinned* [Ecclus. 27:1], and so he provided them everything that was necessary inside and out, lest poverty descend upon them and they seek support for this earthly life to the peril of their souls, and lest because of this he should receive not a reward but a punishment from God, the strict judge of Hell.

1.21. HOW HE MADE A LAME MAN STAND. One day, when he was walking around the oft-mentioned place, his way was blocked by a certain lame man who lived there and who, with his knees bent to the ground, lifted his head from the ground with little hand-held stools and made his way around with his whole body bent over like a quadruped. Moreover, this man was very skilled in every form of woodcarving, as can be seen rather well within the doors of this monastery. When the venerable bishop saw this man, he said to him, "Man, why

---

38 cf. CP 1.32.

39 Presumably these were the knights (probably ministerials) mentioned in CP 1.32. On the condition of these unfree dependents, see cf. pp. 15–16.

40 cf. Ezek. 10:12, Apoc. 4:8. This may be a reference to the idea of unceasing effort.

41 The image of Mary and Martha was often invoked in debates concerning the monastic balance between contemplation and action. See Giles Constable, "The Interpretation of Mary and Martha," in *Three Studies in Medieval Religious and Social Thought* (Cambridge: Cambridge University Press, 1998), 3–141.

APPENDIX 1: THE LIFE OF ST. GEBHARD

do you drag yourself around on your hands and knees, and not walk upright on your feet?" He responded, "You already know, lord, that I am lame by God's judgment and cannot take a single step upright." But Gebhard extended the staff that he held in his hand toward the man and said, "Rise and support yourself on this, and then walk with a proper gait." Arising, he joyfully lifted himself on the staff and began to run with new steps. Oh the ineffable man, comparable to the princes of the apostles, Peter and Paul, of whom one lifted a lame man who lay begging alms *at the beautiful gate of the temple* and the other resurrected Eutychus who fell from a third-story window while sleeping [cf. Acts 3:2–10, 20:9–12]: thus did this beloved man of the Lord make a lame man, who was not lying but crawling on hands and knees, step with his own feet, and resurrected, alive and well, a man who fell from the top of the walls.[42] In this matter it should be considered how holy this man was, and how much merit he had in the eyes of God, for Christ deigned to show through him nothing less than he had through his apostles. For still in present times, even with the charity of the masses waning, Truth deigned to fulfill in this man's faith what he promised to his disciples: *"If you shall ask of the Father in my name, he may give it to you"* [John 15:16].

1.22. ON HIS DEATH.[43] When, however, the Rewarder of all good works resolved to draw his servant from the stormy sea of this world to the gate of eternal peace, he was not found sleeping and beaten by bodily troubles, but when the Lord came and knocked, he met him with a burning lamp [cf. Matt. 25:1–13], and he appeared before the one who is to be exalted, saying with the apostle, "I desire *to be dissolved and to be with Christ*" [Phil. 1:23]. And when the feebleness of his body increased and he perceived that he would soon depart from the world, he asked to be buried in the temple that he himself had built; for at that time he was dwelling in the city of Constance, where this same illness had seized him. When the illness reached his vital organs in the sixteenth year of his episcopacy, on 27 August [995], he went the way of all flesh, and it should truly be believed that he was lifted by angelic hands, returned his owed talent to his Lord two-fold, and deserved to hear from his maker: *"Well done, good and faithful servant, because*

---

42 cf. *Life of Gebhard* 1.12.
43 cf. CP 1.51. Gebhard died on 27 August 995, although the chronicler provides 996 as a date in the CP.

thou hast been faithful over a few things, I will place thee over many things. Enter thou into the joy of thy Lord' [Matt. 25:21]. After his body was bathed and dressed in his priestly vestments, as was the custom, and was placed on a bier and carried to the church, dissension arose over whether he should be entombed in the church that was his bride[44] or, as he himself had requested, in the church that he had built. While they thus quarreled amongst themselves, with some desiring to fulfill his petition and others grieving to be without the remains of such a pastor, the majority – who shouted that they refused to turn away from the remains of their father – triumphed over the minority and decreed that he should be buried in Constance.

1.23. ON HIS SEPULCHER AND THE MIRACLES SHOWN AT HIS FUNERAL.[45] Those assigned to carry the bier to the gate approached and tried to lift the coffin to carry it to the waiting sepulcher. But when they extended their arms toward the bier, they began to tremble and shake violently with tremendous fear, losing all human sense and nearly going mad, and the bier became so heavy that it could by no means be moved by human hands. Then all who were present, terrified by this miracle, began to say that this place for the sepulcher was not ordained by God, and by such a correct divine judgment, they determined that he should be buried where he himself had requested. Then the pallbearers came again and hastily lifted the coffin, and its original weight was so completely altered that they found it nearly weightless to carry.

When they passed out of the gates of the church of Constance, divine mercy deigned to show another miracle no less than the first. For when they left the church, as it is said, a dove flew over all the spectators and, when no one drove it away, it landed on the bier of the oft-mentioned blessed man and did not leave that spot until they had crossed the river and entered the church of St. Gregory. As soon as they entered, the dove that they had seen disappeared and no one managed to spot it afterward. It left them with such a sweet odor that everyone felt refreshed, and no one could recall ever having smelled such an odor as that before. This sweet odor lingered over his holy body for a long time, until it was handed over to be buried with the greatest honor in the middle of this same church. For since he was as simple as a dove, a dove rightly

---

44 i.e., the Church of Constance.
45 For the tomb, cf. CP 1.52.

appeared at his funeral, through which the innocence of his mind and the sincerity of his life was shown. The nostrils of his good sheep were rightly refreshed by a sweet new odor from the remains of the pious shepherd, just as before they had always been refreshed in spirit by his preaching and prayer.[46] Whether it was his blessed soul in this dove, as is also read concerning other saints whose souls have often seemed to enter heaven with the appearance of a dove, or whether some other spirit appeared is unknown to us, but it is known to God, for whom all things are laid bare and uncovered, and who deigned to show to men by this miracle his illustrious servant in heaven.

1.24. THE EPITAPH WRITTEN OVER HIS SEPULCHER.[47] When the soul of the blessed bishop was thus received into heaven and his flesh was honorably committed to the earth, they wrote the following epitaph over his tomb in gold letters:

> *O fated plot of land, spurn the beguiling times*
> *And remember the journey that these ashes attest.*
> *Here lies the honor of our people, and also their sorrow.*
> *He was the prefect of the city, but the profit of the entire world,*
> *He founded a sanctuary and seat of the temple to God.*
> *Graciously forgiving this plot of land, O God,*
> *Justly reward this man, since he loved you.*

1.25. HOW HE APPEARED TO ABBOT PERRIGER AFTER HIS DEATH. Later, the above-mentioned Perriger, the abbot of this same monastery, came to the chapel on a certain night to pray. In the silence of that night, as he was attentively kneeling to pray, blessed Gebhard appeared to him and said to him with a cheerful expression: "Know for certain that I have beseeched before the omnipotent God that none of the brothers serving Christ in this monastery be struck by a second death, but that they all, after undergoing a temporal death, should possess eternal life with Christ."[48] After saying this, he vanished from Perriger's sight, and he was no longer able to see him. For this same holy man, having already achieved victory from the world, did

---

46 cf. CP T.3, where the chronicler describes a crumbling body and rotting liturgical vestments when the tomb is opened for the translation of Gebhard's relics.
47 cf. CP 1.53. The wording of the epitaph is identical in both sources, although the *Life of Gebhard* records only the first epitaph.
48 cf. *Life of Gebhard* 2.6 below for a similar promise later made to another brother.

not forget his brothers still laboring with toils in this world, but as someone[49] said:

> "True love of Christ is the true guardian of the Law and fulfills the commandments of God by loving men."[50]

Remembering his first love, he was an advocate before God for those still serving him on the path of laborers, and he consoled them with the success of the journey to be completed, with the result that the more eager brothers hastened with this consolation down the path of righteousness, on which they had less doubt that they would reach their homeland. Wherefore it is befitting for us also to beseech his aid assiduously, such that by the aid of his merit we might escape the perils of this exile and deserve to enter the homeland of paradise.

1.26. ON THE APPEARANCE OF THIS SAINT. For these same brothers, the venerable man was also an entirely bald-headed hero. Moreover, he was accustomed to fortify his speech by this oath, as he would swear "on my unborn head," since he was not born but cut out from his mother's womb and wrapped in a warm ball of fat, for which reason they say he had a broad bald spot.

1.27. HOW LONG HE WAS BISHOP AND WHEN HE DIED. He held the episcopacy for sixteen years and died in the sixteenth year, on 27 August in the year of the Incarnation of the Lord 996, in the thirteenth year of the reign of august Otto, the third of his name, with our Lord Jesus Christ reigning, for whom one with the Father and the Holy Spirit there is one honor and glory forever and ever. Amen.

HERE ENDS THE FIRST BOOK OF THE LIFE OF BISHOP ST. GEBHARD

Here begins the second book of his miracles[51]

2.0. Therefore, after the Redeemer of humanity transferred his servant Gebhard from the chasm of this world to his celestial home, many virtuous deeds are reported, which our Lord deigned to show through him

---

49 i.e., St. Prosper of Aquitaine (d. c. 455), a student of St. Augustine.
50 Prosper of Aquitaine, *Epigrammata* 1.38: "On the Law of Charity," 636–637.
51 As in the *Life* proper, the late medieval manuscript begins the list of Gebhard's posthumous miracles with a table of contents that are given here as chapter headings.

APPENDIX 1: *THE LIFE OF ST. GEBHARD*

after his blessed soul was freed from the chains of flesh and returned to the Lord who gave it the flesh. And it is not for our knowledge, but for the notice of future generations that it is fitting for me to tell you what great power of his mercy the Lord showed to all who devoutly prayed for aid and grace at his tomb. I will therefore commit to writing certain miracles that the Lord deigned to bestow, but I will pass over others in silence, so that I can satisfy the studious without inflicting the wearied reader with tedium. But I have withheld the names of those from whom I heard these accounts, just as I also did above, lest some barbarism of my words offend and the Latin tongue lose its splendor.

In the flesh of life, the angelic man soldiered for God with the devotion of a contrite heart while he lived and inwardly crucified himself in this flesh. Because Gebhard was the Lord's companion in suffering in this way, he also made him his partner in consolation, not only by rewarding him in the heavenly abodes, but also by openly glorifying him before human eyes, as will be apparent in the clear light of the following accounts.

2.1. ON THE MIST THAT WAS SEEN ABOVE HIS TOMB, AND HOW THE ILLUSTRIOUS MAN APPEARED TO A CERTAIN BROTHER. A certain brother of the oft-mentioned monastery brought himself to the tomb of the holy man Gebhard to pray, and while he was attentively commending himself to God with prayers, he saw a mist covering the entire sepulcher, and he smelled an exceptionally pleasant odor emanating from this mist. After it lingered for a while, it was gradually withdrawn from his amazed and wondering eyes. Regarding this miracle, consider what light and sweet odor his blessed soul enjoyed in heaven, whose bodily decay on earth was also glorified by a such a sweet odor. Indeed, it was these things that the prophet Isaiah foresaw, marveling, *"Who are these, that fly as clouds?"* [Isaiah 60:8]. Rightly did a fragrant mist visit the tomb of this man – whose conversation was always in heaven [cf. Phil. 3:20] and who directed his prayers day and night toward heaven with the perfume of good works, like the incense of the evening sacrifice – so that through this it might be shown more clearly that this man inhabits a most glorious mansion of eternal light.

For indeed, because even in those days some ignorant brothers disregarded his merit and disparaged his sanctity, he appeared before one of them in a vision with ineffable clarity, clothed in priestly garments with a miter on his head and sitting on a raised throne in a very bright mansion. And he said to him, "Behold, brother, you can confirm with your own eyes that in the view of the omnipotent God I am not so contemptible as I seem to be in the estimation of some of your brothers." Indeed, he was looking after the welfare of his brothers in all respects, lest they sin by disparaging him. With God's help, he deigned to manifest his splendor to them so that they might know with how much honor and reverence this worthy man ought to be extolled by men on earth. But the brother to whom he appeared desired that very few of the others know about this vision on account of his humility, so divine clemency deigned to show another miracle at his sepulcher in the case of a possessed man with everyone standing round and watching, as it was later found written quite clearly. Corrected by this miracle, everyone thenceforth extolled the saint with veneration worthy of God, and most eagerly commended themselves to him in their prayers.

2.2. ON THE BLIND MAN GIVEN SIGHT. At another time too, a certain blind man arrived from the *pagus* of Thurgau and stood before the sepulcher of the holy confessor to pray. In accordance with that which he promised through his prophet: *"Call upon me in the day of trouble: I will deliver thee, and thou shalt glorify me"* [Ps. 49:15], in his compassion God looked upon this man *calling upon* him, and through the merit of his servant Gebhard he gave this man, rescued from the shadows of blindness, the light of the sun to see. Moreover, wondering who was there or had been there, he began to move his eyes around, hoping to discover where he was and indeed how this had been done to him. Finally recognizing that he had been left alone, he gave thanks to Christ and his confessor with a great shout, and with immense joy he recounted to everyone how he had recovered the use of his eyes. Those who had seen him arrive blind were rather slow to believe that he could see; but after they discovered the truth, with the greatest outpouring of joy they gave thanks to the God of mercy, who is always marvelous in his saints, for *his mercy endureth forever* over *all who seek him with their whole heart*.[52]

2.3. THAT MANY POSSESSED BY DEMONS WERE FREED BY HIM. Thereafter many demoniacs were freed through him. While they were being led to his tomb, some of these demons said that they

---

52 This is language common in the Psalms. See, for example, Ps. 117:1–4, 118:2, and 137:8.

APPENDIX 1: THE LIFE OF ST. GEBHARD

would not be cast out there, but proclaimed that they would instead be cast out in the presence of St. Conrad in Constance.[53] And when they were brought to Conrad, they said similar things and were frequently freed in the middle of the river as they were about to be brought back to Gebhard. This sign was given so that it might be distinguished clearly by the intervention of which of the two they were freed from the deceiver.[54]

2.4. ON THE HEALING OF A PARALYTIC MAN POSSESSED BY DEMONS. Moreover, a certain servile tenant[55] of this place suffered from paralysis and would languish in his bed for long periods. On a certain day while he was alone in his house with only his wife, he was suddenly seized by a demon and sprang out of bed. He grabbed a cudgel and rushed at his wife, swinging it to beat her, but she bolted away and fled to another small house, calling to her neighbors with loud shouts. Those who heard the woman's shouting came running and found the man, whom they had long known to be paralyzed, completely frenzied. They scarcely managed to restrain him with great effort and could not subdue his raging by any method until, with the combined strength of many men, they carried him to the church tied to a chair and placed him on the tomb of the holy confessor. Following that apostolic pronouncement that *"God is faithful, who will not suffer you to be tempted above that which you are able: but will make also with temptation issue, that you may be able to bear it"* [1 Cor. 10:13], this man was immediately freed by the merits of blessed Bishop Gebhard, and not long thereafter he was drawn from this life.

2.5. ON THE POSSESSED WOMAN. A woman of the village called Schmindorf had long been plagued most cruelly by an exceedingly troublesome demon. She had been brought before many saints but not cleansed. Finally, her friends said that they wanted to take her to blessed Gebhard. Hearing this, the demon was greatly afflicted and said: "And what good will it do if you take me to this man, in whom

---

53 i.e., Bishop Conrad I of Constance, who had recently been made a saint in 1123, and whose relics were housed in the cathedral of Constance.

54 The demoniacs were freed on the second crossing of the Rhine as they returned toward Gebhard, suggesting that it was Gebhard and not Conrad who was responsible for their expulsion.

55 The man in question is specified as a *colonus* – in this period and region a relatively privileged servile tenant whose manorial obligations were fixed at a defined quantity of goods in kind, typically without additional labor obligations.

there is said to be no sanctity? By no means can I be expelled from this vessel through him! For in life he was a pretender and a seducer – how will such a man be able to exert any power over me?" When the wicked being uttered these things to them, they put no faith in the author of falsity, and took the road which led to the place called Petershausen. When the demon perceived this, he became troubled and discouraged, and he began to utter dreadful cries at the heavens and to plague and tear at the woman much more than usual.

Moreover, when they had arrived at this place, she was dragged to the church only with great effort. The demon immediately began to curse the saint of God through the mouth of the woman, shouting over and over: "Woe to you, evil Gebhard! Why do you provoke me?" Then she was led to the sepulcher, but there she was pitifully rent by the enemy and brought back out after only a short time. Next, when the relics of the saints were brought after Mass, she was brought by the force of many men, with some pulling and some pushing. Shrieking loudly and cursing the saint of God by name, the demon incensed them with its unnatural wailing. She was at last placed on the tomb of the holy confessor, albeit with great effort, and the exorcism was recited over her by a priest with all the brothers and many others looking on.

Once she had been freed of the malign spirit, she immediately fell silent and did not utter another shout. When the ancient enemy thus retreated, the woman, whom almost no one dared approach a moment before, fell as if dead and could not move a limb. At last she regained her strength and stood. She covered her bare chest and tearfully exalted God, the Savior, and his confessor Gebhard with as many words as she could. Who can express and who can recount how much tearful joy there was then? For the diverse voices of monks and of people of both sexes and various ages resounded with the sound of bells, all singing a hymn to God, who through his servant rescued the creation of his hands from the grip of the ultimate deceiver. For the praise and glory of his name and that of his confessor Bishop Gebhard, he cleansed this vessel, which had been washed in the sacred font of baptism but polluted by the most impure invader.

Then, with the banner of the Holy Cross and the applause of the people, she was carried across the river to Constance, so that the mother church might rejoice with the daughter who was dead but had been revived, and while rejoicing prepare a spiritual feast, to which she

APPENDIX 1: THE LIFE OF ST. GEBHARD

called together friends and neighbors, saying to them, *"Rejoice with me, because I have found my sheep that was lost"* [Luke 15:6] and next: *"It is fit that we should make merry and be glad: for this my daughter was dead and is come alive again; she was lost, and is found"* [Luke 15:32, adapted].

But that night the evil possessor came again and roused the woman whom it had earlier abandoned, and it poured such venom into her ears, saying: "O beloved vessel, why did you act so wickedly against me? For you rejected me, your ancient possessor, and denied the fidelity you had long kept with me on account of that seducer Gebhard, who expelled me from you. You know this man will not by any means be profitable to you. But come back, I beg you, come back to me! For it is not right that you should receive someone other than me into your vessel. I beg you, do not deny my cohabitation with you, which has been delightful for me for a long time now."

After the ancient serpent hissed in the woman's ears with these and other words of this sort, she woke the religious women among whom she was spending the night, revealed to them the adversary's molestations that she was suffering, and asked that they pray to the Lord for her. This was done, and after she had been marked on the next day with the sign of the Cross and presented with the Gospel that blessed John had written about of the Word that was with God in the beginning, the whole infestation of the impure spirit withdrew so entirely that it never again molested her. She returned home with all joy, praising and glorifying him who brought about this mercy for her, whose glorious name shall be blessed from now until forever.

2.6. HOW GEBHARD APPEARED TO A CERTAIN BROTHER.

In the same monastery there was a certain monk particularly devoted to psalmody,[56] for whom it seemed in a dream as if he stood fast praying before the tomb of Gebhard, the most holy confessor of Christ. The holy bishop thus appeared to this man as he stood there, and as though stepping out of his tomb, greeted him, saying to the fearful man: "Do not be afraid, brother! For I am that Gebhard who constructed this temple for Christ and his confessor Gregory. Therefore, go and tell my brothers so that they may be in good spirit and willingly serve Christ and Pope St. Gregory in my monastery." And he added: "Know for certain that everyone who is found willingly serving in this, my

---

56 This phrasing is also used for Opert the Priest, whose miraculous death is recorded in CP 4.12.

monastery, with a good way of life shall have me and St. Gregory as advocates before God in every temptation and tribulation, and in the last trial of Judgment before the throne of the just Judge, we will lead him to be crowned with eternal life."[57] After saying these things, he disappeared from the monk's sight.

2.7. ON THE CUSTOS OF THE CHURCH. Nor do I think it should be passed over that a certain *custos* of this church was accustomed to extinguish the light of the lamp on Gebhard's sepulcher before dawn, but on a certain night Gebhard appeared to him in his dreams and touched his eye with his finger. An illness immediately took hold of this eye, and the man was quickly rendered one-eyed. And rightly so, so that this man, who deprived the saint of God – who is illuminated with eternal light in heaven – of a portion of physical light on earth, should himself be deprived of a portion of the light by which he made his way.

2.8. ON THE ITCHY BROTHER. In the same oft-mentioned monastery there was another young man, whose arms and legs were afflicted by swelling and very grievous itching, and who could not be helped by any medicine. Since he despaired of any human aid, he gave himself over to the protection of the one who said, *"I will kill and I will make to live: I will strike and I will heal"* [Deut. 32:39]. But because he saw that he was not at all worthy to ask for his aid, he sought an advocate through whose help he could ask for what he desired. For when the Mass was celebrated in the sepulcher of the most holy Bishop Gebhard, this young man often performed the office of the sub-deacon, and he would implore with a devout supplication of his heart that, since he could not be helped by human medicine, he might be healed by divine intercession through the help of this saint. To this end, he promised most devoutly to God and his saints that, if health should be granted to him, he would remain willingly in this same congregation until the end of his life. On a certain day, after the groans and sighs of prayers, he reclined his weary head over the tomb and fell asleep. With a dream stealing in, he saw blessed Gebhard as if stepping out of his crypt, which was nearby, clothed in his episcopal attire and touching the youth with a stick he carried in his hand. He heard Gebhard say: "Be healthy in your arms and legs," after which he disappeared. The youth awoke after seeing this, and within that same hour he began to feel some relief,

---

57 This echoes a similar promise to Perriger in *The Life of Gebhard* 1.25.

APPENDIX 1: THE LIFE OF ST. GEBHARD

according to that which the Psalmist spoke about the Lord, saying, "*He will do* the will *of them that fear him: and* he will hear *their* prayers, *and* make them saved" [Ps. 144:19, loosely]. Therefore, as he himself would later recount, from this hour his arms and legs began to recover their health, until his whole body was soon restored to complete health like a newborn boy.

2.9. ON THE CURING OF A PARALYZED BOY. Since indeed I know that the secret good of the King is hidden away, but that it is best to describe openly God's miracles, which are completely indescribable, and to proclaim these things zealously to Christians, I too will not by any means be silent, for divine piety recently deigned to work a miracle at the sepulcher of the oft-mentioned confessor of Christ. There was in the city of Constance a very poor woman – but full of faith in Christ, as it later became clear – who had a little son who was paralyzed from an early age. This boy had never sat upright and never walked on his feet, but always lay suffering on his side, and by this time the crippled boy had troubled his mother this way for nearly five years. When people congregated from all directions to celebrate the feast of Pope St. Gregory at the tomb of the most pious Bishop Gebhard, the boy's poor mother carried him there in her arms. When this pitiful mother came to the tomb of the blessed bishop, she laid the little boy next to the tomb of the saint and stood beside him praying. Suddenly, the little boy stood up and then sat himself down. Seeing this, the woman was completely overjoyed and gave thanks to the omnipotent God. She hastily rushed to her son, took him in her arms, and carried him to the altar of St. Gregory, where she praised the mercy of the Lord with the most tearful cries of joy, and thus rejoicing returned home.

In the following days the boy began to grow stronger, and after a few days he asked his mother for a pair of crutches. When he had received them, he lifted himself over these in either hand, and after a few more days he walked here and there in the house on his own power. Shoes were then purchased for him, and he began to ask that he be brought back for a second healing. Truly, the mother willingly completed everything the young boy requested. Once shoes had been provided, the woman picked up her son, proceeded to the saint, and prostrated herself in prayer before his tomb. Then, after a little while, the boy laid down his crutches and, with sure steps, joyfully returned home with his mother on his own power.

Behold, father, I willingly completed your orders as well as I could. Nor did I write with my hands anything except that which I heard with my ears from very trustworthy, proven, and senior men. The reader cannot accuse me of consciously transgressing the truth in any respect. If in my ignorance anything is faulted, however, may you, father, be defended by authority and gently correct my error if any reader find fault in this work. Truly, we piously beseech Christ to the end, with Gebhard interceding, that he bestow favor to the delinquent and lead us to enter the celestial kingdom, where he lives and reigns together with the Father and Holy Spirit forever and ever. Amen.

HERE THE LIFE OF ST. GEBHARD ENDS HAPPILY.

Appendix 2

CONCORDANCE OF BOOK AND CHAPTER NUMBERING

Old Numbering (Feger 1956)	New Numbering (Beach, Li, and Sutherland)	Old Numbering (Feger 1956)	New Numbering (Beach, Li, and Sutherland)
P[rologue].1–P.24	same	5.30	A.24
1.1–1.55	same	5.31	A.25
2.1–2.49	same	5.32	A.26
3.1–3.50	same	5.33	A.27
4.1–4.42	same	5.34	A.28
5.1	T[ranslation].1	5.35	A.29
5.2	T.2	5.36	A.30
5.3	T.3	5.37	A.31
5.4	T.4	5.38	A.32
5.5	T.5	5.39	A.33
5.6	T.6	5.40	A.34
5.7	A[ddition].1	5.41	A.35
5.8	A.2	5.42	A.36
5.9	A.3	5.43	A.37
5.10	A.4	5.44	A.38
5.11	A.5	5.45	A.39
5.12	A.6	5.46	A.40
5.13	A.7	5.47	A.41
5.14	A.8	5.48	A.42
5.15	A.9	5.49	A.43
5.16	A.10	5.50	A.44
5.17	A.11	5.51	A.45
5.18	A.12	5.52	A.46
5.19	A.13	5.53	A.47
5.20	A.14	6.1–6.15	5.1–5.15
5.21	A.15	6.16	6.1
5.22	A.16	6.17	6.2
5.23	A.17	6.18	6.3
5.24	A.18	6.19	6.4
5.25	A.19	6.20	6.5
5.26	A.20	6.21	6.6
5.27	A.21	6.22	6.7
5.28	A.22	6.23	6.8
5.29	A.23	6.24	6.9

BIBLIOGRAPHY

Primary sources

Baumann, Francis, Gerold Meyer von Knonau, and Martin Kiem, eds. *Die ältesten Urkunden von Allerheiligen in Schaffhausen, Rheinau und Muri*. Quellen zur Schweizer Geschichte 3. Basel: Verlag von Felix Schneider, 1883.

Bernard of Clairvaux. *Bernard of Clairvaux: On Baptism and the Office of Bishops*. Translated by Pauline Matarasso. Kalamazoo, MI: Cistercian Publications, 2004.

Constable, Giles, trans. *Three Treatises from Bec on the Nature of Monastic Life*. Toronto: University of Toronto Press, 2008.

Constable, Giles, and Bernard Smith, eds. and trans. *Libellus de diversis ordinibus et professionibus qui sunt in aecclesia*. Oxford: Clarendon Press, 1972.

Idung. *Le moine Idung et ses deux ouvrages: "Argumentum super quatuor questionibus" et "Dialogus duorum monachorum."* Edited by R. B. C. Huygens. Spoleto: Centro italiano di studi sull'alto Medioevo, 1980.

Kinnamos, John. *Deeds of John and Manuel Comnenus*. Translated by Charles M. Brand. New York: Columbia University Press, 1976.

McCarthy, T.J.H., trans. *The Chronicles of the Investiture Contest: Frutolf of Michelsberg and his Continuators*. Manchester: Manchester University Press, 2014.

Ortlieb and Berthold of Zwiefalten. *Die Zwiefalter Chroniken Ortliebs und Bertholds*. Edited and translated by Liutpold Wallach, Erich König, and Karl Otto Müller. Lindau: Thorbecke Verlag, 1978.

Otto I of Freising. *Deeds of Frederick Barbarossa*. Translated by Charles Christopher Mierow. New York: Columbia University Press, 2004.

Rivers, T.J, trans. *Laws of the Alamans and Bavarians*. Philadelphia: University of Pennsylvania Press, 1977.

Robinson, I. S., trans. *Eleventh-Century Germany: The Swabian Chronicles*. Manchester: Manchester University Press, 2008.

———. *The Annals of Lampert of Hersfeld*. Manchester: Manchester University Press, 2015.

William of Hirsau. *Willehelmi abbatis Constitutiones Hirsaugienses*. Edited by Pius Engelbert O.S.B. 2 vols. CCM 15. Siegburg: Schmitt, 2010.

Secondary sources

Amitai, Reuven and Christoph Cluse, eds. *Slavery and the Slave Trade in the Eastern Mediterranean (c. 1000–1500 ce)*. Turnhout: Brepols, 2018.

BIBLIOGRAPHY

Arnold, Benjamin. *German Knighthood, 1050–1300.* Oxford: Clarendon Press, 1985.

Bartlett, Robert. *Trial by Fire and Water: The Medieval Judicial Ordeal.* New York: Clarendon Press, 1986.

———. *Why Can the Dead Do Such Great Things? Saints and Worshippers from the Martyrs to the Reformation.* Princeton, NJ: Princeton University Press, 2013.

Beach, Alison I. *Women as Scribes: Book Production and Monastic Reform in Twelfth-Century Bavaria.* Cambridge: Cambridge University Press, 2004.

———. "'Mathild de Niphin' and the Female Scribes of Twelfth-Century Zwiefalten." In *Nuns' Literacies in Medieval Europe: The Hull Dialogue,* edited by Veronica M. O'Mara, Patricia Stoop, and Virginia Blanton, pp. 33–50. Turnhout: Brepols Publishers, 2013.

———. "Shaping Liturgy, Shaping History: A Cantor-Historian from Twelfth-Century Petershausen." In *Medieval Cantors and Their Craft: Music, Liturgy, and the Shaping of History, 800–1500,* edited by Margot Fassler, Katie Bugyis, and Andrew Krabel, 297–309. Woodbridge: Boydell & Brewer, 2017.

———. *The Trauma of Monastic Reform: Community and Conflict in Twelfth-Century Germany.* Cambridge: Cambridge University Press, 2017.

Beach, Alison I., and Andra Juganaru. "The Double Monastery as an Historiographical Problem." In *The Cambridge History of Medieval Monasticism in the Latin West,* edited by Alison I. Beach and Isabelle Cochelin, 561–578. Cambridge: Cambridge University Press, 2020.

Bednarski, Steven, and Andree Courtemanche. "'Sadly and with a Bitter Heart': What the Caesarean Section Meant in the Middle Ages." *Florilegium* 28 (2011): 33–69.

Bedos-Rezak, Brigitte. "Cutting Edge. The Economy of Mediality in Twelfth-Century Chirographic Writing." *Das Mittelalter* 15 (2010): 134–161.

Berszin, Carola. "Kloster, Dorf und Vorstadt Petershausen. Anthropologische Untersuchungen." In *Kloster, Dorf und Vorstadt Petershausen. Archäeologische, Historische und Anthropologische Untersuchungen,* edited by Ralph Röber, 117–190. Stuttgart: Konrad Theiss Verlag, 2009.

Bilgeri, Benedikt. *Bregenz. Geschichte der Stadt. Politik, Verfassung, Wirtschaft.* Vienna and Munich: Verlag Jugend & Volk, 1980.

Blumenthal, Uta-Renate. *The Investiture Controversy: Church and Monarchy from the Ninth to the Twelfth Century.* Philadelphia: University of Pennsylvania Press, 1988.

Brown, Peter. "Society and the Supernatural: A Medieval Change." *Daedalus* 104 (1975): 133–151.

Bynum, Caroline Walker. "Did the Twelfth Century Discover the Individual?" In *Jesus as Mother: Studies in the Spirituality of the High Middle Ages,* 82–109. Berkeley: University of California Press, 1982.

Chenu, Marie-Dominique. "Monks, Canons, and Laymen in Search of the Apostolic Life." In *Nature, Man, and Society in the Twelfth Century: Essays on*

BIBLIOGRAPHY

New Theological Perspectives in the Latin West, translated by Jerome Taylor and Lester K. Little, 202–238. Chicago: University of Chicago Press, 1968.

———. "The Evangelical Awakening." In *Nature, Man, and Society in the Twelfth Century: Essays on New Theological Perspectives in the Latin West*, translated by Jerome Taylor and Lester K. Little, 239–269. Chicago: University of Chicago Press, 1968.

Cochelin, Isabelle. "Customaries as Inspirational Sources." In *Consuetudines et Regulae: Sources for Monastic Life in the Middle Ages and the Early Modern Period*, edited by Carolyn Marino Malone and Clark Maines, Disciplina Monastica 10, 27–72. Turnhout: Brepols Publishers, 2014.

Constable, Giles. "The Ceremonies and Symbolism of Entering Religious Life and Taking the Monastic Habit, from the Fourth to the Twelfth Century." In *Segni e riti nella chiesa altomedievale occidentale, 11–17 aprile 1985*, edited by Centro italiano di studi sull'alto Medioevo, 771–834. Spoleto: Presso la sede del Centro, 1987.

———. "The Interpretation of Mary and Martha." In *Three Studies in Medieval Religious and Social Thought*, 3–141. Cambridge: Cambridge University Press, 1998.

———. *The Reformation of the Twelfth Century*. Cambridge: Cambridge University Press, 1996.

Copeman, William Sydney Charles. *A Short History of the Gout and the Rheumatic Diseases*. Berkeley: University of California Press, 1964.

Cowdrey, H. E. J. *Pope Gregory VII, 1073–1085*. Oxford: Clarendon Press, 1998.

Dollinger, Philippe. *L'évolution des classes rurales en Bavière, depuis la fin de l'époque carolingienne jusqu'au milieu du XIIIe siècle*. Paris: Belles Lettres, 1949.

Fassler, Margot, Katie Bugyis, and Andrew Krabel, eds. *Medieval Cantors and Their Craft: Music, Liturgy, and the Shaping of History, 800–1500*. Suffolk: Boydell & Brewer, 2017.

Freed, John B. *Noble Bondsmen: Ministerial Marriages in the Archdiocese of Salzburg, 1100–1343*. Ithaca, NY: Cornell University Press, 1995.

———. *Frederick Barbarossa: The Prince and the Myth*. New Haven, CT: Yale University Press, 2016.

Geary, Patrick J. *Furta Sacra: Thefts of Relics in the Central Middle Ages*. Princeton, NJ: Princeton University Press, 1991.

Goetz, Hans-Werner. "Die schwäbischen Herzöge in der Wahrnehmung der alemannischen Geschichtsschreiber der Ottonen- und Salierzeit." In *Adel und Königtum im mittelalterlichen Schwaben: Festschrift für Thomas Zotz zum 65. Geburtstag*, edited by Aldres Bihrer, Mathias Kälble, and Heinz Krieg, 127–144. Stuttgart: Kohlhammer Verlag, 2009.

Guidoboni, Emanuela, and Alberto Comastri. "The 'Exceptional' Earthquake of 3 January 1117 in the Verona Area (Northern Italy): A Critical Time Review and Detection of Two Lost Earthquakes (Lower Germany and Tuscany)." *Journal of Geophysical Research* 110 (2005): 1–20.

BIBLIOGRAPHY

Hammond, Kate. "Monastic Patronage and Family Disputes in Eleventh- and Early Twelfth-Century Normandy." In *Anglo-Norman Studies XXXVIII. Proceedings of the Battle Conference 2015*, edited by Elisabeth Van Houts, 67–80. Woodbridge: Boydell & Brewer, 2016.

Haverkamp, Alfred. "Cities as Cultic Centres in Germany and Italy During the Early and High Middle Ages." In *Sacred Spaces: Shrine, City, Land*, edited by Benjamin Z. Kedar and R. J. Zwi Werblowsky, 172–191. New York: New York University Press, 1998.

Heinzer, Felix. *Klosterreform und mittelalterliche Buchkultur im deutschen Südwesten*. Leiden: Brill Publishers, 2008.

Héliot, Pierre, and Marie-Laure Chastang. "Quêtes et voyages de reliques au profit des églises françaises du Moyen-Âge." *Revue d'histoire ecclésiastique* 59 (1964): 789–822.

———. "Quêtes et voyages de reliques au profit des églises françaises du Moyen-Âge." *Revue d'histoire ecclésiastique* 60 (1965): 5–32.

Hotchin, Julie. "Women's Reading and Monastic Reform in Twelfth-Century Germany: The Library of the Nuns of Lippoldsberg." In *Manuscripts and Monastic Culture: Reform and Renewal in Twelfth-Century Germany*, edited by Alison I. Beach, 139–189. Turnhout: Brepols Publishers, 2007.

Jakobs, Hermann. *Die Hirsauer. Ihre Ausbreitung und Rechtsstellung im Zeitalter des Investiturstreites*. Kölner historische Abhandlungen 4. Cologne and Graz: Böhlau Verlag, 1961.

Jansen, Katherine Ludwig. *Peace and Penance in Late Medieval Italy*. Princeton, NJ: Princeton University Press, 2018.

Jestice, Phyllis G. *Wayward Monks and the Religious Revolution of the Eleventh Century*. Leiden: Brill Publishers, 1997.

Kaiser, Reinhold. "Quêtes itinérantes avec des reliques pour financer la construction des églises (XIe–XIIe siècles)." *Le Moyen Age: Revue d'histoire et de philologie* 101 (1995): 205–225.

Kottje, Raymund. "Klosterbibliotheken und monastische Kultur in der zweiten Hälfte des 11. Jahrhunderts." *Zeitschrift für Kirchengeschichte* 80 (1969): 145–162.

Krebs, Manfred. "Quellenstudien zur Geschichte des Klosters Petershausen." *Zeitschrift für die Geschichte des Oberrheins* 48 (1935): 463–543.

Lansel, Peider. *The Raeto-Romans*. Chur: Buchdruckerei Bischofberger, 1937.

Le Goff, Jacques. *The Birth of Purgatory*. Chicago: University of Chicago Press, 1984.

Lea, Henry Charles. *Superstition and Force*. Philadelphia: Lea Brothers, 1892.

Leyser, Karl. "The German Aristocracy from the Ninth to the Early Twelfth Century. A Historical and Cultural Sketch." *Past & Present* 41 (1968): 25–53.

Li, Shannon M. T. "Irimbert of Admont and His Scriptural Commentaries: Exegeting Salvation History in the Twelfth Century." PhD Dissertation, Ohio State University, 2017.

BIBLIOGRAPHY

Loud, G. A. *The Age of Robert Guiscard: Southern Italy and the Norman Conquest.* Harlow, England: Pearson Education Limited, 2000.

Lurie, Samuel. "The Changing Motives of Cesarean Section: From the Ancient World to the Twenty-First Century." *Archives of Gynecology and Obstetrics* 271 (2005): 281–285.

Lynch, Joseph H. *Simoniacal Entry into Religious Life from 1000 to 1260: A Social, Economic, and Legal Study.* Columbus, OH: Ohio State University Press, 1976.

Lyon, Jonathan. "Noble Lineages, Hausklöster and Monastic Advocacy in the Twelfth Century." *Mitteilungen des Instituts für Österreichische Geschichtsforschung* 123 (2015): 1–29.

MacMaster, Thomas J., ed. *A Cultural History of Slavery and Human Trafficking in the Pre-Modern Era (500–1450).* London: Bloomsbury Academic, forthcoming.

Maurer, Helmut. "Schwäbische Grafen vor den Mauern Roms. Zu Heinrichs IV. Eroberung der Leostadt im Juni 1083." In *Adel und Königtum im mittelalterlichen Schwaben: Festschrift für Thomas Zotz zum 65. Geburtstag*, edited by Aldres Bihrer, Mathias Kälble, and Heinz Krieg, 193–204. Stuttgart: Kohlhammer Verlag, 2009.

McCarthy, T. J. H. *Music, Scholasticism and Reform: Salian Germany, 1024–1125.* Manchester: Manchester University Press, 2009.

McDonnell, Ernest W. "The 'Vita Apostolica': Diversity or Dissent." *Church History* 24 (1955): 15–31.

Mews, Constant. "Monastic Educational Culture Revisited: The Witness of Zwiefalten and the Hirsau Reform." In *Medieval Monastic Education*, edited by George Ferzoco and Carolyn Muessig, 182–197. London and New York: Leicester University Press, 2000.

Meyer, Bruno. "Die Äbte des Klosters Fischingen." *Thurgauische Beiträge zur vaterländischen Geschichte* 113 (1977): 95–136.

Miller, Maureen C. *Power and the Holy in the Age of the Investiture Conflict: A Brief History with Documents.* Boston: Bedford/St. Martin's, 2005.

———. "Reform, Clerical Culture, and Politics." In *The Oxford Handbook of Medieval Christianity.* Oxford: Oxford University Press, 2014.

Miscoll-Reckert, Ilse Juliane. *Kloster Petershausen als bischöflich-konstanzisches Eigenkloser. Studien über das Verhältnis zu Bischof, Adel und Reform vom 10. bis 12. Jahrhundert.* Sigmaringen: Jan Thorbecke Verlag, 1973.

Moreira, Isabel. *Heaven's Purge: Purgatory in Late Antiquity.* Oxford: Oxford University Press, 2010.

Nottarp, Hermann. *Gottesurteilstudien.* Munich: Kösel-Verlag, 1956.

Phillips, Jonathan. *The Second Crusade: Extending the Frontiers of Christendom.* New Haven: Yale University Press, 2007.

Radding, Charles A. "Superstition to Science: Nature, Fortune, and the Passing of the Medieval Ordeal." *The American Historical Review* 84 (1979): 945–969.

BIBLIOGRAPHY

Radini, Anita et al. "Medieval Women's Early Involvement in Manuscript Production Suggested by Lapis Lazuli Identification in Dental Calculus." *Science Advances* 5, No. 1 (2019).

Remensnyder, Amy G. *Remembering Kings Past: Monastic Foundation Legends in Medieval Southern France.* Ithaca, NY: Cornell University Press, 1995.

Rennie, Kriston. *Freedom and Protection: Monastic Exemption in France, c. 590–1100.* Manchester: Manchester University Press, 2018.

Rio, Alice. "Self-sale and Voluntary Entry into Unfreedom, 300–1100," *Journal of Social History* 45, No. 3 (2012): 661–685.

———. *Slavery after Rome, 500–1100.* Oxford: Oxford University Press, 2017.

Robinson, I. S. "Pope Gregory VII, the Princes and the Pactum 1077–1080." *The English Historical Review* 373 (1979): 721–756.

———. *The Papacy, 1073–1198: Continuity and Innovation.* Cambridge: Cambridge University Press, 1990.

———. *Henry IV of Germany, 1056–1106.* Cambridge: Cambridge University Press, 2000.

Salter, David. *Holy and Noble Beasts: Encounters with Animals in Medieval Literature.* Woodbridge: Boydell & Brewer, 2001.

Schmid, Karl. *Graf Rudolf von Pfullendorf und Kaiser Friedrich I.* Freiburg im Breisgau: E. Albert, 1954.

———. "Zur Problematik von Familie, Sippe und Geschlecht, Haus und Dynastie beim mittelalterlichen Adel. Vorfragen zum Thema 'Adel und Herrschaft im Mittelalter.'" In *Gebetsgedenken und adilges Selbstverständnis im Mittelalter. Ausgewählte Beiträge. Festgabe zu seinem sechzigsten Geburtstag*, 183–244. Sigmaringen, 1983.

Schneidmüller, Bernd. *Die Welfen. Herrschaft und Erinnerung (819–1252).* Stuttgart: Kolhammar Verlag, 2000.

Schreiner, Klaus. "Mönchtum zwischen asketischem Anspruch und gesellschaftlicher Wirklichkeit. Spiritualität, Sozialverhalten und Sozialverfassung schwäbischer Reformmönche im Spiegel ihrer Geschichtsschreibung." *Zeitschrift für württembergische Landesgeschichte* 41 (1982): 250–307.

———. "Hirsau und der Hirsauer Reform. Spiritualität, Lebensform und Sozialprofil einer benediktinischen Erneuerungsbewegung im 11. und 12. Jahrhundert." In *Hirsau. St. Peter und Paul. 1091–1991*, 153–204. Stuttgart: Konrad Theiss Verlag, 1991.

———. *Gemeinsam leben: Spiritualität, Lebens- und Verfassungsformen klösterlicher Gemeinschaften in Kirche und Gesellschaft des Mittelalters.* Edited by Mirko Breitenstein and Gert Melville. Berlin and Münster: LIT Verlag, 2013.

Schulz, Knut. "Zum Problem zur Zensualität im Hochmittelalter." In *Beiträge zur Wirtschats- und Sozialgeschichte des Mittelalters. Festschrift für Herbert Helbig zum 65. Geburtstag*, edited by Knut Schulz, 86–127. Cologne: B, 1976.

BIBLIOGRAPHY

Stump, Philip H. *The Reforms of the Council of Constance: 1414–1418*. Leiden: Brill Publishers, 1994.

Stalley, R. A. *Early Medieval Architecture*. Oxford: Oxford University Press, 1999.

Sutherland, Samuel S. "Mancipia Dei: Slavery, Servitude, and the Church in Bavaria, 975–1225." PhD Dissertation, Ohio State University, 2017.

Tanner, Norman P., ed. *Decrees of the Ecumenical Councils*, 2 vols. Washington, DC: Georgetown University Press, 1990.

Temkin, Owsei. *The Falling Sickness: A History of Epilepsy from the Greeks to the Beginnings of Modern Neurology*, 2nd ed. Baltimore, MD: Johns Hopkins University Press, 1994.

Thomas, David and Alex Mallet, eds. *Christian–Muslim Relations: A Bibliographical History*, Vol. 3 (1050–1200). Leiden: Brill Publishers, 2011.

Tüchle, Hermann. *Kirchengeschichte Schwabens*. 2 vols. Stuttgart: Schwabenverlag, 1950.

Vanderputten, Steven. *Monastic Reform as Process: Realities and Representations in Medieval Flanders, 900–1100*. Ithaca, NY: Cornell University Press, 2013.

———. "Monastic Reform in the Early Tenth to Twelfth Century." In *The Cambridge History of Medieval Monasticism in the Latin West*, edited by Alison I. Beach and Isabelle Cochelin, 599–617. Cambridge: Cambridge University Press, 2020.

Vauchez, André. *Sainthood in the Later Middle Ages*. Cambridge: Cambridge University Press, 1997.

Walther, Helmut G. "Gründungsgeschichte und Tradition im Kloster Petershausen vor Konstanz." *Schriften des Vereins für Geschichte des Bodensees und seiner Umgebung* 96 (1978): 31–67.

Weinfurter, Stefan. *The Salian Century: Main Currents in an Age of Transition*. Philadelphia: University of Pennsylvania Press, 1999.

Werner, Wilfried. *Die mittelalterlichen nichtliturgischen Handschriften des Zisterzienserklosters Salem*. Wiesbaden: Reichert Verlag, 2000.

Widemann, Josef, ed. *Die Traditionen des Hochstifts Regensburg und des Klosters St. Emmeram*. Quellen und Erörterungen zur bayerischen Geschichte. Herausgegeben von der Kommission für bayerische Landesgeschichte bei der Bayerischen Akademie der Wissenschaften. Neue Folge, Bd. 8. Munich: C.H. Beck'sche Verlagsbuchhandlung, 1942.

Wolfram, Herwig. *Conrad II, 990–1039: Emperor of Three Kingdoms*. College Park, PA: Pennsylvania State University Press, 2006.

Wollasch, Joachim. "A propos des fratres barbati de Hirsau." In *Histoire et société. mélanges offerts à Georges Duby*, Vol. 3, 37–48. Aix-en-Provence: Université de Provence, 1992.

Wood, Susan. *The Proprietary Church in the Medieval West*. Oxford: Oxford University Press, 2006.

Woods, David. "The Origin of the Legend of Maurice and the Theban Legion." *Journal of Ecclesiastical History* 45, No. 3 (1994): 385–394.

BIBLIOGRAPHY

Zösmair, Josef. "Geschichte Rudolfs des letzten der alten Grafen von Bregenz." *Schriften des Vereins für Geschichte des Bodensees und seiner Umgebung* 44 (1915): 25–39.

Zotz, Thomas. "Der südwestdeutsche Adel und seine Opposition gegen Heinrich IV." In *Welf IV. – Schlüsselfigur einer Wendezeit*, edited by Dieter R. Bauer and Matthias Becher, Zeitschrift für bayerische Landesgeschichte 24, Series B, 333–359. Munich, 2004.

———. *Adel und Königtum im mittelalterlichen Schwaben: Festschrift für Thomas Zotz zum 65. Geburtstag*. Edited by Aldres Bihrer, Mathias Kälble, and Heinz Krieg. Stuttgart: Kohlhammer Verlag, 2009.

INDEX

Note: 'n.' after a page reference indicates the number of a note on that page. Parentheticals following names indicate Latin variants in spelling found in the CP manuscript.

Aaron, priest from Kamberg 149–150
Aasen 170
abbots, apostolic model 31
Abel, Otto 19, 157
Adalgod of Märstetten (Adilgoz) 60
Adalhard, uncle of Gebhard
    (Adilhardus) 63–64
Adalheid, mother of Count Rudolf of
    Ramsberg (Adilheide) 186
Adalheid of Dillingen 47n.40
Adalheid of Winterthur-Kyburg
    (Adilheida) 46
Adalheid, noblewoman
    (Adelheida) 77
Adalheid, religious woman of
    Petershausen (Adilheit) 162
Adelaide of Savoy 89n.93
Admont, monastery 11, 13
Adrian IV, Pope 179n.7
advocates, role of 6
Aegidius, Saint 175
Afra, Saint 103, 104, 145, 165
Agapitus, Saint 154, 158, 175
Agatha, Saint 103, 104, 145, 155,
    165, 175
Agaunum, monastery 185
Agnes, Saint 158, 175
Agricius, Saint 146
Ahausen 43
Aichstetten 63, 114
Ailingen 147
Albert I, Archbishop of Mainz
    (Adilbertus, Adelbertus)
    123–124, 134–135

Albert, Abbot of Petershausen
    (Adelbertus) 77, 78, 144, 189
Albert, Abbot of Schaffhausen
    (Adilbertus) 116
Albert, Abbot of Wessobrunn
    (Adilberonus) 119
Albert, Count (Adilbertus) 187
Albert, Count of Calw 6, 8
Albert, Count of Mörsberg
    (Adilbertus) 116
Albert, Count of Winterthur
    (Adilbertus) 46
Albert, monk of Petershausen
    (Adelbertus) 158–159
Albert of Achalm 47
Albert of Tal, priest (Adilbertus) 187
Albert, son of Liutfrid
    (Adilbertus) 46
Alberweiler 82
Aldo, Bishop of Piacenza 125–126
Alexander I, Pope 154
Alexander III, Pope 178
Alexander, Saint, son of Felicity 103,
    145, 146
Alexandrian Schism 178–179n.7
Allmannsweiler 80
Altar of St. Peter 158
Altar of the Holy Cross 154
Altdorf, monastery 130n.13
Altenrhein 61
Altheim 164
Altman, Abbot of Kastl
    (Altmannus) 120
Amand, Saint 154

INDEX

Ambrose, Saint 145
Amilhard, monk of Petershausen (Amilhardus) 124
Amizo, *custos* of Petershausen 139–140
Anastasius, Saint 104, 145
Andelsbuch 112–113, 114, 115
Andreas Berlin, Abbot of Petershausen 190
Andrew the Apostle 103, 104, 145, 154, 175, 188
Anianus, Saint 154
Anslechiswilare 61
Antony, Saint 146
ants, infestation 144–145
Apollinaris, Saint 146, 154, 171, 175
apostolic life (*vita apostolica*) 25–26
Arnold, Abbot of Petershausen (Arnoldus) 78, 144, 189
Arnold, brother of Count Rudolf of Ramsberg (Arnoldus) 187
Arnold of Heiligenberg, anti-Bishop of Constance (Arnoldus, Arnolfus) 117, 118, 119, 120
Arnold of Kriessern (Arnolt) 187
Arsenius, Saint 145
art and architecture 52–54, 66–67, 68–69, 102–104, 145–147, 152–153, 164–165, 170
Aubertus, Saint 171
Augustine, Saint 145, 175
autodedition *see* self-donation
Azala, freewoman 133
Azala of Pfrungen, religious woman of Petershausen 132, 134, 135–136

Balbina, Saint 188
Barbara, Saint 103, 146, 175
Barbatian, Saint 154, 155
Bartholomew the Apostle 103, 104, 145, 146, 154, 165, 175, 188
Basil, Saint 146

Basilla, Saint 146
bearded brothers 10–11, 84, 102, 104, 136–137, 149, 163, 180, 183
beggars 37
Benedict, Saint 104, 146, 154, 158, 175, 188
Benno of Spaichingen 133
Berengar II, Count of Sulzbach 119n.70
Berengar of Arnach (Berngarius) 159, 160
Berg 76
Bernard, deacon (Bernhardus) 78
Bernard, monk teacher of Petershausen (Bernhardus) 100, 104, 105–109
Bernard of Clairvaux 165, 166n.33, 168n.43
Bernold of St. Blasien 2, 11, 71, 85n.69, 86n.75, 87n.82, 93n.115, 94n.121, 116n.56, 117nn.64-65, 133n.27
Bernold, prior of Neresheim (Bernoldus) 121
Bertha, Countess of Bregenz (Berhta) 115, 137
Bertha, daughter of King Rudolf (Berhta) 114
Bertha, *inclusa* 169
Bertha, mother of Theodoric (Berhtam) 100
Bertha of Savoy/Turin 89n.93
Berthold II, Duke of Carinthia/
Berthold I, Duke of Zähringen (Berhtoldus, Bertholfus) 86, 87, 88
Berthold II, Duke of Swabia and Zähringen (Bertholdus, Bertolfus) 118, 170
Berthold, Abbot of Petershausen (Bertoldus, Bertholdus, Bertolfus, Bertholfus) 53, 130–131, 132, 139, 140, 142–144, 189

INDEX

Berthold, advocate of Azala of Pfrungen (Bertholdus) 135
Berthold of Lustenau (Bertoldus) 187
Berthold of Reichenau 2, 78n.34, 84nn.65–66, 86–87n.80, 86n.75, 89n.94
Berthold of Zwiefalten 3, 71
Bertrada, wife of Herman of Hirschegg (Perhterada) 83
Beuren 76
Bichtlingen 169
Bigenhausen 82, 114–115
Billafingen 48, 62
bishops, apostolic model 35
Blaise, Saint 103, 145, 146, 154, 165, 175
Bodman 43
Boethius, Saint 154
Boniface, Saint 145, 175
Boos 79, 142, 147
Bregenz 43, 113–116
Bregenzer (Udalrichinger) 38–39
Breitenbach 63
Brigid, Saint 155
Brugg 61
Buchhorn 43
Burchard III, Duke of Swabia (Burchardus) 64, 75
Burchard, nobleman (Burchardus) 83
Burchard of Hausen (Burchardus) 169
Burkhard, Abbot of Petershausen (Burkardus) 189
Burkhard Lüczler, Abbot of Petershausen (Burkardus) 189

Caecilia, Saint 175
Callixtus I, Pope 146, 154, 158, 175, 188
Callixtus II, Pope 135, 136, 151n.2
Callixtus III, Pope 179n.7
Candidus, Saint 145, 146, 154

canons, aspostolic model 34–35
Cantianilla, Saint 146
Carl, Bishop of Constance (Karolus) 85
Carpophorus, Saint 154
Castus, Saint 154
Casus Sancti Galli (Ekkehard IV of St. Gall) 3
Cecilia, Saint 103, 104, 145, 146, 155
censuales (liberti tributarii) 16, 164n.22
Chapel of St. Andrew 104, 174
Chapel of St. John the Baptist 79, 146, 173, 178
Chapel of St. Martin and St. Oswald (double chapel) 145, 174, 175–176
Chapel of St. Mary 103, 174–175, 176
Chapel of St. Mary Magdalene and St. Fides (double chapel) 146, 173, 174
Chapel of St. Michael 51, 104, 174
Charlemagne 38, 42–43
charters *see* privileges
cherubim, as monastic model 27–28
chirographs 139
Chrisantus, Saint 154
Christopher, Saint 103, 146, 154, 158
Christophorus Funk, Abbot of Petershausen 190
Chronicle of Ottobeuren 3
Chronicle of Petershausen (CP)
  authorship 4–5, 177–178
  compared to contemporary chronicles 2–4
  compared to *Life of St. Gebhard* 38, 191–192
  manuscript 17–18, 151, 156–157, 184
Chuzzo, advocate (Chuzonus) 51
Civitate, Battle of (1053) 46n.35
Clement I, Pope 158, 175
Clement III, anti-Pope 86–87, 91, 95, 117

228

INDEX

Clementia of Zähringen 180n.13
Cluny, monastery 7, 8
coloni 16, 211n.55
concubines 100
Conrad I, Abbot of Petershausen
  (Kounradus, Counradus,
  Chounradus)
  appointment at Petershausen
    143, 189
  character 185
  death and burial 183
  monastery improvements and
    management 59, 145, 149,
    152–154, 158–159, 163, 164–165,
    173–174, 182–183, 185
  monastery possessions sold and
    spent by 138, 142, 147, 164,
    181, 183, 185
Conrad I, Bishop of Chur
  (Kounradus, Counradus) 56,
  136, 181
Conrad I, Bishop of Constance
  (Chuonradus, Counradus,
  Kounradus) 48, 82, 151n.2,
  196, 211
Conrad I, Bishop of Würzburg 188
Conrad I, Duke of Zähringen
  (Counradus) 168
Conrad II, Abbot of Petershausen
  (Cuonradus) 189
Conrad II, Bishop of Chur
  (Counradus) 158
Conrad II, King of Italy (Kounradus,
  Counradus) 94
Conrad III, Abbot of Petershausen
  (Cuonradus) 189
Conrad III, King of Germany
  (Counradus) 89, 165–166, 167
Conrad of Frickingen
  (Counradus) 134
Conrad of Heiligenberg, advocate
  of Constance and Petershausen
  (Counradus) 164, 179, 185
Conrad, Saint 145, 165, 175
Constance, Council of (1094)
  133n.27
Constance, Council of
  (1414–1418) 190
Constantius, Saint 154
Constitutiones Hirsaugienses
  (Constitutions of Hirsau)
  8, 9, 99
conversae see lay sisters
conversi see lay brothers
Cornelius, Saint 146
Cosmas, Saint 103, 146, 154,
  158, 175
Crescentius, follower of
  Henry IV 90
Crispin, Saint 154
Crispinian, Saint 154
crusades 165–168
Cuno I of Rott, Count of Vohburg
  (Couno) 92
Cuno, Abbot of Altdorf
  (Cuono) 130
Cuno of Altshausen, Abbot of
  Rheinau (Cuono) 104, 109–111
Cuno, Count of Achalm and
  Wülflingen (Cuono) 100
Cuno of Linzgau (Cuono) 132
Cuno of Linzgau, son of Cuno
  (Cuono) 132
Cuno, son of Wezil (Cuono) 133–134
Cyriacus, Saint 103, 145, 146, 175
Cyricus, Saint 154
Cyril, Saint 145, 146

Damascus, siege of 167
Damian, Saint 103, 146, 154,
  158, 175
Danketsweiler 81
Daria, Saint 155
demonic possessions 210–213
Denis, Saint 154
Desiderius, Saint 146, 154

INDEX

Diedo, hermit 112
Diemo of Bregenz 187
Diepirga, mother of Gebhard 43, 47, 195
Diepold II, Margrave of Vohburg, Lord of Diengen (Diepoldus) 90
Diethelm, Abbot of Petershausen (Diethelmus) 189
Diethelm Wissz, Abbot of Petershausen (Diethalmus) 190
Dietrich, hermit (Dietericus) 169
Digna, Saint 146, 154, 155
Dionysius, Bishop 175
Dorylaeum, second battle of (1147) 166n.34
Dotternhausen 122–123
Dussnang 61, 73–74

earthquakes 131
Ebbo, monk of Petershausen (Eppo) 104
Ebbo of Heiligenberg (Eppo) 83
Eberhard I, Bishop of Constance (Eberhardus) 77–78, 161
Eberhard, Abbot of Petershausen (Eberhardus) 189
Eberhard, advocate (Eberhardus) 51
Eberhard, blind man (Eberhardus) 140
Eberhard, Count (Eberhardus) 77
Eberhard, Count of Bodman (Eberhardus) 82
Eberhard, Count of Nellenburg (Eberhardus) 88
Eberhard, layman (Eberhardus) 125
Eberhard, monk of Petershausen (Eberhardus) 104
Eichstetten 61
Eigilward, son of Rudiger (Eigilwardus) 179
Einsiedeln, monastery 6, 52
Ekkehard IV of St. Gall, *Casus Sancti Galli* 3

Ekkehard of Aura 2
Eleanor of Aquitaine 167
Eleven Thousand Virgins 145, 146, 165, 175, 188
Elisabeth, wife of Count Rudolf of Ramsberg 187
Ellimbold, Abbot of Petershausen (Ellimboldus, Ellenboldus) 76, 189
Elster, Battle of the (1080) 91–92
Embrico, Bishop of Augsburg (Imbrico) 89
Emerita, Saint 146
enclosed (*inclusi/ae*) 36, 169
enclosure and reclusion, apostolic model 28–30
Epfendorf 61, 64–66, 75
episcopal proprietary monastery 1n.1
Erasmus, Saint 145, 154
Erchimbold, Abbot of Petershausen (Erchenboldus, Erchimboldus) 76, 189
Erimbreth, nobleman 76–77
Erlach, monastery 141n.50
Erlafried, Count of Calw 5
Ernest, Margrave of Austria (Ernist) 88
Eschen 76
Escherichsweiler 83, 170
Ettishofen 134
Eugenia, Saint 158
Eugenius III, Pope 165, 168n.43
Eugenius, Saint 175
Eunomia, Saint 103, 104
Eutropia, Saint 103, 104, 145, 165
Eutyches, Saint 175
Exuperius, Saint 146

Fabian, Pope 145, 154, 175
famine 53, 142, 164, 168n.44
Feger, Otto 19, 20, 157
Felicity, Saint 103, 146, 155
Felix, Pope 104, 146, 154, 175

INDEX

Fidelis, Saint 154, 188
Fides, Saint 138n.43, 146, 163n.15
  see also Chapel of St. Mary
    Magdalene and St. Fides
fires 138–140, 163, 171–173, 178
Fischbach 149
Fischingen, monastery 149
Flarchheim, Battle of (1080) 91n.104
Folchnand, priest (Folchnandus) 141
Folmar, Abbot of Petershausen
    (Folmarus, Volmarus)
    76–77, 189
Folmar, monk of Petershausen
    (Folmarus) 169
Forchheim 89
forgeries 50n.50, 57–58n.74, 60n.88
Fortunata, Saint 103, 165
Frederick I, Duke of Swabia
    (Fridericus) 89, 92
Frederick I, Holy Roman Emperor
    178–179n.7, 179
Frederick II of Hohenstaufen, Duke
    of Swabia (Fridericus) 89,
    124, 134
Frederick, Abbot of Einsiedeln 6
Frederick, Archbishop of Cologne
    (Fridericus) 124
Frederick, nobleman (Fridericus) 119
free commoners 15
freedom, monastic 7–8, 56–57,
    62, 70–71, 79, 128–129, 130,
    142–143
Frickingen 147–148
Frimmenweiler 81
Frutolf of Michelsberg 2, 78n.34,
    85n.67, 87n.80, 87n.82
furta sacra (relic theft) 192, 202–203

Gall, Saint 103, 104, 146, 154, 158,
    165, 175
Gaminolf, Bishop of Constance
    (Gamenoldus) 196–197
Gams 76

Gaugericus, Saint 154
Gebhard I, Abbot of Petershausen
    (Gebehardus) 4–5, 184–185,
    188, 189
Gebhard II, Bishop of Constance
    (Gebehardus, Kebehart)
    appointed as bishop 196, 197
    on Bernard 109
    birth by excision 47, 195
    character and appearance 193,
      197–198, 208
    childhood 196
    death and burial 67–69, 205–207
    donation of ministerials and
      servants 41, 60, 61, 203–204
    imaginative genealogy 14,
      38–39, 42–43
    inheritance dispute 45–48, 198
    miracles, while living 54–55, 105,
      199–200, 202–203, 204–205
    miracles, posthumous 111,
      157–158, 169, 173, 206–215
    monastery location search
      and establishment 1, 49–50,
      198–199, 200
    property donations and
      acquisitions 48–49, 50, 51,
      59–62, 63–65, 74
    relic acquisitions 55–56, 58–59,
      200, 202
    translation of 152–155
Gebhard III, Bishop of Constance
    (Gebehardus) 52, 95–96, 99,
    101–103, 113–114, 117, 118,
    120, 121, 133
Gebhard Dornsperger, Abbot of
    Petershausen (Gebehardus) 190
Gebhard, forefather of CP chronicler
    (Gebehardus) 104–105
Gebhard, priest scribe
    (Gebehardus) 187
Gebhard, Saint 146, 154, 158, 165,
    175, 188

INDEX

Gebino, Abbot of Wagenhausen, uncle of CP chronicler 5, 80, 121, 124, 146–147, 149, 168–169
Gebino of Pfrungen 81–82
Gebino, son of Cuno of Linzgau 132–133
Gelasius II, Pope 131
Genesius, Saint 158, 175
George, Saint 103, 104, 146
Gerald, bearded brother/monk of Petershausen (Geroldus) 83–84, 170
Gerald, cleric and subdeacon (Geraldus) 105
Gerald, son of Gisilfrid of Teuringen (Geraldus) 148
Gerbert, Martin 17
Gereon, Saint 146, 188
Gerhoch of Reichersberg 11, 13
Gering, priest (Gerungus) 164
Gero, Count of Pfullendorf (Ger) 82–83
Gervasius, Saint 145
Gießelmacher 79
Giordano da Clivio, Archbishop of Milan 131
Gisela, donor (Gisila) 164
Giselmar, servant (Gisilmarus) 133
Gisilfrid of Teuringen (Gisilfridus) 148–149
Gorgonius, Saint 146
Gotistiu, wife of Wolfrad of Weiler 79
Gottlieben 60, 61
Gottschalk, son of Swiggerr (Goteshalchus) 77
Gotzhalm, monk of Petershausen (Gozhalmus) 104
Gozold, layman (Gozoldus) 125
Grabs 76
Gregory V, Pope 73–74
Gregory VII, Pope 85–86, 88–91, 92–93, 94–95

Gregory VIII, anti-Pope 131
Gregory, Bishop of Portus 202
Gregory, martyr saint 154, 175
Gregory the Great, Pope 55–56, 59, 154, 165, 175, 188, 202
guesthouses 33
Guiscard, Robert 46n.35
Gundelinde, Saint 146
Gundelo of Constance 164

Hadwig, wife of Duke Burchard III of Swabia (Hadiwich, Hadewic, Hadewiga, Hadiwiga) 64–65, 75
Haidgau 169
Hardt, Hermann von der 17
Hartman I, Count of Dillingen (Hartmannus) 46, 101, 120
Hartman II, Count of Dillingen (Hartmannus) 46
Hartman, *inclusus* (Hartmannus) 169
Hasenau 115
Hasungen, monastery 101
Hausen 63
Heggelbach 48, 62
Heistergau 43
Helias, ministerial 175
Henry I, Abbot of Petershausen (Heinricus) 189
Henry II, Abbot of Petershausen (Heinricus) 189
Henry II, Holy Roman Emperor 74–75, 188
Henry III, Abbot of Petershausen (Heinricus) 189
Henry III, Duke of Saxony (Heinricus) 179–180
Henry IV, Abbot of Petershausen (Heinricus) 189
Henry IV, Holy Roman Emperor
character description 84–85
excommunicated 85–86, 93, 95
investitures and alliances 86–87, 91, 94, 117, 118nn.66-67

INDEX

military campaigns 88, 89–92, 93
   pardoning and death 120
   royal charter for Hirsau 8
   supported by Liutold, brother of Theodoric 101
Henry V, Holy Roman Emperor 94n.118, 119–120, 121, 123–124, 131, 135
Henry, advocate of priest Gering (Heinricus) 164
Henry, monk priest and guest-master of Petershausen (Heinricus) 188–189
Henry, monk priest of Petershausen (Heinricus) 187
Henry, monk scribe of Petershausen (Heinricus) 104
Henry, priest at St. Mary of Rötsee (Heinricus) 158
Henry of Heiligenberg (Heinricus) 118, 122–123, 133
Henry of Hirschegg (Heinricus) 134
Henry of Lützelburg, Bishop of Semgallen (Heinricus) 188
Henry of Neufrach (Heinricus) 180
Henry of Zwiefalten, Abbot of Neresheim (Heinricus) 140
Henry Selmy, Abbot of Petershausen (Hainricus) 189
Heraclius, Saint 154
Herbert, *custos* of Petershausen (Heribertus) 137, 158
Herdwangen 82
Herman I, Bishop of Constance (Herimannus, Heremannus) 150, 165, 174, 175, 178, 184
Herman, advocate (Heremannus) 77
Herman, monk priest of Petershausen (Herimannus) 138
Herman, nobleman (Herimannus) 83

Herman of Reichenau 2
Herman of Salm/Luxembourg, anti-King of Germany (Herimannus) 92, 94
Herman, prior of Petershausen (Herimannus) 173
Herman the Elder of Hirschegg (Herimannus) 80, 83, 185
Hermes, Saint 154
hermits 36, 112, 169
Hilaria, Saint 103, 105, 145
Hildebold, Bishop (Hiltiboldus) 60, 65
Hildegard, wife of Count Ulrich I of Bregenz 39n.3, 42n.17
Hippolytus, Saint 103, 145, 146, 158, 165, 175
Hirsau, monastery 5–6, 174
Hirsau reform
   arrival at Petershausen 99–100
   as book-oriented 12–14, 127n.100
   CP chronicler's constructed narrative 95–96, 97, 99–102
   historical overview 5–9
   ideals and spirituality 9–12
Höchst 61
Höchstädt, Battle of (1086) 92
Hohentwiel, monastery 64n.96
Holy Innocents 158, 175
Homburg on the Unstrut, Battle of (1075) 88
Honstetten 116
Hostia, Saint 146
Hugo, canon of Constance (Hugonus) 152
Hugo, provost of Constance 164
Hyacinth, Saint 154, 175
Hylarion, Saint 145

inclusi/ae 36, 169
Innocent I, Pope 145, 146
Innocent II, Pope 163

INDEX

Investiture Controversy
  in Hirsau context 6, 10
  impact on Constance and
    Petershausen 117–120, 121,
    124, 133–135
  major events and military conflicts
    85–95, 116–117, 120–121,
    123–124
Irimbert, Abbot of Admont 13–14
Irmingard, noblewoman
  (Irmingarda) 77

Jacob the Apostle 146, 154, 175, 188
Jakobs, Hermann 9n.28
Jettenhausen 148
Johann I, Abbot of Petershausen
  (Johannes) 189
Johann II, Abbot of Petershausen
  (Johannes) 189
Johann Amfeld, Abbot of
  Petershausen (Johannes) 190
Johann Fryg, Abbot of Petershausen
  (Johannes) 190
Johann Hir, Abbot of Petershausen
  (Johannes) 190
Johann Merk, Abbot of Petershausen
  (Johannes) 190
John XV, Pope 55, 56, 58n.76,
  200–202
John the Baptist 146, 154, 158,
  165, 175
John the Evangelist 103, 146, 158,
  175, 188
John, martyr saint 146, 175
John, official of holy Lateran Palace
  57, 202
Judetenburg 79
Jude the Apostle 175
Judinta, *inclusa* 169
Julian, Saint 154

Kappel 116
Kastl, monastery 119, 120

Kempten, monastery 159
knights 15, 175, 204
Krebs, Manfred 50n.50
Kreuzlingen, community of regular
  canons 143n.58

Lambert, Bishop of Constance
  (Lampertus) 70, 73–76
Lambert of Birchtlingen
  (Lampertus) 122–123
Lambert of Hersfeld 2, 71, 72,
  78n.34, 86n.75, 88n.85, 89n.94
Lambert, Saint 154
Langensalza, Battle of (1075) 88
Lanzilin, bearded brother of
  Petershausen (Lanzilinus) 163
Laurentinus, Saint 154
Lawrence, Saint 103, 188
lay brothers (*conversi*) 10–11, 84,
  102, 104, 136–137, 149, 163,
  180, 183
lay sisters (*conversae*) 12
Leo I, Pope 154
Leo IX, Pope 6, 46
Leonard, Saint 145, 175, 188
Leonida, Saint 146
Libellus de diversis ordinibus et
  professionibus qui sunt in
  aecclesia 26–27
libertas see monastic liberty
liberti tributarii (*censuales*) 16,
  164n.22
Lienz 76
Life of St. Gebhard, CP comparison
  38, 191–192
Liggersdorf 48, 62
Lindau, monastery 45
Lippertsreute 179
Lippoldsberg, monastery 13
liturgy, in Hirsau-oriented
  monasticism 12–13
Liutfrid, Count of Winterthur
  (Liutfridus) 45–48, 198

INDEX

Liutold, Abbot of Petershausen (Liutoldus) 82, 100, 144, 189
Liutold, brother of Theodoric (Liutoldus) 100–101
Liutold of Eppenstein, Duke of Carinthia (Liutoldus) 87
Liutolf, Count of Achalm (Liutolfus) 133–134
Louis I, Grand Duke of Baden 17
Louis VII, King of France 165–166, 167
Louis, Count of Pfullendorf (Ludewicus) 113
Lucia, Saint 155, 158, 175
Luke the Evangelist 145
Lull, Saint 175
Lutwangen 61

Magnus, Saint 103, 104, 165, 175, 188
Makko, ministerial 61
Manilius, Felix 191
Manuel I Comnenus, Byzantine Emperor 166
Marcellus, Pope 146, 154
Marcian, Saint 154
Margaret, Saint 145, 175, 188
Marquard, brother of Gebhard (Marquardus) 45–46, 47–48, 59, 198
Marquard, brother of Theodoric (Marquardus) 100–101
Marquard, hermit (Marquardus) 169
Martin Brülin, Abbot of Petershausen 190
Martin, Saint 104, 145, 146, 158, 162–163, 175
Mary Magdalene 145, 146, 154, 155, 163n.15, 165, 175, 188
Mary, Mother of God 103, 104, 154, 161, 165, 174–175, 188, 197
Maternus, Saint 154

Matilda, daughter of Emperor Henry III 78n.34, 89n.93
Matilda, noblewoman of Constance (Mathilda, Mahthilda) 187
Matilda of England, Empress 135
Matilda, purchaser of church columns (Mahtilt) 178
Matthew the Apostle 146, 158, 165, 175
Maurice, Saint 80n.51, 103, 104, 145, 146, 154, 158, 175, 185, 188
Mauritius Burdinus, anti-Pope Gregory VIII 131
Maximin, Bishop Saint 103, 104, 146
Maximinus, Saint 154
Maximus, Saint 154, 175
Meginrat, religious woman of Petershausen 162
Meginzo, son of Cuno of Linzgau 132
Meinrad, Abbot of Petershausen (Meginradus, Meinradus) 70–71, 78–79, 81, 104, 113–114, 144, 189
Meinrad, Saint 52n.56
Mellrichstadt, Battle of (1078) 90
Meribod, *inclusus* (Meribotus) 169
Metellus, Saint 146
Michael the Archangel 104, 154, 175
Miller, Maureen 10
Mimmenhausen 83, 169–170
ministerials 15, 41, 60, 61, 175, 204
miracle stories 44–45, 104–105, 157–158, 161, 199–200, 202–203, 204–205, 206–215
see also visions
monasticism, apostolic model 27–34
monastic liberty (*libertas*) 7–8, 56–57, 62, 70–71, 79, 128–129, 130, 142–143
Mülheim 61

Neresheim, monastery 120–122, 140
Neufrach 83, 170

235

INDEX

Neuheim 60, 61, 182
Nicander, Saint 154
Nicetius, Saint 146
Nicholas, Saint 103, 104, 145, 146, 154, 158, 165, 175, 188
Nicholaus Roschach, Abbot of Petershausen 190
Noting, Bishop of Vercelli 5
Numia, Saint 146
Nur ad-Din 165n.28, 167n.40

obedientiaries 139
Oberdorf 48–49, 62
Oberwangen 61, 73–74
Oggelshausen 79
Opert, bearded brother of Petershausen (Opertus) 125, 132
Opert, father of Witigo (Opertus) 148
Opert, man of Count Ulrich X (Opertus) 115
Opert, monk priest of Petershausen (Opertus) 137
Ortlieb of Zwiefalten 3, 12
Oswald, Saint 145, 163n.15
Othmar, Saint 175
Otto I, Bishop of Constance 70–71, 85, 94, 95, 96
Otto I, Holy Roman Emperor 44n.25, 45
Otto II, Holy Roman Emperor 197
Otto III, Holy Roman Emperor 59–60, 64–65, 73–74, 200
Otto, Abbot of Petershausen 99–100
Otto, Bishop of Freising 167
Otto, Bishop of Ostia 95, 96
Otto, nobleman 119
Otto of Nordheim, Duke of Bavaria 87
Otto, priest 185

Otzo, Count Ulrich VI of Bregenz (Houtzo, Outzo, Ouzo) 39, 43–45, 195
Owingen 61

Pancras, Saint 103, 146, 154, 158, 188
Pancratius, Saint 175
Pantaleon, Saint 104
Paschal II, Pope 120, 121, 124, 131
Patrialia, Saint 188
Paulinus of Nola 103, 104, 146
Paul, martyr saint 146, 165, 175
Paul the Apostle 103, 104, 146, 154, 158, 165, 175, 188
Pechilda, mother of Witigo 148
Pelagius, Saint 103, 104, 145, 154, 158, 165, 175, 188
Pergentinus, Saint 154
Perriger/Pezilin, Abbot of Petershausen (Berricherus, Periggerus, Perricheru; Bezilinus, Pezilinus) 51, 67, 72–73, 189, 203, 207
Peter the Apostle 103, 104, 112, 141, 145, 154, 158, 165, 175, 188
Pfrungen 132–134, 135–136
Philip the Apostle 59, 145, 146, 154, 171, 175, 185, 200
pilgrims, apostolic model 37
Pleichfeld, Battle of (1086) 93
Polycarp, Saint 154
possessions, demonic 210–213
Premonstratensians 26
Primus, Saint 146
privileges
    of Dussnang 73–74
    of Epfendorf (994) 64–66
    of Frickingen (1135) 147–148
    of Oberdorf 48–49
    of Petershausen 55, 56–57, 200–202
    of Pfrungen (1121) 135–136

INDEX

of Rheingemünd (1164) 186–187
of Riedlings (1043) 76–77
of Rötsee 122–123
of Thayngen (995) 51
of Uhldingen (1058) 77–78
of Worndorf (993) 59–60
proprietary monastery 1n.1
Protasius, Saint 145
Protus, Saint 154, 175
Purgatory 106n.35

Quiriacus, Saint 146

Ratpero, hermit (Ratperonius) 122, 159–162
Raymond of Poitiers, Prince of Antioch 167
recluses 36, 169
reclusion and enclosure, apostolic model 28–30
Regilind, religious woman of Petershausen (Regillinda) 162–163
Regula, Saint 145, 146
regular canons, apostolic model 34–35
Reichenau, monastery 1, 50, 100
Reinbald, layman (Reginboldus) 125
relics 55–56, 58–59, 80, 103–104, 145–146, 165, 171, 173–174, 185, 188, 200, 202
religious women 12, 30–31, 162–163, 169
Repperweiler 61
Reute 83, 170
Rheingemünd 185–187
Richinza, wife of Henry of Hirschegg 134
Rieden 63
Riedlings 76–77
Riggenweiler 81
Rinhart 61
Robinson, I. S. 91

Rot 61
Rötsee 122–123, 158–161
Routhard, monk priest of Petershausen (Routhardus) 112
Rudiger, nobleman (Roudigerus) 179
Rudolf, Duke of Swabia, anti-King of Germany (Roudolfi, Roudolfus) 86, 88–90, 91–92
Rudolf, Count (Roudolf) 78
Rudolf, Count of Bregenz (Roudolfus) 115, 145
Rudolf, Count of Ramsberg (Roudolfus) 185–187
Rudolf, monk priest of Petershausen (Roudolfus) 185
Rudolf of Güttingen (Roudolfus) 187
Rule of St. Benedict 9, 25, 128
Rumold, Bishop of Constance (Rumaldus, Roumaldus) 78n.34, 85, 133
Rupert, first monk of Petershausen (Roupertus) 51–52
Rupert, monk teacher of Petershausen (Roupertus) 100
Rupert of Deutz 11–12
Rupert of Otterswang (Roupertus) 142
Rupert of Teuringen (Roupertus) 148, 149, 187
rural clerics, apostolic model 35

St. Emmeram, monastery 6, 8, 41
St. Gall, monastery 3
St. George in the Black Forest, monastery 169–170
St. Peter, monastery 174
St. Peter's basilica (Rome) 1
St. Ulrich in Augsburg, monastery 101
Saturninus, Saint 146
Sauldorf 61
Saxon Rebellion (1073–1075) 88
Schaffhausen, monastery 13, 116, 141

INDEX

Schiggendorf 164
Schlatt 61
Schmid, Karl 185n.10
Scholastica, Saint 158, 175
Schwäblishausen 79
Sebastian, Saint 103, 146, 154, 158, 165, 175, 188
Second Crusade (1147–1149) 165–168
Second Lateran Council (1139) 163
self-donation (autodedition) 164n.22
Sergius, Saint 146
servi cottidiani 16, 17, 40, 50–51n.52, 61n.91, 133n.24, 133n.26
servile class and servitude
  concubines 100
  in medieval Germany 15–17, 40, 133n.24, 133n.26, 164n.22, 211n.55
  at Petershausen 50–51n.52, 61n.91, 102–103n.29, 211
Servilian, Saint 145
servi manentes 16
Siegfried II, Bishop of Augsburg (Sigifridus) 93
Sigbod, monk of Hirsau, Abbot of Neresheim (Sigiboto) 122
Sigfrid, Abbot of Petershausen (Sigefridus, Sigifridus) 76, 189
Sigfrid, *custos* of Petershausen (Sigifridus) 125, 132, 138, 139
Sigfrid of Weiler (Sigifridus) 79–80
Sigger, monk priest of Petershausen (Sigiherus) 111
Sigger, monk teacher of Petershausen (Sigiherus) 104
Sigger, nobleman (Siggerus) 73
Siggo, Abbot of Petershausen 78, 144, 189
Sigismund, Saint 145
Simon the Apostle 103, 104, 165, 175
simony 66n.101
Sisinnius, Saint 146

Sixtus, Saint 145
slaves, in Swabian society 16
solitaries 36, 112, 169
Sophia, Saint 154, 155
Stein, monastery 64, 141
Steinbach 63
Stephen I, Pope 103, 146
Stephen the Protomartyr 103, 145, 146, 165, 175, 188
Stetten 61
Sulpitius, Saint 145
Swigger, donor (Swiggerus) 77–78
Sylvester, Pope 175

Tägerwilen 60, 61, 169
Tassilo III, Duke of Bavaria 119n.68
Teuringen 43, 148
Thayngen 51, 61
Theban legion 80n.51, 185
theft 54, 137–138, 181, 192, 202–203
Theiter, priest (Tiethere) 76
Theodoric, Abbot of Petershausen (Theodericus, Theoderich)
  anniversary celebration 182–183
  appointment at Petershausen 100, 101–102, 189
  biographical sketch and character 100–101, 102, 127
  building renovations 102–104, 144
  death 125–126, 144
  investiture controversy involvement 118–119, 120
  library enhancement 126–127
  property acquisitions 112–116, 120–121, 122–123
  in visions 132, 141
Theophanu, wife of Emperor Otto II 59n.83
Thiemo, Archbishop of Salzburg 116–117
Thomas the Apostle 146, 175, 188
Tiburtius, Saint 146, 154
tonsure 32–33

INDEX

Torpeiadech, Saint 188
Tractatus de professionibus monachorum 26–27
trial by ordeal 137–138
Trithemius, Johannes 7
Trutlind, noble woman (Triutlint) 149
Turand, ministerial (Turandus) 61
Tuta, wife of Ebbo of Heiligenburg (Touta) 83
Tuto, nobleman (Touto) 116

Überlingen 43
Udalrichinger (Bregenzer) 38–39
Uhldingen 77–78
Ulrich I, Abbot of Petershausen (Uolrico, Uodalricus) 188, 189
Ulrich I, Abbot of Zwiefalten 142
Ulrich I, Bishop of Augsburg (Oudalricus) 58, 103, 146, 159, 165, 175
Ulrich I, Bishop of Constance (Oudalricus) 46, 59n.77, 121, 122, 124, 126, 131, 134, 140, 141, 142–143
Ulrich I, brother-in-law of Charlemagne 39n.3, 42n.17
Ulrich II, Abbot of Petershausen (Uodalricus) 189
Ulrich II, Bishop of Constance (Oudalricus) 145, 149, 153–154
Ulrich VI, Count of Bregenz (Oudalricus) 39, 43–45, 195
Ulrich VII, Count of Bregenz (Oudalricus) 45–46, 47–48, 198
Ulrich IX, Count of Bregenz (Oudalricus) 77, 82
Ulrich X, Count of Bregenz (Oudalricus) 112–116
Ulrich XI, Count of Bregenz (Oudalricus) 115
Ulrich, advocate (Oudalricus, Oudelricus) 48

Ulrich, Count of Gammertingen (Oudalricus) 47
Ulrich of Eppenstein, Patriarch of Aquileia, Abbot of St. Gall (Oudalricus) 117
Ulrich of Zell 8
Ulrich, Prior of Ursberg, Abbot of Fischingen and Mehrerau 182n.19
University of Heidelberg, *Codex Salemitani* IX 42a 17–18, 191
Unstrut, Battle on the (1075) 88
Urban II, Pope 94n.118
Ursus, priest 80–81
Ursus, Saint 146
Uto, Abbot of Wagenhausen 141, 149

Valens, Saint 145
Valentinus, Saint 145, 146
Valerius, Saint 146
Verena, Saint 103, 146
Victor IV, Pope 178
Victor, Saint 146
Vigilius, Saint 146
Vincent, Saint 103, 146, 188
violence 109–111, 136–137, 160, 180, 181
Virgin Mary 103, 104, 154, 161, 165, 174–175, 188, 197
visions 99, 105–109, 111, 112, 131–132, 141, 162–163, 168–169, 209–210, 213–215
vita apostolica see apostolic life
Vitalis IV Candiano, Patriarch of Grado 54
Vitalis, Saint 146
Vitus, Saint 146, 154, 158, 175
Vratislaus II, Duke of Bohemia 90, 91

Wagenhausen, monastery 116, 141, 149
Walbertsweiler 61

INDEX

Walburga, Saint 146, 154, 155, 175
Walcher, *inclusus* (Walcounus) 169
Walfrid, Abbot of Hohentwiel (Walfridus) 64
Walter, Abbot of Petershausen (Waltharius) 76, 189
Walter, monk of Petershausen (Waltherus) 135
Waltram, Abbot of Fischingen (Waltrammus) 149, 168
Wangen 164
Warman, Bishop of Constance (Warmannus) 160–161
Wegesaza 76–77
Weiland, Ludwig 19, 157
Weingarten, monastery 130n.13
Welf, Duke of Bavaria (Welfonus) 86, 88, 93, 114
Welf of Ravensberg (Welfonus) 87
Welfesholz, Battle of (1115) 124n.93
Wenceslaus, Saint 104
Wendish Crusade (1147) 168
Werner, Count of Habsburg (Wernherus) 114–115
Werner, monk of Petershausen (Wernharius) 100, 105
Werner, nobleman (Wernherus) 83
Werner of Altshausen (Wernharius) 104, 122, 131, 140–141
Werner of Epfindorf, anti-Abbot of Petershausen (Wernherus) 119, 121
Werner, servant of Petershausen (Wernherus) 152–153
Wessobrunn, monastery 119
Wezil, cleric of Constance 179
Wezil, son of Cuno of Linzgau 132–133
Wibert, Archbishop of Ravenna (Wipertus) 86–87, 91, 95, 117
Wicpert, Saint 175
Wido, Bishop of Chur (Wito) 131, 136
William I, King of Sicily 179n.7
William, Abbot of Hirsau (Willihelmus; Willihalmus) 6, 7–8, 95–96, 99, 100, 101
Winhard, hermit (Winihardus) 169
Winnenden 80
Winterthur 43, 45–46
Wiserich, monk of Petershausen (Wisericus) 135
Witigo, priest 147–148
Wolfarn, nobleman (Wolfarnus) 83
Wolfrad, layman (Wolveradus) 137
Wolfrad, monk cellarer of Petershausen (Wolferadus) 136–137
Wolfrad, monk priest of Petershausen (Wolferadus) 131–132
Wolfrad of Weiler (Wolveradus) 79
women, religious 12, 30–31, 162–163, 169
Worndorf 59–60
Würzburg, Battle of (1086) 93

Zengi, Imad ad-Din 165n.28
Zwiefalten, monastery 3, 12, 13, 140, 174

EU authorised representative for GPSR:
Easy Access System Europe, Mustamäe tee 50,
10621 Tallinn, Estonia
gpsr.requests@easproject.com